To our parents

John and Irene Dimitry

and

Thomas and Margaret Mott

this book is dedicated

with affection and gratitude

Introduction to

Fortran IV Programming

Introduction
to
Fortran IV
Programming

DONALD L. DIMITRY

IBM Corporation

THOMAS H. MOTT, JR.

Rutgers University and
Stevens Institute of Technology

HOLT, RINEHART and WINSTON

New York / Chicago / San Francisco / Toronto / London

Preface

The purpose of this text is to consider — in detail although at an elementary level — the Fortran language. The text is designed for both the person without any previous computer training and the novice programmer. Although the text is designed for the beginning student, the Fortran language is presented to its fullest capabilities. If a student masters the ideas presented in this text he could consider himself a competent programmer. The authors believe that presenting many examples to illustrate the salient points of the discussion is the key to a good programming text. All of the examples presented have been run on a computer to insure their correctness. Problems included at the end of chapters are designed to give the reader the opportunity to show his understanding of the material presented in the chapter.

The final chapter of the text includes twenty-five problems. Flow charts and programs for ten of the problems are presented. These problems were chosen to illustrate the basic concepts of programming and to demonstrate the techniques used to program commonly occurring problems. The remaining fifteen problems are left as exercises for the reader.

It is the opinion of the authors that a complete mastery and appreciation of the fundamentals of Fortran programming is possible only with a thorough understanding of how the computer functions and of how basic programming concepts are implemented at the level of machine-language programming. The first three chapters of the text are designed to supply the reader with a thorough understanding of these underlying concepts. However, the reader who is interested only in Fortran programming may proceed directly to Chapter IV and return to the first three chapters at a later opportunity.

Fortran, like ordinary languages, suffers from the existence of many "dialects" or versions. It is extremely difficult to describe in a text the rules of the language as they pertain to every version of Fortran in existence today. We have chosen to describe the most recent version of Fortran, Fortran IV, as it is defined for the IBM 7040-7044 computer systems. However, once the reader has learned the Fortran IV language, it is a relatively simple matter to learn the rules for the other versions of Fortran, most of which are a subset of Fortran IV. We have attempted to indicate to the reader all of the areas of the Fortran IV language which might differ from Fortran II, a version of Fortran in wide use today.

We are deeply indebted to Mr. Daniel N. Leeson of the IBM Corporation, Professor William C. Lynch of Case Institute of Technology, and Professor Howard N. Schmeising of the Illinois Institute of Technology for their excellent critical reviews of the manuscript. Many of their valuable suggestions have been incorporated in this text. We also wish to thank our colleagues, Professors F. G. Fender, S. Baxendale, D. R. King, J. Martin, L. Miller, and Mrs. R. Ralph for their counsel and advice. We are also indebted to Mrs. Helen C. Bowen for her careful typing of a difficult manuscript, and to Mrs. Geraldine Ritter for her help in keypunching the problems and examples.

Finally, we owe a debt of gratitude to our wives, without whose forbearance this book could not have been written.

WESTFIELD, NEW JERSEY
PRINCETON, NEW JERSEY
FEBRUARY 1966

Donald L. Dimitry
Thomas H. Mott, Jr.

Contents

Introduction to

Fortran IV Programming

1

Introduction to Digital Computers

Twenty years ago the slide rule and desk calculator were the principal tools available for anyone desiring to perform complex numerical computations. Today the use of the digital computer for this purpose is commonplace. The series of technological developments that brought about this change and provided man with an unprecedented tool for shaping his environment already ranks among the outstanding achievements in the history of scientific progress.

One of the key disciplines comprising the core of this new technology is *computer programming*. Like the computer field generally, programming technology has experienced many important advances. It will be the purpose of this book to consider in detail, although at an elementary level, one major advance in programming technology. This concerns the development of a programming language which is user-oriented in the sense of closely resembling the user's own language for stating and solving problems. Called Fortran, the programming language resembles the language of elementary mathematics and provides a convenient way of programming computers to solve mathematical problems of a numerical nature. Its significance as a user-oriented language will be fully brought out in Chapter 3, where it will be contrasted with machine-oriented programming languages.

Before we turn to a study of the essentials of Fortran, it is advisable for the reader to have some knowledge concerning the organization and operation of the *modern electronic digital computer*. In what follows we shall strive to offer a simple yet adequate explanation of how and why digital computers work as they do. With this material as background the reader can approach the chapters on Fortran programming with a better understanding and appreciation of the basic concepts underlying computer programming.

A GENERAL DESCRIPTION OF A MODERN DIGITAL COMPUTER

1.1 Finite Discrete Methods

The development of modern mathematical analysis has produced a new class of methods and procedures for solving a variety of problems confronting the physical and social scientist and engineer. Known by the general name of "finite, discrete methods," most of the new methods are also distinguished by specific names such as "linear programming" † and "operations research." Typical of the range of problems to which the new methods can be applied are techniques for controlling inventory in a parts department, scheduling jobs in an assembly plant, allocating resources in a manufacturing process, optimizing blending mixtures in a refinery/cracking process, or determining optimal routes in a transportation network to minimize shipping cost. It is beyond the scope of this text to consider specific details of the various mathematical techniques for solving such problems. What is important here is that all the methods alike employ a *finite number of steps*, and all the methods operate upon data that is represented in *discrete, as opposed to continuous, form*. Hence we use the name "finite, discrete" to characterize the new methods as a whole.

With the advent of the high-speed digital computer there has occurred a widening interest in the application of both finite, discrete methods and the older methods of numerical analysis to scientific and engineering problems. As a result, increasing numbers of problems are being solved with the use of digital computers; and as new applications of these methods are sought, the prospects grow for still larger numbers of problems to be solved.

1.2 Digital versus Analog

A major characteristic of the modern digital computer, then, is its ability to cope with problems that are solvable by finite, discrete methods. This ability derives from the fact that the digital computer operates on data represented by *discrete sets of digits*. This is in contrast to the class of computing machines called *analog computers* which operate on data represented in a continuous form in terms of some measurable physical quantity (such as voltage, current, or shaft rotation) that varies in proportion to the actual data it represents.

The difference between analog and digital computation can be illustrated

†The term "linear programming" applies to a class of *mathematical* techniques for maximizing (or minimizing) a given function subject to certain linear constraints. This should not be confused with the activity of *programming* a computer, which is an altogether different and distinct process.

by considering two distinct ways in which it is possible to compare the amounts of various commodities. Two methods, which might be described as *measuring* and *counting*, are available. The digital computer deals with numbers, each of which is represented as a finite sequence of digits, and performs comparisons and the operations of arithmetic by a counting process. The analog computer operates without doing any counting at all. The results are derived directly from the magnitudes of the quantities involved by a process of measurement without ever expressing them numerically at any stage.

An illustration of a simple analog device is the mercury thermometer. The mercury is enclosed within a confined space. Its volume is measurable and changes with a change in the temperature. A scale correlates changes in the volume of mercury with changes in the air temperature. Since our interest lies wholly in digital computation, we shall say nothing more about measuring and about analog computers.

1.3 High-Speed Computation

In dealing with discrete sets of digits the digital computer, in essence, can perform only a few simple operations. Basic among them is the capacity for distinguishing between two identifiable physical states. Thus it is able to determine whether the polarity of a signal line is "high" or "low," the direction in which a ferrite core is magnetized, whether a transistor diode is in the "active" state or "inactive." The computer is also able to keep track of this binary (two-state) information and move it from one place to another for the purpose of effecting desired changes in the states of the various components. The fact that these and similar operations, which are performed automatically within the computer, are very simple is compensated for by the extremely *high speeds* at which the computer performs them. Literally thousands, even millions, of such operations are carried out each second by the computer.

This feature of the digital computer — its capacity for high-speed computation — has made it possible for the methods of mathematics to be applied to problems previously considered beyond the reach of solution — problems requiring such extensive numerical calculations that a person or group of persons could not complete them in a lifetime of labor on desk calculators.

1.4 The Computer Program: a Series of Machine-Language Commands

From the very simple operations described above, often called "subcommands" by some computer designers, are fashioned certain elementary arithmetic and logical operations. Referred to as "machine language instructions" or "commands," the latter enable the computer to perform automatically by a predetermined and fixed sequence of the subcommands such operations as addition, subtraction, multiplication, division, distinguishing between a sequence of digits representing a nonnegative integer and one representing an integer less than zero, and so forth.

Although most digital computers have the ability to perform considerably more complex operations than those cited above, such as evaluating the natural logarithm of a number or approximating the roots of a polynomial equation, very few digital computers have a *built-in* (that is, hardware) ability to perform them. Any one of these machines can be used to approximate roots or produce a table of natural logarithms, but it can carry out such complex operations only by following a proper sequence of the elementary machine language instructions.

Such a sequence of basic machine instructions, specifically arranged to accomplish a given task, is called a program. The program provides the control under which the computer operates in executing the series of machine instructions called for by the nature of the task.

1.5   The Stored-Program Machine

Some computers are designed with a fixed, built-in program to solve a specific type of problem. These are known as *special-purpose* computers and are a useful and economical device from the standpoint of solving the same problem over and over again for different sets of data. For example, a machine designed only to compute payroll information, or to perform only inventory control, falls in the category of special-purpose computers. The majority of modern high-speed digital computers, however, belong in the category of *general-purpose* computers. These are machines that can be programmed to solve a wide range of problems.

Since the general-purpose computer can act upon more than one program, it is important to consider the facilities that are available in the general purpose computer for changing from one program to another. When the computer must accept the program as formulated by the user and can do little if anything at all to alter or modify by its own means the given sequence of instructions, the computer is said to be *externally programmed*. The earlier generations of digital computers are general-purpose machines of this type. Change of programs for these machines is usually accomplished by means of removable plugboards or punched paper tape for changing internal switch settings, which thus alter the hardware configuration of the machine.

A program for a modern digital computer, however, is stored within the computer in the same form as its data. As a result, the modern digital computer can operate upon the instructions of a program just as it can operate on data and can change and modify the program during the course of its actual execution. For this reason the modern digital computer is referred to as an *internally programmed* or *stored-program* machine. New programs are stored in these machines usually by means of an "executive program" or "monitor"† stored in the machines. A more concise picture of just how a stored-program machine operates will be postponed until we have come to the section on the internal organization of the digital computer.

1.6   The Properties of a General-Purpose Computer

The repertoire of basic machine instructions varies among general-purpose digital computers. Identical sets of instructions are seldom if ever found among them; nor is the same instruction (say, the add instruction) executed in the same way by two different machines. This does not mean, however, that general-purpose digital computers are not similar in their main operating features; for they are, although they may differ in the design and implementation of these features. A machine may be properly classified as a general-purpose digital computer, provided it can perform the following operations:

1. Move information from one place to another and find information already stored.

2. Perform basic arithmetic operations.

3. Make simple tests and decide which of two or more possible procedures to follow, basing such decisions on intermediate results, which may not be initially known.

4. Follow a prescribed sequence of operations.

5. Change the predetermined sequence of operations to be performed, depending upon the results of intermediate operations.

6. Perform more complex operations by repetition of basic instructions and simple tests, possibly modifying (changing) the instructions in the course of repeating them.

7. Store in the computer, for later use, the results of the operations.

How these operations are performed will be made clear in the next section on the organization of a digital computer.

†A description of monitors is deferred until Section 3.13.

THE ORGANIZATION OF A MODERN DIGITAL COMPUTER

1.7   Over-all Organization

In order to carry out the operations listed above, the modern highspeed digital computer typically uses (*a*) *storage* elements which hold information, (*b*) *arithmetic* and *control* elements which operate on and control the flow of information, and (*c*) *input/output* elements which receive and display information. Although the manner in which these various elements are organized depends on the specific make of computer and may vary from computer to computer, a typical organization of the major functional units of a digital computer is shown schematically in Fig. 1.1.

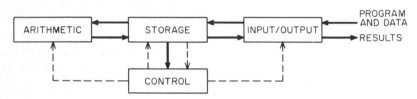

FIGURE 1.1   Block diagram showing a typical organization of the functional units of a digital computer. Heavy arrows represent data (information) flow. Broken arrows represent control signals.

To illustrate the interplay that occurs among the major functional units shown in Fig. 1.1, a sequence of operations that the computer typically follows in executing a program to solve a problem will be described. It is beyond the scope of this text to discuss these operations in sufficient detail that they can be understood in all their complexity. However, enough details are presented to provide the reader with a broad understanding of the internal operation of a digital computer. The sequence of operations in the execution of a program is as follows:

Step 1. First, the method of solution for solving the problem is programmed. That is, it is converted into a sequence of machine language instructions, which becomes the program to be executed. The program, along with the data to be used for obtaining a solution, is then entered into the storage unit of the computer via the input device.

This is indicated in Fig. 1.1 by the heavy arrows from PROGRAM and DATA to STORAGE. Entering the program and data into storage is accomplished under supervision of the control unit, which is indicated by the broken arrow in Fig. 1.1 from CONTROL to INPUT/OUTPUT.

Step 2. Once in storage, the program is then made available to the control unit for interpretation and eventual execution of the instructions.

This is indicated in Fig. 1.1 by the broken arrows between STORAGE and CONTROL.

Step 3. Next, under supervision of the control unit, the arithmetic unit performs the following three operations:

a. It obtains the data from storage. This is indicated in Fig. 1.1 by the heavy arrow from STORAGE to ARITHMETIC.

b. It operates on the data in accordance with the method of solution prescribed by the program. This is indicated by the broken arrow from CONTROL to ARITHMETIC in Fig. 1.1.

c. It returns the results of the prescribed operations to storage. This is indicated by the heavy arrow from ARITHMETIC to STORAGE.

Step 4. Finally, under instruction from the program, the results of operating upon the data are transferred to the output medium. This is indicated in Fig. 1.1 by the heavy arrows from STORAGE to RESULTS.

We shall now describe in greater detail the major functional units of the digital computer and some of their important characteristics.

1.8   Input/Output

The function of the input/output unit is to move information that is external to the computer into the storage unit, and vice versa. This involves the *transmission* of information, and the *transformation* of information.

Transmission of Information

There exists a variety of peripheral devices that serve as input/output units. The most common types of such devices are card readers and punches, paper-tape readers and punches, printers, magnetic-tape stations, and magnetic disks. The majority of digital computers make use of some combination of these devices for entering information into the computer and obtaining output of the results.

Inscription of the information to be entered into the computer is ordinarily done off-line† on a key-punch machine, Flexowriter, or similar device. Once the preparation of input data is complete and the programmer has access to the computer, the appropriate on-line peripheral device will take the inscribed information and enter it into the computer storage. On output the computer itself inscribes information from storage onto a specified medium (punched cards, punched paper tape, or magnetic tape, for exam-

†"Off-line" is a term used to denote operations that do not require the use of the computer.

ple), which can then be taken later to an appropriate off-line device for final recording without requiring further use of the computer.

Many computers employ a card reader and card punch as their main input/output devices. However, for very high-speed digital computers the operating speeds of these devices are too slow for efficient operation. These computers are likely to employ magnetic tape for input and output of information and perhaps a high-speed printer as an optional output unit. This is done to speed up the input/output process as much as possible and minimize the waiting time (time required to transfer information between the input/output media and storage) before information is ready for processing. It requires off-line auxiliary devices for transcribing punched cards or paper tape onto magnetic tape for input and converting magnetic tape output into a suitable form for direct recognition.

Although direct communication with the computer by means of a console typewriter or control panel is usually available, this method of communication is extremely slow. For this reason it is better if this method is used only sparingly for such purposes as program testing and debugging.

Transformation of Information

Communication with the digital computer requires that information be reduced to a set of symbols that can be read and interpreted by the computer. The basic operation of all digital computers consists of distinguishing between two identifiable physical states. This means that the information to be processed by the computer must be represented internally by a set of symbols consisting of the digits zero (0) and one (1). This explains why there is usually a disparity between the external form of information and its representation as stored within the computer. In its external form the information may be numerical or alphabetic in character, but it must undergo a transformation into binary form during its transmission from outside of the computer to internal storage.

In order to facilitate the transformation of information between internal and external form the majority of input/output equipment is designed to accept some form of binary coding. The choice of binary coding has also been found to have advantages from the standpoint of simplicity of equipment design. These facts explain why alphabetic and numeric information is represented, on punched cards, for example, by the presence or absence of holes in specific locations of the card. A discussion of binary coding is presented in Chapter 2.

Cards

The punched card is the most commonly used medium for entering information into computer storage. Information is recorded as small holes punched in specific locations of the card, as shown in Fig. 1.2. Transmission of information inscribed on the card is accomplished by passing the card through a card reader, which senses the presence or absence of holes by mechanical or optical means and converts them into electrical pulses for transmission into the computer.

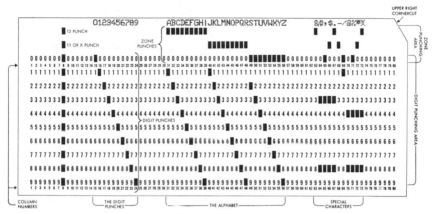

FIGURE 1.2   Fortran character code for punched cards.

Several kinds of punched cards and character codes for inscribing information on them are currently in use. We shall describe in this section one type of punched card and character code in common use. This punched card is divided into 80 columns and 12 rows. The latter provide twelve punching positions for each column. Ten of the twelve punching positions are numbered 0–9; two more punching positions are present, but unnumbered, between row 0 and the top edge. These are referred to as the 11 (or X or minus) and 12 (or plus) punching positions, the latter being closer to the top edge. Each column of the card is used to represent a digit, a letter, or a special character. Thus the card may contain up to 80 individual characters of information. In the Fortran character code shown in Fig. 1.2, decimal digits are represented by a single punch in a column, alphabetic characters by two punches in a column, and special characters by one, two, or three punches in a single column.

A special key punch machine containing a keyboard similar to that of a typewriter is used to encode information into punched cards. Some key punches have an additional facility for printing the character above the column into which it is punched.

Paper Tape

Information is recorded on paper tape in much the same manner as on punched cards. Here, information is inscribed as a special arrangement of punched holes along the length of the paper tape. Several kinds of paper tape and character codes for inscribing information on them are currently in use. Figure 1.3 shows a character code that is in common use for eight-channel paper tape. Eight parallel tracks running the length of the paper

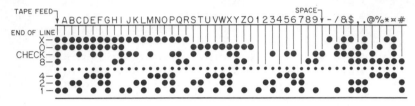

FIGURE 1.3   Commonly used character code for eight-channel paper tape.

tape serve as channels along which information can be recorded. One column of eight punching positions (one for each channel) across the width of the tape is used to code either a numeric, alphabetic, or special character. The lower four channels of the tape (excluding the feed holes) are labeled 1, 2, 4, and 8, and are used to record decimal digits. The decimal digits 1 through 9 are represented as a punch or punches in these four positions. The sum of the positional values indicates the digit punched: a hole in channel 1 represents the digit one; a combination of a 1 and 2 punch represents the decimal digit three; and so on. The X and 0 channels are used in combination with the four numeric channels to record alphabetic and special characters. The presence of a hole in the topmost channel (EL — end of line) indicates the end of a record of information on the tape.

Several checking systems are available to insure that each letter or digit is recorded correctly on tape. A commonly used system is the odd-parity check. This consists of each column of the tape always having an odd number of holes. The check channel is used for this purpose and will automatically have a hole punched when the number, letter, or special character has an even number of holes. Whether used as input or output, each column of the tape is scanned to make certain that this condition has been satisfied. If an even number of holes in any column is sensed, this condition is detected as an error and indicated to the machine operator.

Paper tape is a continuous recording medium as compared to cards, which are fixed in length. This tends to make the task of locating and correcting mistakes on punched paper tape somewhat cumbersome. It also helps to explain why the punched card is the preferred and most commonly used medium for entering information into the computer, since cards with errors are easily removed from a deck and repunched.

Paper tape can be prepared on Flexowriters, which are machines similar to key punches. Punched paper tape is read into the computer through a paper tape reader that senses the presence or absence of holes in a manner similar to that for card readers.

Magnetic Tape

The principle used to record information on magnetic tape is substantially the same as for paper tape. The tape is divided into parallel channels extending along the length of the tape. Sensing of information is accomplished by means of a "read/write" head, which has the ability to sense the presence of magnetic spots in any one of the channels. A character of information is represented by small magnetized sections of the channels located vertically across the width of the tape. The direction of magnetization (clockwise or counterclockwise) determines whether a section is storing a binary 0 or 1, which corresponds to the absence or presence of holes in punched paper tape. Figure 1.4 illustrates a coding scheme used for seven-channel magnetic tape. The absence of a vertical mark in a channel denotes magnetization in a counterclockwise direction.

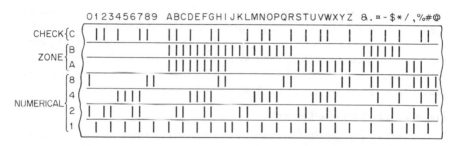

FIGURE 1.4   Representation of information on seven-channel magnetic tape.

A single character of information can be represented by a column of several magnetized sections (one for each channel) across the width of the tape. As a consequence, the number of characters that can be recorded on a fixed length of magnetic tape is determined by the closeness with which the magnetized sections can be placed one after another. Placing them closer and closer together is called *packing* the tape. The number of characters that can be packed on a given length of tape is called the *density* of the tape. Most magnetic tape units provide the user with an option of recording information at high or low density.

A principal advantage of magnetic tape, in addition to its fast operating speed, is that the information on it may be changed when necessary, whereas information stored in paper tape and punched cards cannot be altered.

1.9   Storage

The function of the storage unit of the computer is to hold the initial data, the program of instructions, intermediate and final results before output, and any other information pertinent to the solution of the problem at hand.

Registers

As illustrated earlier, a digital computer must have the capability of having access to where information is stored so that it can be referred to and replaced as desired.

In order to provide for this capability information is represented internally as finite sequences of digits which are stored within the machine in physical devices known as *registers*. The sequence of digits stored in a register is referred to as a *word*. A register, then, is simply a storage device for holding an ordered array of digits, the array of digits being called a word. The storage unit of a computer consists of large numbers of such registers.

In many present-day computers arrays of different kinds of physical devices serve as registers. Thus a register may be composed of an array of tiny magnetic cores residing in identical locations of the core memory planes, or it may consist of a group of identically positioned magnetized spots on the layers of a thin-magnetic-film unit, or a sequential grouping of magnetized spots on a magnetic drum. In addition to these devices, an array of tiny current- or voltage-operated electronic devices called flip-flops may also serve as a register for holding information.

Fixed versus Variable Length

The number of digits that are stored in a register defines both the length of the register and the length of the word stored in it. Depending upon its design, a computer may operate entirely upon *words of fixed length*, entirely upon *words of variable length*, or a combination of both.

In a variable-word-length operation it is customary to refer to the basic unit of information that can be stored and operated upon singly as a *character* instead of a word. A character is, of course, of fixed length, and it is understood that a variable-length word consists of a sequence of characters that is of any length practical to store and manipulate within the storage capacity of the computer. The reader should remember, however, that whether a computer employs all fixed-word-length operations, variable-word-length operations, or a combination of the two, is strictly a matter of the design of the hardware of the computer.

It is always good advice for the programmer to acquaint himself with the characteristics of the particular computer he is using in order to take maximum advantage of the hardware features that are available to him.

The Basic Properties of Registers

Depending upon the particular functions with which they are involved, every register in a digital computer can be classified as belonging to one or more of the following groups:

> Input/output registers
> Storage registers
> Control registers
> Arithmetic registers

However, no matter to what group it belongs or to what purpose it is put, every register of a digital computer shares two basic properties, known as the *read property* and the *write property*.

1. The Read Property

Copies can always be made of a word stored in a register by means of a reading operation that does not alter the word.

2. The Write Property

A new word can always replace the current word stored in a register by means of a writing operation.

In addition to these two basic properties shared by all registers of the computer, every *storage* register shares a third property known as the *address property*.

3. The Address Property

Every storage register is uniquely identifiable by an integer known as its address.

In any digital computer every storage register will be found to have assigned to it a fixed, permanent address that distinguishes it from all other registers in the computer. By means of this numerical address, which serves the same purpose as a street address or house number, the programmer may specify to the computer exactly where to locate a piece of data or instruction needed in the solution of a problem.

As will become evident in later chapters, the three aforementioned properties of registers are absolutely fundamental to programming. Without these properties, programming a digital computer would prove virtually impossible.

The Content and Address of Registers

It is conventional to refer to the word stored in a register as the *content* of that register. Every register in a digital computer has associated with it a content, which is the sequence of digits stored in the register. Moreover, all addressable registers have a second sequence of digits associated with them — namely, the *address* of the register. *It is of utmost importance to avoid confusion between the two sequences of digits associated with a register.* Fortunately, a standard notation to distinguish between the two sequences has been developed and will be followed in this text.

Parenthesis Notation

Let α represent the address of any addressable register. Then the symbol (α) — that is, α enclosed within parentheses — will represent the content of the register whose address is α.

For example, if the sequence of digits, 66573, is stored in the register whose address is 01425, we can refer to the digits stored at this location simply by the notation (01425). In other words, we shall interpret

$$(01425) = 66573$$

to mean that the register whose address is 01425 contains the digits 66573.

The notation is also useful in referring to the contents of registers that do not have assigned numerical addresses. For such registers it will suffice to enclose within parentheses the name or some other symbol identifying the register in order to refer to its content. Thus the five digits, say, in the five-digit register whose name is X can be referred to by the notation (X). Extensive use of this application of the notation is made in what is called *symbolic* programming, and will be discussed further in Chapter 3.

The Dual Role of a Storage Register

One of the essential characteristics of a modern digital computer as a stored-program machine is that a person cannot, in general, tell whether a sequence of digits stored in a register represents a data word or an instruction word, or for that matter, an address of a data word or instruction word. Indeed, any storage register may store either an instruction word or a data word at different times during the course of a computation. Thus, several interpretations can be placed upon the content of a storage register. We turn now to consider the interpretation that the content of a storage register represents an instruction to the control unit.

1.10   Control

It is the function of the control unit to (*a*) obtain instructions from the storage unit in the correct sequence, and (*b*) activate the necessary control mechanisms for the proper execution of each instruction. We shall refer to these two main functions of the control unit as the *fetch function* and the *execute function*. Together they constitute the general mode of operation of the computer. Figure 1.5 shows a flowchart of the general operation cycle for a stored-program digital computer. The "execute" phase of the control

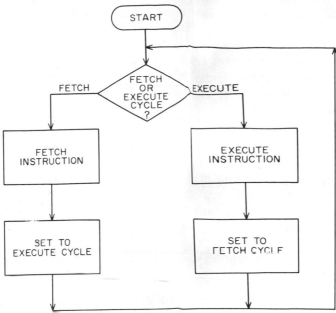

FIGURE 1.5   Basic control cycle of a digital computer.

cycle will be considered first; the question of how the control unit determines the exact order in which instructions are to be fetched for execution will be deferred until later.

The Execute Cycle

In order to determine how the control unit causes an instruction to be executed once it is located and obtained, it is first necessary to examine the structure of the sequence of digits that have been interpreted by the control as an instruction.

It will be found that any sequence of digits that serves as an instruction word can be divided into subsets. One subset of digits will represent a numerical code for the particular operation to be performed, and the remaining digits will generally specify the addresses or locations in storage of the operands and perhaps the location at which the result is to be delivered. In some instructions the actual operand, rather than the address of an operand, may appear.

Instruction Formats and Types of Addressing Systems

The division of the digits into subsets, which defines the structure of the instruction word, is often referred to as the *format* of the instruction word. Instruction formats vary from computer to computer.

The particular subset of digits that designates a specific operation is known as an *operation code* (or more briefly, *op code*), and the remaining portions of the instruction word are commonly referred to as *addresses*. The number of addresses used in the instruction format provides a convenient way to classify a computer. Thus we often hear of single address computers, two-address computers, and so on.

The *single address* computer is exemplified by an instruction of the following form:

$$23 \qquad u$$

This instruction consists of two parts; 23 is the operation code and u denotes the address of an operand. An exact description of this command might be "Clear the accumulator,† then add the number at address u to the number in the Q register† and store the sum in the accumulator." The control unit of the computer would be constructed to interpret and execute instructions of this form in exact accordance with the above description.

In a *two-address* system an ADD instruction might take the form

$$21 \qquad u \qquad v$$

where 21 is the operation code and u and v represent addresses of any storage registers. Here the control unit of the computer might be constructed to interpret this instruction as "Clear the accumulator, then add the number at address v to the number at address u and store the sum in the accumulator." Provided that the control unit was suitably constructed, an alternate interpretation might be "Add the number at address v to the number at address u and store the sum at address u."

There are also computers that use *three-address* and *four-address* instruction formats. Three addresses, u, v, w, are used in such instructions as "Add the number at address u to the number at address v and store the sum at address w." A fourth address is used in some computers as the address of the next instruction. This relieves the programmer of the necessity to locate instructions in sequence.

It should be kept in mind that not all instructions require use of the address portion, and any integer placed there will be ignored by these instructions. Other instructions make use of the address part of the instruction, but for some purpose other than denoting the addresses of storage locations.

The Program Control Register

Once it has been determined that a given sequence of digits in storage is to be interpreted as an instruction word, the control unit causes transfer of the

†The accumulator and Q register are special arithmetic registers. See Section 1.11 for a description.

:art of a program the control unit places in the program address
: storage address of the first instruction to be executed in the pro-
n, when this instruction is fetched from storage and has under-
hering by the program control register, the content of the pro-
ess register is incremented by a fixed amount; this results in its
the next higher address above that of the initial instruction.
cution of the initial instruction is complete, control is trans-
he fetch cycle, whose job is to locate the instruction digits stored
lress contained in the program address register and to transfer
e program control register as the next instruction to be executed.
it that the current instruction is a jump instruction and the instruc-
executed next is located elsewhere than at the next higher address,
it instruction itself resets the program address register to the cor-
ss of the next instruction.
this manner that, after the initial instruction in the program has
uted, the control unit can determine the sequence of storage
for obtaining succeeding instructions in the program. The con-
is able to do this because the sequence is defined by the stored
ns themselves.
mary, the function of the control unit is to (a) fetch an instruction
ecified location in storage, (b) perform the operation indicated by the
n on the operands specified by the instruction, and (c) determine
ss of the location from which the next instruction can be obtained.
of executing the current instruction and fetching the next instruc-
petitively performed until a current instruction causes the comput-
). This statement of course implies that there is a stored list of in-
s and a stored group of operands on which the instructions are to

1.11   Arithmetic

function of the arithmetic unit to perform the fundamental arith-
erations and a variety of logical operations, the exact number and
ending on the particular computer. The logical operations would
include the ability to compare numbers, test signs, shift digits
ne arithmetic registers, form logical products, and so on.
ler to be able to carry out its repertoire of arithmetic and logical
ns the arithmetic unit of the computer is provided with a set of
irithmetic registers for the storage of the operands as well as inter-
and final results of its operations. The most important of these reg-
the *accumulator*, which, in an addition or subtraction, holds the
rand before the operation and the sum or difference after the opera-
augment the function of the accumulator and permit it to perform

word to a special control register designed to s
execution. Although the function of this regis
puters, the name assigned to it will vary w
A commonly used name is *program control re*
when the instruction word is stored in this regi
instruction digits is deciphered. The particular
the operation to be performed is decoded, and
activate the proper circuits in the arithmetic
specified operation. The remaining digits of the
in order to arrange for transmission of opera
specified in the address portion of the instructio
vice versa.

We have indicated briefly how the program c
itiate the necessary events that result in the prop
tion. We turn now to the other main function
viding the proper sequence in which instruction
done in the fetch cycle of operation.

The Fetch Cycle

The programmer is responsible for determining th
of instructions are to be executed when he writes
the proper order of execution, instructions are ge
in adjacent storage locations. The computer is con
the sequence specified by the program. *A cardina*
ming is that instructions are to be executed sequenti
they occur) unless indicated otherwise by the prese
in the program. This implies a class of so-called "ju
are found in every repertoire of machine-language
instruction is, in effect, a command to ignore the se
structions and to take some command other tha
following as the next instruction to be performed. T
ditional, or it may be predicated upon the outcome
dition.

The Program Address Register

In addition to executing the current instruction,
vides the facility for determining what sequence of d
interpreted as the next instruction to be executed. T
plished by means of a special control register whose
address of that storage register which contains the
performed. The specific name assigned to this registe
of computer, but it is commonly referred to as the *pr*
This register functions primarily as a counter, as will

At the
register th
gram. Th
gone deci
gram add
containin
When ex
ferred to
at the ad
them to t
In the eve
tion to be
the curre
rect addi

It is in
been exe
addresses
trol unit
instructi

In sun
from a s
instructi
the addr
The cycl
tion is r
er to sto
structio
operate.

It is the
metic o
kind de
typically
within

In or
operati
special
mediat
isters i
first op
tion. T

repeated additions and subtractions, as are required for multiplication and division, there will usually be some auxiliary arithmetic registers, such as a Q register, for holding products and quotients.

In executing an arithmetic or logical instruction, the control unit obtains the operands from storage locations specified in the address portion of the instruction and makes them available to the arithmetic registers. Control also selects an appropriate subset of the total operations that the arithmetic unit can perform on digits stored in its registers, and causes the selected operations to be performed sequentially in a manner that produces the end result of the instruction.

Problems

1.1 Describe three practical problems arising in industry for which solutions might be obtained by use of finite, discrete methods of analysis. Could the methods of solution be programmed?

1.2 What is the basic difference between a digital computer and an analog computer?

1.3 Explain the concept of a stored-program digital computer. Why is it considered one of the most significant advances ever made in the design of digital computers?

1.4 Name the basic capabilities that have been ascribed to general-purpose digital computers.

1.5 What are the classical subsystems of a digital computer?

1.6 In what ways does a register differ from a word?

1.7 Name the three basic properties possessed by all storage registers. Explain the statement that programming would be virtually impossible without these properties.

1.8 Is (04617) = 04617 contradictory? Explain.

1.9 What are the basic components of an instruction word? Can an instruction word contain its own address in the address portion of the word?

1.10 What is the minimum number of instructions that would be needed to add three numbers using a single-address computer? Using a two-address computer?

1.11 How does the control unit of a computer distinguish a sequence of digits which is an instruction and one which is an operand?

1.12 In what sense is the order in which the control unit executes a series of instructions defined by the stored instructions themselves? Explain.

References

1. PHISTER, MONTGOMERY, *Logical Design of Digital Computers.* New York. John Wiley and Sons, Inc., 1958.

2. RICHARDS, R. K., *Arithmetic Operations in Digital Computers.* Princeton, N. J.: D. Van Nostrand, Inc., 1955.

3. SCHMIDT, R. N. and W. E. MEYERS, *Electronic Business Data Processing.* New York: Holt Rinehart and Winston, Inc., 1963.

4. STEIN, M. L. , and W. D. MUNRO, *Computer Programming: A Mixed Language Approach.* New York: Academic Press Inc., 1964.

5. WARFIELD, J. N., *Principles of Logic Design.* Boston: Ginn and Company, 1963.

2

Number Systems and Codes

2.1 Numbers and Counting

Numbers have long played an important role in human affairs. Numerical computations are essential for trade and commerce, for bookkeeping and accounting, for scientific investigation, and for many other purposes. One of the earliest methods of counting, still practiced today, is based on the *tally system* whereby any number N is expressed by a row of N marks or tallies. However, this system has the disadvantage of being extremely unwieldy for expressing large numbers and does not lend itself well to arithmetic operations.

Another method of counting, known to primitive man, consists of matching the objects to be counted with some familiar set of objects — such as fingers, toes, small sticks, or stones — that serve as counters. When the number of objects being counted is in excess of those in the basic counting group, the additional objects are accounted for by matching afresh with the basic counting group until it is once more exhausted, and so on. From this method of counting, known as multiplicative counting, has developed a type of number systems called *positional*. Positional systems afford a compact and reasonably convenient notation for expressing arbitrarily large numbers, and more important, the execution of arithmetic operations and computations in such systems becomes relatively simple.

When a positional notation system is used, the value of each digit in the number is determined by the digit, the position of the digit in the number, and the *base* or *radix* of the number representation system. The radix or base is defined as the number of different digits which can occur in a given position in the number. In the decimal system the base is equal to 10. Other number systems using positional notation have other bases. For instance, the binary number system with a base 2, has only two digits that can occur in each position in any binary number. These are the digits 0 and 1.

An outstanding example of a positional number system in widespread use today is, of course, the base 10 or *decimal* system. This system, which is familiar to everyone, has many advantages — including the ease with which arithmetic operations are performed. This advantage is characteristic of positional number systems generally, and is not due to any special property of decimal numbers. Number systems other than base 10 offer the same advantage, but they are less familiar to us. Because of the on-off nature of the physical devices used in computers, it is not surprising that the positional number system with base 2 should prove highly convenient for the purposes of computer-oriented computation. This chapter will be devoted to a consideration of some of the fundamental concepts underlying number systems, with particular attention directed to binary and octal systems.

2.2   *Positional Notation*

In the decimal system numbers are represented as sums of powers of 10, each power weighted by an integer between zero and nine inclusive. For example,

$$682 = 6 \times 10^2 + 8 \times 10^1 + 2 \times 10^0$$

Such numbers are said to be expressed in a number system with base 10 because there are ten basic digits $(0,1,2, \ldots, 9)$ from which the number system is formulated. This manner of representing numbers as sums of weighted powers of 10 is an instance of *positional notation*. Its name derives from the fact that each digit designates a value which depends in part on the position it occupies in the number representation. For example, in the three decimal numbers 682, 628, and 286, the digit 2 signifies respectively 2, 2×10, and 2×100.

Generally, any positive integer $N = a_n a_{n-1} \ldots a_2 a_1 a_0$ can be represented in the decimal system by

$$a_n a_{n-1} \ldots a_2 a_1 a_0 = a_n \times 10^n + a_{n-1} \times 10^{n-1}$$
$$+ \cdots + a_2 \times 10^2 + a_1 \times 10^1 + a_0 \times 10^0$$

where $0 \leq a_i \leq 9$.

The same principle applies with equal validity to decimal fractions by using negative powers of ten. Thus

$$0.139 = 1 \times 10^{-1} + 3 \times 10^{-2} + 9 \times 10^{-3}$$

and any decimal fraction $M = 0.a_{-1}a_{-2} \ldots a_{-m+1} a_{-m}$ is expressible as

$$0.a_{-1}a_{-2} \ldots a_{-m+1} a_{-m} = a_{-1} \times 10^{-1} + a_{-2} \times 10^{-2}$$
$$+ \cdots + a_{-m+1} \times 10^{-m+1} + a_{-m} \times 10^{-m}$$

where $0 \leq a_{-i} \leq 9$.

The general decimal number $N + M$ thus becomes

$$a_n a_{n-1} \ldots a_2 a_1 a_0 \cdot a_{-1}a_{-2} \ldots a_{-m+1} a_{-m} = \sum_{i=-m}^{n} a_i \times 10^i \qquad (0 \leq a_i \leq 9)$$

It is possible to express any number N in a system using any base b. We shall follow the convention of writing such a number as N_b, where the subscript b designates the base of the system in which the number is expressed. The subscript b shall be omitted whenever the context makes clear the base that is being used. The convention of always expressing b in base 10 will be followed.

Thus the general formula for expressing

$$N_b = a_n a_{n-1} \ldots a_2 a_1 a_0 \cdot a_{-1}a_{-2} \ldots a_{-m}$$

is given by

$$N_b = a_n \times b^n + a_{n-1} \times b^{n-1} + \cdots + a_2 \times b^2 + a_1 \times b^1$$
$$+ a_0 \times b^0 + a_{-1} \times b^{-1} + \cdots + a_{-m+1} \times b^{-m+1} + a_{-m} \times b^{-m}$$

$$N_b = \sum_{i=-m}^{n} a_i \times b^i$$

where b is any integer greater than 1, and $0 \leq a_i \leq b - 1$.

The only values of the base b that we shall have occasion to consider are 10, 8, and 2. The number systems that use these bases are called decimal, octal, and binary, respectively.

2.3 The Binary System

A major use of computers involves the capability to perform extensive numerical computations. Because of the on-off nature of many of the electronic components, the design of digital computers is considerably simplified if the binary number system is used to represent numbers and the arithmetical operations are carried out using binary arithmetic. A discussion of binary arithmetic is outside the aims of this text and will not be included here.

In the binary number system each number is represented by means of a sequence of the digits 0 and 1. As an example, let us consider the binary number $(101101)_2$ and express it in expanded form as a sum of powers of 2, each power weighted by the digit 0 or 1.† Thus we have

$$(101101)_2 = 1 \times 2^5 + 0 \times 2^4 + 1 \times 2^3 + 1 \times 2^2 + 0 \times 2^1 + 1 \times 2^0$$

Binary fractions can be expressed similarly by using negative powers of 2. The first digit to the right of the binary point indicates the number of halves (2^{-1}), the next digit indicates the number of quarters (2^{-2}), the following digit represents the number of eighths (2^{-3}), and so on. Thus

$$(0.1011)_2 = 1 \times 2^{-1} + 0 \times 2^{-2} + 1 \times 2^{-3} + 1 \times 2^{-4}$$

The general binary number $(a_n a_{n-1} \ldots a_1 a_0 \cdot a_{-1} a_{-2} \ldots a_{-m})$ becomes

$$a_n \times 2^n + a_{n-1} \times 2^{n-1} + \cdots + a_1 \times 2^1 + a_0 \times 2^0$$
$$+ a_{-1} \times 2^{-1} + a_{-2} \times 2^{-2} + \cdots + a_{-m} \times 2^{-m}$$

$$\sum_{i=-m}^{n} a_i \times 2^i \qquad a_i = \{0, 1\}$$

2.4   The Octal System

A disadvantage of the binary system is that lengthy sequences of zeros and ones are required if one is to express large numbers in the system. Moreover, human beings generally find it awkward to manipulate such expressions. Fortunately, however, there is a quick and speedy way to convert binary numbers to numbers that are less cumbersome by using the octal system. This explains the interest in octal numbers among programmers who code in binary machine languages. The method of binary-to-octal conversion is presented in Section 2.5.

The octal system, which uses a base of 8, represents numbers by means of the digits 0,1,2,3,4,5,6,7. In an octal number, each digit represents a multiple of a power of eight and the number itself represents the sum of such multiples. The first digit to the left of the octal point represents the number of units (8^0), the next digit indicates the multiples of eight (8^1), the following digit represents the number of sixty-fours (8^2), and so on. For example, the octal number 5076 may be expressed as follows:

$$(5076)_8 = 5 \times 8^3 + 0 \times 8^2 + 7 \times 8^1 + 6 \times 8^0$$

The general form of expansion for any octal number

$$a_n a_{n-1} \ldots a_1 a_0 \cdot a_{-1} a_{-2} \ldots a_{-m}$$

†It is common practice when using several bases to append the particular base associated with a given number as a subscript. Thus, $(10110)_2$ is binary 10110, $(546)_{10}$ is decimal 546, and so on.

where the a_i has admissible values $0,1,2,3,4,5,6,7$, is given as follows:

$$a_n \times 8^n + a_{n-1} \times 8^{n-1} + \cdots + a_1 \times 8^1 + a_0 \times 8^0$$
$$+ a_{-1} \times 8^{-1} + a_{-2} \times 8^{-2} + \cdots + a_{-m} \times 8^{-m}$$

$$\sum_{i=-m}^{n} a_i \times 8^i \quad a_i = \{0,1,\ldots,7\}$$

The representation in binary, octal, and decimal of the integers from zero to twenty appears in Table 2.1.

TABLE 2.1   Integers in Binary, Octal, and Decimal Form

Base 2	Base 8	Base 10	Base 2	Base 8	Base 10
0	0	0	1010	12	10
1	1	1	1011	13	11
10	2	2	1100	14	12
11	3	3	1101	15	13
100	4	4	1110	16	14
101	5	5	1111	17	15
110	6	6	10000	20	16
111	7	7	10001	21	17
1000	10	8	10010	22	18
1001	11	9	10011	23	19
			10100	24	20

CONVERSION SCHEMES

In order to make use of different positional number systems it is necessary to be able to convert a number expressed in one base into the correct representation of the number in another base. Several techniques for accomplishing this will now be considered. The procedure that is described in Section 2.8 is a general method for converting from an arbitrary base b_1 to another arbitrary base b_2. It has the added merit that only decimal arithmetic is required in carrying out the conversion process.

2.5   Binary-to-Octal Conversion

Binary-to-octal conversion is based on a very simple relationship between base 2 numbers and base 8 numbers. This depends upon the fact that $2^3 = 8$. From Table 2.1 we see that the following correspondence exists between groups of three binary digits (bits)† and octal digits:

Binary	000	001	010	011	100	101	110	111
Octal	0	1	2	3	4	5	6	7

†The word *bit* is commonly used as a contraction for *binary digit*.

Thus it is evident that if a binary number is separated into groups of three digits, the resulting decimal value of each group cannot exceed 7. Since the octal system uses the digits 0 through 7 only, the value of each group of three binary digits will be the corresponding octal representation.

To convert any binary number to octal form, the binary digits are taken in groups of three in each direction starting at the binary point and are expressed as appropriate octal digits to give the corresponding octal number. For example, 110010111 in binary form is equivalent to 627 in octal form, and 10101.1011 in binary form corresponds to 25.54 in octal form. It is equally easy to convert octal numbers to binary notation. The reverse of this procedure is then followed; that is, each octal integer is converted to three binary digits.

Because the conversion between octal and binary is so simple, many programmers find it useful to treat the octal expression as a convenient shorthand for the corresponding binary number.

2.6   Binary/Octal-to-Decimal Conversion

Conversion of numbers from an arbitrary base b_1 to the decimal system is carried out by expanding the numbers as sums of weighted powers of base b_1 (see Section 2.2). To obtain the decimal equivalents of such numbers one simply adds up the terms of each expansion using decimal arithmetic.

Binary-to-decimal conversion may be carried out by expansion in powers of two. Thus

$$(101110.1011)_2 = 1 \times 2^5 + 0 \times 2^4 + 1 \times 2^3 + 1 \times 2^2 + 1 \times 2^1$$
$$+ 0 \times 2^0 + 1 \times 2^{-1} + 0 \times 2^{-2} + 1 \times 2^{-3} + 1 \times 2^{-4}$$

$$= 32 + 0 + 8 + 4 + 2 + 0 + \frac{1}{2} + 0 + \frac{1}{8} + \frac{1}{16}$$

$$= 46\frac{11}{16}$$

$$= 46.6875$$

Octal-to-decimal conversion is carried out in a similar fashion by expansion in powers of eight. Thus

$$(5076)_8 = 5 \times 8^3 + 0 \times 8^2 + 7 \times 8^1 + 6 \times 8^0$$

$$= 2560 + 0 + 56 + 6$$

$$= 2622$$

Because of the simplicity of binary-octal conversion it is often more convenient, when converting binary numbers to decimal, to convert first from binary to octal, and then from octal to decimal. For example, the binary number 101110.1011 in the preceding example is readily seen to be equivalent to the octal number 56.54. Conversion of this number to decimal yields

$$(56.54)_8 = 5 \times 8^1 + 6 \times 8^0 + 5 \times 8^{-1} + 4 \times 8^{-2}$$

$$= 40 + 6 + \frac{5}{8} + \frac{4}{64} = 46\frac{11}{16}$$

$$= 46.6875$$

This procedure illustrates that the computation involved in the conversion of an octal number to decimal form is roughly a third of that involved in converting the equivalent binary form to decimal.

2.7   *Decimal-to-Binary/Octal Conversion*

In converting from the decimal system to a number system with an arbitrary base b_1, the integer (whole) and fractional parts of the decimal number are converted separately. First, consider the portion to the left of the decimal point. The general conversion procedure is to divide the integer part of the decimal number to be converted by b_1, thus obtaining a quotient and a remainder. The remainder, call it r_0, is the *least significant (rightmost)* digit of the integer part of the required number N_{b_1}. This quotient is then divided by b_1, yielding a new quotient and a new remainder, r_1. This process is continued until a zero quotient is obtained, yielding a final remainder r_n. The result of the conversion is given by

$$r_n r_{n-1} \ldots r_2 r_1 r_0$$

which represents the integer part of the required number N_{b_1}.

Now consider the portion of the decimal number to the right of the decimal point. The general conversion procedure here is to multiply the fractional part of the decimal number by b_1. The resulting product consists of an integer part, call it p_{-1}, and a fractional part, call it f_{-1}. Then p_{-1} is the *most significant (leftmost)* digit of the fractional part of the required number N_{b_1}. The next most significant digit is formed by multiplying f_{-1} by b_1 to obtain a new product consisting of an integer part p_{-2} and a fractional part f_{-2}. Remaining digits are formed by repeating this process. The process may or may not terminate and is repeated either until f_{-m} becomes 0 or until a desired number of digits is reached. The result of the conversion is given by

$$p_{-1} p_{-2} \ldots p_m$$

which represents the fractional part of the required number N_{b_1}.

Decimal-to-binary conversion is carried out by dividing the integer part of the decimal number by 2 successively and multiplying the fractional part by 2 successively in accordance with the foregoing procedures. A convenient form for carrying out the conversion is illustrated in the following example.

EXAMPLE 1

Convert the decimal number 46.6875 to binary form. The conversion is done in two stages.

1. Computation for conversion of the integer part of the decimal number is given as follows:

$$
\begin{array}{ll}
2)\underline{46} & \text{(remainder)} \\
2)\underline{23} & 0 = r_0 \\
2)\underline{11} & 1 = r_1 \\
2)\underline{5} & 1 = r_2 \\
2)\underline{2} & 1 = r_3 \\
2)\underline{1} & 0 = r_4 \\
0 & 1 = r_5
\end{array}
$$

Thus decimal 46 is equivalent to binary 101110.

2. Computation for conversion of the fractional part, 0.6875, is as follows:

$$
\begin{array}{ll}
0.6875 \times 2 = \underline{1}.3750 & p_{-1} = 1 \\
0.3750 \times 2 = \underline{0}.7500 & p_{-2} = 0 \\
0.7500 \times 2 = \underline{1}.5000 & p_{-3} = 1 \\
0.5000 \times 2 = \underline{1}.0000 & p_{-4} = 1
\end{array}
$$

The decimal fraction 0.6875 is thus seen to be equivalent to the binary fraction 0.1011. Combining the two results above yields

$$(46.6875)_{10} = (101110.1011)_2$$

In a similar fashion, decimal-to-octal conversion involves a series of divisions in which each successive quotient is divided by eight (the base of the octal system), and a series of multiplications in which each successive product is multiplied by eight. The remainders of each division then comprise the integer part of the octal number and the integer parts of the successive products comprise the fractional part of the octal number.

EXAMPLE 2

Convert the decimal number 46.6875 to octal form.

1. Computation for conversion of the integer part of the number to octal is given below:

$$8)\underline{46} \quad \text{(remainder)}$$

$$8)\underline{5} \qquad 6 = r_0$$

$$0 \qquad 5 = r_1$$

Decimal 46 is thus equivalent to octal 56.

2. Conversion of the decimal fraction 0.6875 to octal proceeds as follows:

$$0.6875 \times 8 = \underline{5}.5000 \quad p_{-1} = 5$$

$$0.5000 \times 8 = \underline{4}.0000 \quad p_{-2} = 4$$

Decimal 0.6875 is thus equivalent to octal 0.54. Hence

$$(46.6875)_{10} = (56.54)_8$$

The conversion of a fraction from one base to another does not always terminate. This will be true whenever it is not possible to represent the fraction exactly in the new base with a finite number of digits. An example of a process which fails to terminate is the conversion of the decimal fraction 0.3 to octal. The conversion of this fraction expressed to six octal places is shown below:

$$0.3 \times 8 = \underline{2}.4$$

$$0.4 \times 8 = \underline{3}.2$$

$$0.2 \times 8 = \underline{1}.6$$

$$0.6 \times 8 = \underline{4}.8$$

$$0.8 \times 8 = \underline{6}.4$$

$$0.4 \times 8 = \underline{3}.2$$

Hence 0.231463 represents an approximation to six octal places of the decimal fraction 0.3.

2.8 A General Conversion Procedure

It is possible to convert between any two arbitrary bases using only decimal arithmetic. The procedure makes use of the conversion methods described in Sections 2.6 and 2.7, and is as follows: To convert a given number from an arbitrary base b_1 to another arbitrary base b_2, first convert the number to its equivalent decimal form by the method of expansion, and then convert the resulting decimal expression to base b_2 by the method of successive divisions and multiplications. Only decimal arithmetic is required in the conversion process.

EXAMPLE

Convert the number $(402.361)_7$ to base 4.

The conversion is done in two steps. First, the number is converted to decimal form by expansion in powers of 7:

$$(402.361)_7 = 4 \times 7^2 + 0 \times 7^1 + 2 \times 7^0 + 3 \times 7^{-1} + 6 \times 7^{-2} + 1 \times 7^{-3}$$

$$= 196 + 0 + 2 + \frac{3}{7} + \frac{6}{49} + \frac{1}{343}$$

$$\approx 198.554$$

The decimal number 198.554 is then converted to base 4 by dividing the integer part of the decimal number by 4 successively and multiplying the fractional part by 4 successively in the following manner:

$$4\overline{)198} \qquad \text{(remainder)} \qquad 0.554 \times 4 = \underline{2}.216$$

$$4\overline{)49} \qquad\qquad 2 \qquad\qquad 0.216 \times 4 = \underline{0}.864$$

$$4\overline{)12} \qquad\qquad 1 \qquad\qquad 0.864 \times 4 = \underline{3}.456$$

$$4\overline{)3} \qquad\qquad 0$$

$$0 \qquad\qquad 3$$

Hence

$$(402.361)_7 \approx (198.554)_{10} \approx (3012.203)_4$$

CODING

2.9   Coded Binary Systems

Because of the on-off nature of the switching devices used in computers, there is an advantage in representing numbers in binary form inside the computer and using binary arithmetic to carry out arithmetic operations. However, since the decimal number system is more familiar and more widely used than the binary system, many computers are designed to accept data expressed in a decimal form and to convert this data automatically to a binary form. Computers that use the decimal number system for the machine coding of information are known as "decimal" computers, in contrast to "binary" computers, which require machine coding of information in binary or octal form.

There are several ways to represent decimal numbers in binary form. One way is to use the binary number system (discussed in Section 2.3) and convert the decimal number *as a whole* into its equivalent binary form. Thus the decimal number 348 translates into the binary number 101011100. This method of using the binary system to represent decimal numbers in binary form is often called *straight binary coding*. It is the method of conversion used in binary computers.

Another way to represent decimal numbers in binary form, which avoids the task of converting the number as a whole into binary, is to represent each *decimal digit* by a code of four (or more) binary digits. There are many such codes available to represent decimal digits. These representations, known as *binary-coded decimal schemes*, require at least four binary digits to represent all the integers from zero to nine inclusive. A unique combination of the binary digits is used to represent each decimal digit; so if four binary digits are used then there will be six out of the sixteen possible combinations that are unused. The six unused combinations may be used in an extended code to represent special characters, such as a minus sign or a symbol representing an arithmetic operation.

In general, any arbitrary assignment of combinations of binary digits to decimal digits can be made provided that every integer from zero to nine is uniquely represented; therefore it is possible to construct many different binary decimal codes in this manner. The conversion of each digit in a decimal number into a binary-coded decimal digit is simpler than that from decimal numbers to binary numbers (as required in straight binary coding), but it should be noted that this advantage is gained at the cost of forming longer numbers, since more bits are required in the conversion. Moreover, only a very few of the many possible binary decimal codes have ever been used in any computer, since the rules for doing arithmetic based on binary-coded decimal numbers are usually much more complicated than the rules of ordinary binary arithmetic.

Two of the more common binary-coded decimal (BCD) codes are the *8-4-2-1* and *excess-three* codes. In 8-4-2-1 coding the assignment of binary digits to decimal digits is such that each set of four binary digits represents the straightforward binary equivalent of the corresponding decimal digit. Under this assignment the digit positions in the binary representation correspond to successive powers of two. For this reason the code is referred to as 8-4-2-1 code. The code is shown in Table 2.2. Since four binary digits are needed to represent each decimal digit, exactly four times as many digits will be required in the conversion of a decimal number. The decimal number 56 would be represented in 8-4-2-1 coding as 01010110, and the decimal 937 would be represented as 100100110111.

TABLE 2.2 Common Binary Codes

Decimal Digits	Straight Binary Code	8-4-2-1 BCD Code	Excess-Three BCD Code
0	0	0000	0011
1	1	0001	0100
2	10	0010	0101
3	11	0011	0110
4	100	0100	0111
5	101	0101	1000
6	110	0110	1001
7	111	0111	1010
8	1000	1000	1011
9	1001	1001	1100

The excess-three (XS-3) code is obtained from the 8-4-2-1 code by adding to each 8-4-2-1 representation of the decimal digits the binary value of a decimal 3, which is 0011, to form the corresponding XS-3 representation. This code is shown in Table 2.2. The decimal number 56 would be represented as 10001001, and the decimal number 937 would be represented as 110001101010.

In both 8-4-2-1 and XS-3 coding odd and even numbers can be distinguished by reference to the right-most digit. Also, XS-3 coding has the interesting property that representation of the 9's complement of a given decimal number is formed by complementing the corresponding XS-3 representation of the original decimal number. Thus the 9's complement of 56, namely 43, would be represented as the complement of 10001001, or 01110110. This property is useful in carrying out arithmetic operations based on excess-three representation.

An extra binary digit, called a *parity bit*, is often used in the coding of each decimal digit to determine whether the computer is malfunctioning by gaining or losing a binary digit. The parity bit is automatically assigned a value 0 or 1 so that the total number of 1's in each binary-coded decimal digit is even or odd depending upon the parity rule used. The computer is designed to test the total number of 1's in a binary-coded decimal digit and to signal an error condition if the total number is not odd (or even depending upon the parity rule used). Further discussion of codes for parity checking as well as for error detection and correction is beyond the scope of this text.

2.10 Scientific Notation and Floating-Point Numbers

In scientific and engineering applications it is common to encounter operations on numbers that may vary widely in magnitude. If a computer is used and if the results are to be meaningful, several factors should be considered. One concerns the *precision* with which numbers can be expressed and manipulated conveniently inside a computer. Design considerations place limits on the size of numbers which can be stored by computers. How then is the computer to handle data outside the range of these limits? Second, for results to be *accurate* it is desirable to retain as many significant digits as possible during the calculations. And third, to insure *correct* calculations, the decimal points of all numbers should be properly aligned for any given calculation.

Scaling

A convenient way to overcome the above difficulties is to use *scaling* during a calculation. For example, consider the following four sums:

5461000.0	54.61	0.5461	0.0005461
1327000.0	13.27	0.1327	0.0001327
6788000.0	67.88	0.6788	0.0006788

Eight places for decimal digits are required to hold all these numbers in the manner shown. But suppose only a maximum of *four* places were available for holding decimal digits. By scaling, that is, by applying a *scale factor*— a power of ten — to each number, we may treat these sums as follows:

0.5461×10^7	0.5461×10^2	0.5461×10^0	0.5461×10^{-3}
0.1327×10^7	0.1327×10^2	0.1327×10^0	0.1327×10^{-3}
0.6788×10^7	0.6788×10^2	0.6788×10^0	0.6788×10^{-3}

In this form four places are sufficient to treat the significant figures without rounding them off. It is necessary to provide for storage of the scale exponents $7, 2, 0, -3$. But since the base of the exponent is always 10, it need not be stored.

To add two numbers, they are adjusted until their scale exponents are equal, then the significant digits are added and their sum is stored as well as the adjusted scale exponent. To multiply, the two strings of significant digits are multiplied and their scale exponents are added to obtain a product. To divide, the significant digits of the dividend are divided by the significant digits of the divisor to give the significant digits of the quotient. The scale exponent of the quotient is obtained by subtracting the scale exponent of the divisor from the scale exponent of the dividend.

To preserve the maximum number of significant digits, numbers are often scaled so that the most significant nonzero digit of the number appears immediately to the right of the decimal point after scaling. Such numbers are said to be *normalized*. The second set of numbers in the foregoing example are all in normalized form. Although numbers may be initially normalized by scaling, the results of calculations are not necessarily normalized. For example,

$$
\begin{array}{r}
0.1805 \\
-0.1003 \\
\hline
0.0802
\end{array}
$$

Floating-Point Numbers

Scaling thus affords a convenient way of using a computer to carry out operations on numbers that may vary widely in magnitude. However, in complicated calculations the job of scaling can be a very time-consuming and laborious task. Most large-scale digital computers are equipped to perform scaling operations automatically during computation. For this purpose, numbers may be expressed in a special format similar to the normalized form.

Two types of arithmetic are commonly employed in computers. *Integer* (or *fixed-point*) arithmetic is used when arithmetic operations are carried out on numbers that are restricted to integer values only. When calculations are performed on numbers which take decimal values the arithmetic is called *floating-point*.

The notation used in floating-point arithmetic to represent numbers internally in the computer is basically an adaptation of the scientific notation used widely today. In scientific work, numbers of very large or very small magnitude are usually expressed as normalized fractions times a power of ten. That is, the number is scaled so that the decimal point is placed immediately to the left of the most significant nonzero digit. The fraction is called the *mantissa*, and the power of 10, used to indicate the number of places the decimal point was shifted, is called the *characteristic*.

Correspondingly, a *floating-point* number contains two parts: the digits of the number, called the *mantissa*, and the exponent expressed as a two-digit *characteristic*. The size of the mantissa varies among computers. If a number in a floating point operation is represented in scientific notation as

$$0.yyyyyyyy \times 10^{ww}$$

a typical format for representing the number in floating point form inside the computer is shown in Fig. 2.1. Here C represents the characteristic and

$$\underbrace{YYYYYYY}_{M} \quad \underbrace{WW}_{C}$$

FIGURE 2.1 Typical format of a floating point number.

M the mantissa. The form of the original number is $M \times 10^C$. The sign of the original number is always associated with the mantissa, and suitable provision for it should be made in the format. Similarly, provision must be made for expressing the sign of the exponent. A common technique is to add 50 to the exponent ww to obtain the characteristic WW. By adding this amount to all exponents, the two digits WW can represent the range of numbers from 10^{-50} to 10^{49}, and a sign for the exponent need not be stored. Table 2.3 illustrates the conversion of numbers from ordinary decimal notation to the floating point form shown in Fig. 2.1.

TABLE 2.3   Conversion of Decimal Numbers to Floating-Point Form

Number	Normalized	Mantissa Size (digits)	Floating Point Form
378.92561	0.37892561×10^3	8	3789256153
−6783.9	$−0.67839 \times 10^4$	8	−6783900054[a]
−0.00056733	$−0.56733 \times 10^{-3}$	5	−5673347
−0.43987652	$−0.43987652 \times 10^0$	5	−4398750[b]
1.0	0.1×10^1	4	100051[a]
$−9.43 \times 10^{-14}$	$−0.943 \times 10^{-13}$	4	−943037[a]

[a] Low-order zeros added to increase mantissa to desired length.
[b] Mantissa truncated to reduce size to desired length.

In addition to the advantages of uniformity inherent in scientific notation, the use of floating-point numbers in a calculation eliminates the necessity of analyzing operations to determine the position of the decimal point in intermediate and final results, since the decimal point is always immediately to the left of the high-order (most significant) digit in the mantissa.

2.11   Alphabetic Coding

It is a common practice in business-data processing — where the task is often as much editing, translating, and manipulating nonnumerical data as it is performing numerical calculations — to require the use of alphabetic or letter symbols. Alphabetic characters are more difficult to represent in binary form since they are more numerous than decimal digits — twenty-six letters and a dozen or so special characters — and there are no easy conversion schemes, such as the method of successive divisions and multiplications, for representing them in binary form. Fortunately, however, binary decimal codes are well suited for this purpose and can be easily adapted to encode alphabetic characters. Information that may consist of both decimal numbers and alphabetic characters is sometimes called *alphameric* information. This information is usually encoded in binary form either by expanding the number of binary digits used in a binary decimal code or by using two decimal digits to represent an alphameric character.

If the first approach is followed, a binary-coded decimal representation in which four binary digits represent sixteen characters can be extended to six binary digits to represent 2^6 or 64 characters. Using six binary digits for each character makes it possible to represent the twenty-six letters of the alphabet, the decimal digits 0–9, and twenty-eight other special symbols such as punctuation marks, etc. A binary-coded decimal representation expanded in this manner would be known as a *binary-coded alphameric code*.

In the second approach two decimal digits are used to code alphameric characters. If a four-digit binary-coded decimal representation is used to represent each decimal digit, then one alphabetic character might be represented by a two-digit number. This is known as *double-numeric coding* or a *two-for-one* scheme. For example, "B" might be assigned the decimal number 42 and coded as 01000010 in 8-4-2-1 coding. When numbers are to be used, they too must be coded in this double digit representation: "0" might be assigned the decimal number 70 and coded as 01110000, "1" assigned the decimal number 71 and coded as 01110001, and so forth. Double-numeric coding is rather inefficient for alphameric characters because each character is represented by eight binary digits, whereas six binary digits are sufficient to represent 64 different characters. Also, use of this type of alphameric coding entails two modes of operation for entering and extracting data from the computer: a numeric mode for processing numerical data only and an alphameric mode for processing alphameric data. It is the programmer's responsibility to provide for the appropriate mode.

Problems

2.1 Convert the octal number 374 to binary form.

2.2 Convert the binary number 1101011.0011 to decimal form.

2.3 Convert the following octal numbers to decimal form:

     a) 2000   *b*) 51.622

2.4 Convert the following decimal numbers to octal form and binary form:

     a) 3046   *b*) 0.46875   *c*) 49.9375

2.5 Convert $(2043)_5$ to its equivalent form in the base-3 number system.

2.6 Convert $(1022)_3$ to its equivalent form in the base-7 number system.

2.7 Write the following numbers in scientific notation using a normalized mantissa:

     a) 0.000437   *b*) 43.7×10^{-9} *c*) 437.0×10^5

2.8 Write the following numbers in the normalized floating-point format described in the text, using a fixed mantissa size of five digits:

     a) 8.3   *b*) 0.006   *c*) 7.392×10^{-4} *d*) 684.5793

2.9 (*a*) Sum the following three numbers using ordinary decimal arithmetic. (*b*) Scale the numbers so that the exponents are all equal to 10^5 and the mantissas contain four significant digits. (*c*) Sum the numbers in scaled form and compare with the original sum. (*d*) Discuss the loss in accuracy from rounding off.

       0.000465
       69.7
      23498.82

2.10 Write the decimal number 1436 in the following binary-coded decimal systems:

a)   8-4-2-1   b)   excess-three

References

1. FLEGG, H. G., *Boolean Algebra and Its Application*. Glasgow: Blackie & Son, Ltd., 1964.

2. McCLUSKEY, E. J., JR., *Introduction to the Theory of Switching Circuits*. New York: McGraw-Hill, Inc., 1965.

3. ORE, OYSTEIN, *Number Theory and Its History*. New York: McGraw-Hill, Inc., 1948.

4. RICHARDS, R. K., *Arithmetic Operations in Digital Computers*. Princeton, N. J.: D. Van Nostrand, Inc., 1955.

3

Programming Digital Computers

This chapter serves as a general introduction to computer programming. Its purpose is to relate the discussion of the previous two chapters on the organization and operation of digital computers to the study of Fortran, which begins with the next chapter. Three important types of computer programming are considered: (*a*) machine-language programming, (*b*) symbolic programming, and (*c*) machine-independent programming. As these topics are discussed, the general nature of programming, and the role assigned therein to the computer, will become clearer. The order in which the above topics are discussed reflects two major innovations that have occurred in the programming field. The significance of these innovations is discussed in the sections on symbolic programming and machine-independent programming.

As implied by the name, machine-independent programming involves the use of computer languages that are designed to reflect the structure inherent in problems rather than the structure and organization of any computer. These languages are *problem-oriented* in the sense that they closely resemble the language and operations for solving problems from given problem areas. A major advantage problem-oriented languages offer over symbolic and machine languages is that programs written in them may, in principle, be run on any computer. In practice, variations among computers are reflected in these languages, causing them to be not as machine-independent as might be desired. Fortran is the most widely used problem-oriented language; it exists in the form of several different versions (dialects), which are available for use on different computers.

MACHINE LANGUAGE PROGRAMMING

In order for a computer to solve a problem there must be available a *language* for instructing the computer on how to obtain a solution. The language must be in terms in which the programmer can formulate a set of instructions that when executed by the computer will produce a solution. The language may be designed for a specific computer, in which case no other computer will be able to execute the instructions, or it may be of a more general type that can be used on a number of computers of different design. Languages of both kinds are called *computer languages* or *programming languages* and can be classified as belonging to one of the following three categories:

> Machine languages
> Symbolic languages
> Problem-oriented languages

Both machine and symbolic languages are programming languages that are *machine-dependent* in the sense that they are designed for use on computers of a specific design. Programs written in these languages can be executed only on computers of identical design.

Problem-oriented languages are *machine-independent;* theoretically, programs written in these languages may be executed on any computer. We say "theoretically" because two important yet related qualifications must be added in order to make the statement entirely correct. First, as noted in the introductory paragraphs, variations in the design of computers are reflected in problem-oriented languages. So that programs written in, say, version A of a problem-oriented language for computer X may not necessarily run on computer Y, which uses version B of the same language. Second, if programs written in a problem-oriented language are to be executed on a given computer, there must exist for that computer a translation *program*, called a *compiler*, which translates these programs into the machine language of that computer. This second consideration basically accounts for why there exist different versions of a problem-oriented language such as Fortran. A discussion of compilers must be deferred until after the topic of machine language programming is considered. We shall return to the subject in Section 3.12.

Before we turn to a discussion of machine language programming, one further general comment, related to the above remark, should be made. This concerns the basic role which machine language assumes in programming; namely, *programming computers would prove impossible without the existence of machine languages.* No program can be executed on a computer without its first being translated into the machine language of that computer. No matter what language the program is written in or how dissimilar that language is to machine language, there are no exceptions to this require-ment.

This statement does not imply that the programmer writing in Fortran, for example, must always convert his programs into machine language, for he does not — it is the function of the compiler to perform the conversion automatically for the programmer. What is implied is that the capabilities of a symbolic or problem-oriented language are necessarily determined by the capabilities inherent in machine language. To express the matter differ-ently, whatever can be accomplished by a program written in a problem-oriented language can be done by a program written in machine language. The converse statement is false, however. To be sure, writing programs in problem-oriented languages offers major advantages, some of which will be enumerated near the end of this chapter when the limitations of ma-chine language programming are discussed. There would be no purpose for the development of a language like Fortran if there were none. But the point to be made here is that such basic programming concepts as *loops*, *indexing*, and *the ability to call subroutines*† are present in languages like Fortran only because they have their counterparts in machine language programming. Thus, while it is possible to learn a machine-independent language like Fortran and to write programs in it without knowing any-thing about the structure and operation of digital computers, it nonetheless increases one's knowledge of the language to know how some of the basic ideas of the language are implemented in machine language. Indeed, without this understanding, some aspects of Fortran may appear strange and puzzling to the user. The remainder of this section is devoted to illus-trating basic programming concepts at the level of machine language pro-gramming.

3.1   Machine Languages

Associated with every digital computer is a repertoire of hardware instruc-tions that define the total set of operations the computer is capable of per-forming. It is this set of instructions that comprises the *machine language* of the computer.

Machine languages vary among computers depending on the design of the computer. Identical sets of machine instructions are seldom if ever found among them; nor is the same command (say, the machine language instruc-tion for addition) ever executed in the same way by computers of different design. This does not mean, however, that digital computers are not similar in their main operations. For they are, although they may differ in the de-sign and implementation of these operations. Thus some computers may

---

†A discussion of these concepts will be considered in later sections of the text.

employ an instruction format based on a single-address system, whereas a two-, three-, or perhaps four-address system may be used in other computers. Nonetheless, despite individual differences among machine languages, the total set of basic operations that these languages are capable of performing is much the same for all general-purpose digital computers.

Types of Machine Commands

The instructions comprising the machine language of a computer can be classified by the nature of the operations performed. A typical classification would include the following five types:

Internal data-transfer instructions
Arithmetic instructions
Program control instructions
Logical instructions
Input/output instructions

Data-transfer instructions move numbers between registers in the storage unit and the arithmetic unit. A typical operation performed by these instructions is to copy the content of one register and store it in a second register. This basic operation is made possible by virtue of the READ, WRITE, and ADDRESS properties common to all storage registers of a computer (see Section 1.9).

Arithmetic instructions perform the familiar operations of addition, subtraction, multiplication, and division.

Program control instructions cause a change of control in the program if certain conditions are satisfied. Typical of this type of instruction is the so-called jump instruction, which is a machine-language command to ignore the sequential order of the instructions in the program and to take some instruction other than the one immediately following as the next instruction to be performed. The jump may be unconditional, or it may be predicated upon the outcome of a test condition.

Logical instructions perform such operations as obtaining the logical sum or logical product of two binary numbers as well as operations in which the content of a register is shifted to the left or to the right by an indicated number of places. Logical instructions are useful for extracting a certain portion of a word from its storage location as well as for performing Boolean operations.

Input/output instructions move information between the input/output equipment and the internal storage of the computer.

Instruction Format

Every machine language instruction has associated with it an *operation* and one or more *operands*. As stored internally, each instruction consists of a sequence of binary or decimal digits, depending on whether the computer is a binary or decimal machine. As was pointed out in Section 1.10 the structure of a machine instruction is determined by the manner in which the sequence of digits is divided into subsets. One subset of digits represents the numerical code for the operation performed by the instruction, and the remaining digits generally specify the addresses or locations of the operands in storage. The subset of digits designating the operation is known as the *operation code* (or *op code*) of the instruction, and the remaining subsets of digits are commonly referred to as "addresses." The op code and address portions together comprise the *format* of the instruction word.† Instruction formats usually vary from computer to computer.

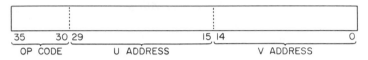

| 35 | 30 | 29 | 15 | 14 | 0 |
| OP CODE | | U ADDRESS | | V ADDRESS | |

FIGURE 3.1   Typical format of an instruction word for a two-address binary computer of fixed word length (36 bits).

A typical format of an instruction word is shown in Fig. 3.1. Here it is assumed that the format illustrates the structure of an instruction word for a two-address binary computer that operates upon words of a fixed length of 36 bits each. Bits 30–35 are used to designate the operation code of an instruction and bits 15–29 and 0–14 are employed to hold the addresses of the two operands specified by the instruction.

A Set of Typical Machine-Language Instructions

In order to provide an illustration of machine language programming, several machine commands of an actual computer are introduced. The computer chosen for this purpose is the Univac Scientific Computer 1105. In terms of instruction repertoire this computer is representative of most large-scale digital computers. Not only are many of its characteristics the same as those of other machines, but the format of its instruction words is typical of a two-address binary computer, which is a commonly used type. For the purpose intended here, only a narrow subset of the repertoire of machine language commands available to the 1105 programmer will be described. These include three data-transfer instructions, two arithmetic instructions, and three program control instructions, all of which are basic to many programs and suffice for many simple problems. The use of these instructions is illustrated later in several sample programs.

†In some instructions the format may include provisions for specialized features such as indexing and indirect addressing.

In the description of the instructions, which follow, this ordering of information is observed: first the numerical operation code expressed as an octal number is given; then the instruction name in full; then an abbreviated form for the instruction; and last, the description. The "u" and "v" appearing in the abbreviated form of the instruction refer to addresses of storage registers where the operands are stored. Bits 15–29 and 0–14 in the instruction word are used to designate "u" and "v" respectively. In the following descriptions the phrase "u address" is used as an abbreviation for "the register whose address is u"; "(u)" means "the content of the u address"; and "→" means "transmit," such as (u) → v or "transmit the content of the u address to the v address."

11   TRANSMIT POSITIVE   TP u v. Replace the content of the v address with the content of the u address. In other words, (u) → v.

15   TRANSMIT U ADDRESS   TU u v. Replace the 15 bits of (v), designated by bits 15 through 29 (see Fig. 3.1), with the corresponding bits of (u), leaving the remaining 21 bits of (v) undisturbed.

16   TRANSMIT V ADDRESS   TV u v. Replace the rightmost 15 bits of (v), designated by bits 0 through 14 (see Fig. 3.1), with the corresponding bits of (u), leaving the remaining 21 bits of (v) undisturbed.

21   REPLACE ADD   RA u v. Form in the accumulator AC† the sum of (u) and (v), then replace (u) with (AC). (u) + (v) → u.

35   ADD AND TRANSMIT   AT u v. Add (u) to (AC), then replace (v) with (AC). (AC) + (u) → v.

41   INDEX JUMP   IJ u v. Form in AC the difference (u) minus 1. If (AC) is negative, continue the present sequence of instructions by taking the instruction immediately following IJ u v as the next instruction. If (AC) is zero or positive, replace (u) with (AC), and take (v) as the next instruction.

45   MANUALLY SELECTIVE JUMP   MJ j v. If j = 0, take (v) as the next instruction. On the computer console are 3 two-way switches called MJ1, MJ2, and MJ3 respectively. If j = 1, 2, or 3, and the correspondingly numbered MJ switch on the console has been set, take (v) as the next instruction. If the switch is not set, take the instruction immediately following MJ j v as the next instruction.

57   PROGRAM STOP   PS u v. This instruction causes the computer to stop; the u and v addresses are meaningless insofar as stopping the program and may be used for other purposes.

The operations of the foregoing instructions are summarized in Table 3.1. Sample programs will be presented later in which we will make use of these

†AC is the symbolic name for the accumulator.

instructions. In order to provide an adequate understanding of these programs, the reader should refer to the table and familiarize himself with the operation of the instructions.

These instructions have the format shown in Fig. 3.1. A machine-language program consists of a series of machine instructions stored sequentially in adjacent storage registers. Thus, if a TRANSMIT POSITIVE instruction appears in a program and is stored in a given 36-bit register in storage, the content of that register might appear as shown in Fig. 3.2. Bits 30–35 comprise the operation code of the instruction, in this case 001001 which is the

FIGURE 3.2 Format of a TRANSMIT POSITIVE instruction.

binary equivalent of octal 11, the assigned numerical code for TRANSMIT POSITIVE. Bits 15–29 and 0–14 comprise, respectively, the u address and v address portions of the instruction. In Fig. 3.2 the u address is 000000111 000000, which is octal 00700, and the v address is 000000111000110, which is octal 00706. Since in the illustration the computer is a binary machine, all computer operations are performed on binary numbers, and the machine instructions themselves must be expressed as binary numbers in order for the computer to execute them. However, to facilitate the task of

TABLE 3.1 Summary of Sample Machine-Language Instructions

Op Code	Name	Format	Remarks
11	TRANSMIT POSITIVE	TP u v	$(u) \to v$
15	TRANSMIT U ADDRESS	TU u v	Bits 15–29 of (u) → Bits 15–29 of (v)
16	TRANSMIT V ADDRESS	TV u v	Bits 0–14 of (u) → Bits 0–14 of (v)
21	REPLACE ADD	RA u v	$(u) + (v) \to u$
35	ADD AND TRANSMIT	AT u v	$(AC) + (u) \to v$
41	INDEX JUMP	IJ u v	$(u) - 1 \to AC$. If $(AC) < 0$, continue present sequence. If $(AC) \geq 0, (AC) \to u$ and take (v) as next instruction.
45	MANUALLY SELECTIVE JUMP	MJ 0 v	Take (v) as next instruction.
57	PROGRAM STOP	PS – –	Stops the computer.

coding, most binary computers are designed to accept coding expressed in octal form. Thus, it would be acceptable to have the TRANSMIT POSITIVE instruction appear in a *program* as an octal rather than binary number. The octal representation of the instruction in Fig. 3.2 is 110070000706, where 11_8 is the operation code of the instruction and 00700_8 and 00706_8 are the u and v addresses, respectively. When executed by the computer, this instruction would cause the content of the storage register whose address is 00706_8 to be replaced with the content of the storage register whose address is 00700_8. In the event that the programmer desires to know the decimal equivalent of these octal numbers it is his responsibility to convert them. When programming in machine language for binary computers that accept octal coding, all numbers are required to be coded in octal form, *including any numerical data that may have been expressed originally in decimal form.* These data must be converted by the programmer to octal form. Thus a machine language program for a binary computer will appear as a sequence of octal numbers. The convention of coding in octal form will be followed in the sample programs to be presented below.

3.2   Sample Problem

We have seen that a computer can execute a program only if the program is in the form of a sequence of machine language instructions. Such programs are called machine language programs, and the activity of writing them is called machine language programming, the techniques of which are best learned by studying a number of sample programs written to solve specific problems. To illustrate some of these techniques a simple summation problem is considered. Several ways of analyzing the problem will be offered to illustrate the manner in which a problem may be broken down into component parts. The analyses result in different machine language programs for solving the problem on a computer. The programs are designed to illustrate certain fundamental concepts of programming which have their counterparts in problem-oriented languages, such as Fortran.

The problem for whose solution machine language programs will be constructed is as follows:

Form the sum $C = A + B$ of two n-dimensional vectors, A and B, whose elements are assumed to be in storage. The problem of adding two n vectors may be restated in the following way. Assume two tables of values, each containing n entries, are stored in the computer. Let these table entries be denoted by a_i and b_i, $i = 1, 2, \ldots n$. Then the problem is to form the sum

$$c_i = a_i + b_i \qquad i = 1, 2, \ldots n$$

of corresponding table entries.

As a *first analysis* of the problem one sees that the equation

$$a_1 + b_1 = c_1$$

can be evaluated in two steps:

Step 1. Place the value of a_1 in the accumulator (AC).

Step 2. Add the value of b_1 to the AC and store the sum in c_1. Further, one sees that if the two steps are repeated n times using new values of a_i and b_i each time, the entire set of equations can be solved in a perfectly straight-forward fashion.

Although it is always helpful to analyze a problem into a sequence of steps, in preparing the problem for computer solution it is often useful to

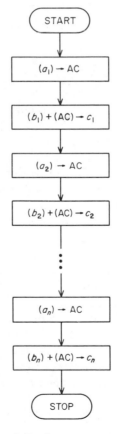

FIGURE 3.3   Flowchart of first analysis of vector summation problem.

translate the analysis into the graphic form of a *flowchart*. This is a graphical representation of the sequence (flow) of operations that are to be performed, where all paths of the sequence are indicated. Many programmers believe that drawing a flowchart of the analysis tends to clarify one's thinking about the problem and helps to eliminate errors from the analysis. Certainly flowcharts aid in communicating one's ideas to others. A flowchart of the first analysis of the vector summation problem is drawn in Fig. 3.3.

3.3   A Machine-Language Program

In order to obtain a computer solution of the vector summation problem a machine language program incorporating the analysis of the problem, together with the data, must be available for execution by the computer. Such a program consists of a sequence of machine language instructions, which are assigned adjacent storage locations and which are specifically arranged to carry out the steps of the analysis.

In writing a program to carry out the analysis above, a moment's reflection will reveal that the operations implied in Steps 1 and 2 of the analysis can be performed by the TRANSMIT POSITIVE and ADD AND TRANSMIT instructions, respectively. Thus if it is assumed that the value of a_1 is stored in the register whose address is 00500, the value of b_1 is stored in the register whose address is 00600, and the value of c_1 is to be stored in the register whose address is 00700, the following set of instructions would evaluate the first equation:

$$\text{TP} \quad 00500 \quad 32000$$

$$\text{AT} \quad 00600 \quad 00700$$

where the octal number 32000 represents the address of the accumulator.

It is obvious that if the u address of the TRANSMIT POSITIVE instruction and the u and v addresses of the ADD AND TRANSMIT instruction were suitably modified the necessary number of times to correspond to the addresses where successive values of the a_i, b_i, and c_i are located, a series of these instructions would evaluate the entire set of equations.

However, before the program can be completed, two additional items of information are necessary. First, the exact number of equations must be known, as well as the addresses of all the registers for storing the values of a_i, b_i, and c_i. Second, the programmer must decide where in storage to locate the program. For this he needs some knowledge about the storage capacity of the computer and the number of digits used to specify the address of a storage register. For obvious reasons octal numbers are used to specify addresses of registers in binary computers. For purposes of illustration it is assumed that the computer whose instruction set was partially described in the preceding paragraphs has available 2^{15} (about 32,000) addressable storage locations, so that a five-digit octal number suffices to identify any addressable storage location in the computer.

We are now in a position to write a machine-language program that will carry out the first analysis of the vector summation problem. (See Table 3.2.) It is assumed that *five* equations are given, and the values of the a_i and b_i are stored in successive locations starting at 00500 and 00600 respectively. The values of the c_i are to be stored in successive locations starting at 00700. The program is written to begin at location 00400. The remarks do not constitute part of the program.

TABLE 3.2   Machine-Language Program to Sum Vectors (1)

Location	Contents		Remarks
00400	11	00500 32000	$(a_1) \rightarrow$ AC
00401	35	00600 00700	$(a_1) + (b_1) \rightarrow c_1$
00402	11	00501 32000	$(a_2) \rightarrow$ AC
00403	35	00601 00701	$(a_2) + (b_2) \rightarrow c_2$
00404	11	00502 32000	$(a_3) \rightarrow$ AC
00405	35	00602 00702	$(a_3) + (b_3) \rightarrow c_3$
00406	11	00503 32000	$(a_4) \rightarrow$ AC
00407	35	00603 00703	$(a_4) + (b_4) \rightarrow c_4$
00410	11	00504 32000	$(a_5) \rightarrow$ AC
00411	35	00604 00704	$(a_5) + (b_5) \rightarrow c_5$
00412	57	00000 00000	STOP

3.4   Indexing and Program Loops

The first analysis of the vector summation problem consists of a straightforward repetition of the two basic steps outlined in Section 3.2. These two steps, which are performed repeatedly on a given set of data until all the numbers are processed, may be summarized as follows:

1. $(a_i) \rightarrow$ AC
2. $(AC) + (b_i) \rightarrow c_i$

Translation of the analysis into a computer program was discussed in Section 3.3. However, the machine-language program (shown at the end of that section) for carrying out the analysis suffers from the serious defect that *the program is extremely wasteful of storage space.* This waste arises from the fact that the length of the program varies directly with the number of summations to be evaluated. Thus, if the data consisted of two vectors whose dimensions were *1000* instead of 5, as assumed, a machine language program consisting of no less than 2000 steps would be required to carry out the vector summation. We are, therefore, faced with the question of whether it is possible to write a program for the vector summation problem whose length is independent of the dimensions of the vectors to be added. Actually, the question is part of the larger question of whether it is possible to express a repetitive type of analysis in an abbreviated form that avoids a straightforward repetition of the basic steps of the analysis. Fortunately, affirmative answers to both questions are possible. To demonstrate the truth of this statement, it is necessary to consider the basic concepts of *loops* and *indexing*, which are introduced later in this section.

In the first analysis, if the data consist of two n-dimensional vectors, A and B, whose sum is to constitute the vector C, the set of operations necessary to form each component of C appears n different times in the analysis. The $2n$ steps that thus constitute the analysis are as follows:

$$1. \quad (a_1) \rightarrow AC$$
$$2. \quad (AC) + (b_1) \rightarrow c_1$$
$$3. \quad (a_2) \rightarrow AC$$
$$4. \quad (AC) + (b_2) \rightarrow c_2$$

$$\cdot$$
$$\cdot$$
$$\cdot$$

$$2n - 1. \quad (a_n) \rightarrow AC$$
$$2n. \quad (AC) + (b_n) \rightarrow c_n$$

A Second Analysis of the Vector Summation Problem

In effect, the foregoing analysis consists of applying to pairs of numbers (a_i, b_i) in a repetitious fashion a set of operations which (1) places the first number a_i in the accumulator and (2) adds to the accumulator the second number b_i and stores the result c_i in a specified location. If a running count is kept of how many times the operations are applied to such pairs of numbers, the procedure stops after the count reaches n. The count must be checked after each application of the operations. In this manner the sum of the first pair of numbers would be computed and stored appropriately, and a check made of the count. Then the same operations would be applied to the second pair of numbers, and a check made of the count. The procedure would continue in this manner until a check of the count revealed that the operations have been applied to n pairs of numbers. The steps by which the complete sequence of operations can be carried out are as follows:

Step 1. Set the count equal to 1.

Step 2. For the first pair of numbers not yet operated upon, place the first number in the accumulator.

Step 3. Add to the accumulator the second number and store the sum in a specified location.

Step 4.   Add 1 to the count.

Step 5.   Check the count; if it is n or less, continue at Step 2; if it is greater than n, stop.

Observe that the procedure is explicit; hence, when the steps are translated into machine language the computer can perform the required number of summations. The manner in which Steps 2 and 3 are formulated permits their use both initially and after each return to Step 2. Thus, they can be used to sum the first pair of numbers and also to sum all succeeding pairs of numbers. In fact, the whole procedure has been formulated in such a manner that the same sequence of operations is performed on all the data.

The five steps listed constitute a *second* analysis of the vector summation problem. To translate the steps into a form appropriate for use on a computer, it is helpful to introduce additional notation. Steps 2 and 3, the core of the analysis, are concerned with the "current pair of numbers" (that is, the pair whose sum is being computed "now"). If the ith pair of numbers, a_i and b_i, is the pair under consideration, the count of the pairs of numbers already summed is i at the conclusion of Step 3. The use of the subscript i permits succinct identification of the particular pair of numbers being operated upon at a given stage of the analysis. With this notation Steps 2 and 3 can be restated symbolically in the following fashion:

Step 2. $(a_i) \rightarrow \mathrm{AC}$

Step 3. $(\mathrm{AC}) + (b_i) \rightarrow c_i$

As the value of the subscript i changes, the significance of Steps 2 and 3 changes accordingly so that they can be used both initially and after each return to Step 2. In this manner, as i takes on successive values from 1 to n, the operations implied in Steps 2 and 3 are performed on successive pairs of numbers, thus permitting sequencing through all the pairs of numbers. With this notation it is possible to restate the five steps of the second analysis of the vector summation problem in a more concise form which corresponds closely to the operations that a computer can perform. Restated, the five steps become

Step 1. $1 \rightarrow i$

Step 2. $(a_i) \rightarrow \mathrm{AC}$

Step 3. $(\mathrm{AC}) + (b_i) \rightarrow c_i$

Step 4. $(i) + 1 \rightarrow i$

Step 5.   If $(i) \leq n$, continue at Step 2; if $(i) > n$, stop.

In the foregoing analysis the variable i is used both as a subscript and as a count of the number of times a set of operations is performed. The use of a count that is associated with a subscripted variable is termed *indexing*. The subscript itself often serves as the index or count, and its value is important not only in allowing the repetition of a set of operations but also in providing initialization of the index and allowing termination of the count. In the foregoing analysis the initial value of the index is 1 (as determined by Step 1). A set of operations is then performed in which use is made of the current (in this case, initial) value of the index (Steps 2 and 3). Next, the value of the index is increased by adding 1 to it (Step 4). Finally, a check is made of the index against a constant n (Step 5). If the new value of the index is n or less, the set of operations is repeated for the new value of the index (continue at Step 2); otherwise the analysis terminates.

In this manner the necessity for listing the complete set of operations required to form the sum of two vectors A and B is avoided simply by allowing for a repetition of the set of operations for forming the sum of a single pair of components, a_i and b_i. In other words, by the use of indexing, the second analysis circumvents the need of actually listing all the summation operations required for all pairs of components of A and B. Rather, it suffices to list the summing operations only for a single pair of components of the vectors, since the same operations are performed on all such pairs. One consequence of introducing indexing into the analysis is that the length of the analysis no longer varies with the amount of data of the problem. Thus it does not matter whether the vectors to be summed are of dimensions 1000 or 5; the number of steps required to formulate an analysis of the problem remains the same. This is the principal advantage of the second analysis of the vector summation problem over the first analysis.

For machine language programming the manner in which indexing is introduced into an analysis depends largely upon the computer to be used. Because indexing is useful in analyzing problems of a repetitive nature, all general-purpose digital computers have machine language instructions that perform such operations as setting and modifying indexes and checking them against constant values. Since the basic function of indexing is to control the analysis of a problem, the machine language instructions that perform the operations are classified as *program control* instructions.

Typical of program control instructions that perform indexing operations is the INDEX JUMP instruction described in Section 3.1. When this instruction is used to perform an indexing operation, the initial value of the index is stored by the programmer in a register whose location is specified by the u address of the instruction. Each time the instruction is executed, the value of the index is *decreased* by 1 and a check is made in the accumulator to determine whether the resulting value of the index is negative or nonnegative. If nonnegative, control is transferred to the instruction whose address is designated by the v address of the jump instruction; otherwise the instruction immediately following the jump instruction is executed next. Since different computers perform indexing operations in different ways, an analysis that uses indexing will often have to be modified slightly if it is to be appropriate for different computers.

In some computers special registers called *index registers* are available to hold index values. In other computers ordinary storage registers are assigned by the programmer to perform this function. In the latter case a simple data-transfer instruction often suffices to set the initial value of the index.

As an illustration of how the technique of indexing may be implemented at the level of machine language programming, a sample program that incorporates the second analysis of the vector summation problem will be considered. The program will consist of machine language instructions drawn from Table 3.1. One of the first requirements to be met in translating an analysis into a computer program is to make certain that the analysis is expressed in a form appropriate for the instructions. In the analysis under consideration a slight modification of the indexing is required. The modification is based on a knowledge of the manner in which indexing is performed by the INDEX JUMP instruction. If this instruction is used to control a repetitious set of operations, it is seen from the description of the instruction found in Table 3.1 that the initial value of the index must always be a positive number j and the terminal value is 0. The set of operations which the index is controlling will then be repeated $j + 1$ times. Thus, if a set of operations is desired to be performed exactly n times, the initial value of the index must be $n - 1$. The index will then be decreased by 1 each time the INDEX JUMP instruction is executed as long as the value of the index is 0 or positive. †

Using the above knowledge about the operation of the INDEX JUMP instruction, it is a simple task to modify the indexing in the second analysis of the vector summation problem so that it corresponds to the operation of this instruction. When the indexing is thus modified, the five steps of the analysis become

Step 1. $1 \rightarrow i$; $n - 1 \rightarrow k$

Step 2. $(a_i) \rightarrow AC$

Step 3. $(AC) + (b_i) \rightarrow c_i$

Step 4. $(i) + 1 \rightarrow i$; $(k) - 1 \rightarrow k$

Step 5.   If $(k) \geq 0$, continue at Step 2; if $(k) < 0$, stop.

The differences between the modified version, shown above, and the original version of the second analysis will now be considered. As noted

†This presumes that the INDEX JUMP is performed *after* each repetitive sequence of steps If the test is made beforehand, the initial value of the index must be one greater.

earlier, the purpose of the modification is to render the analysis in a form appropriate for use with the INDEX JUMP instruction. Were our intention to implement the indexing with a program control instruction whose operation is different from the INDEX JUMP, the analysis would have to be modified accordingly. In the modified analysis, the index is the variable k and serves the same purpose as the index i of the original analysis; that is, both serve to count the number of times the summation operations are performed (Steps 2 and 3). A glance at Step 4 of the two analyses reveals the essential difference between the two indexes. In the original analysis, at the conclusion of Step 3 the value of i represents the number of summations *already performed*, whereas in the modified analysis the value of k represents the number of summations *still to be performed*. In a manner of speaking, index i "counts up" and index k "counts down." Thus the initial value of index k is $n - 1$ and the final value is 0, which allows for termination of the summation operations after they have been performed n times. Associated with the index k in the modified analysis is the variable i, which serves as a subscript. Starting with a value of 1, i is incremented by 1 every time the index k is decreased. Thus, i serves to identify the ith components of the vectors A and B, namely, a_i and b_i. To indicate that after a_i and b_i are summed, a_{i+1} and b_{i+1} are to be summed next, an operation on the subscript is required:

$$(i) + 1 \rightarrow i$$

This is accomplished in Step 4 at the same time that the index k is decreased by 1. Thus, after the count has reached 0, exactly n pairs of components will have been summed.

Loops

Closely associated with the concept of indexing is that of *program loop*. Both concepts play a fundamental role in analyses that are repetitious in nature (that is, where either calculations are performed repeatedly on many sets of data or the analysis itself involves iteration). Because most computer applications involve analyses of this kind, indexing and looping have received much attention in the development of programming languages. A knowledge of how these concepts are implemented at the level of machine language programming is fundamental to a basic understanding of many aspects of machine-independent programming. For example, the Fortran DO statement, the Algol FOR statement, and the Cobol PERFORM statement, to cite three major problem-oriented language statements, all presuppose these concepts in the sense that none of the three statements are executable on computers that do not have the ability to execute machine language programs containing indexing and loops. Chapter 10 is devoted to a detailed discussion of the DO statement in Fortran.

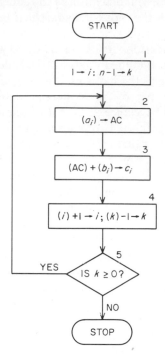

FIGURE 3.4   Flowchart of second analysis of vector summation problem.

The subject of program loops is best introduced by reference to a flow-chart. For this purpose a flowchart of the modified analysis of the vector summation problem is presented in Fig. 3.4. The main part consists of five boxes, numbered on the right for illustrative purposes and containing the steps of the modified analysis of the vector summation problem. Thus, box 1 contains the first step of the modified analysis, box 2 the second step, and so on. A comparison of the flowcharts in Figs. 3.3 and 3.4 shows that the flowchart of the first analysis of the vector summation problem (Fig. 3.3) consists of a straightforward sequence of pairs of almost identical boxes, whereas the flowchart of the second analysis (Fig. 3.4) indicates a return to an earlier box. This is evident from the fact that one of the two paths leaving box 5 is a return to box 2, and an arrow is so drawn. The result of this return is a closed path encompassing boxes 2, 3, 4, and 5.

The term *loop* is applied to such a closed path in a flowchart. The action of performing the operations in a loop is called *looping*, and one traversal of a loop (that is, looping *one* time) is called a *loop cycle*. In Fig. 3.4, a return to box 2 causes the summation operations to be repeated on a new pair of components for a_i and b_i.

Within a loop some means must be provided for its eventual termination. This is usually accomplished by including within the loop an operation that requires a test condition to be met during each cycle. In Fig. 3.4 the test is made in box 5, where the value of the index k serves this purpose; when k is less than 0, the path taken on leaving box 5 is downward, and the looping terminates.

A loop is introduced into a flowchart whenever a repetitious process is present in the analysis of the problem. A flowchart may have several loops, and loops may be *nested* within one another. The latter situation arises

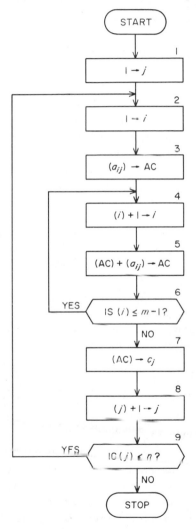

FIGURE 3.5 Flowchart for summation of m vectors of n dimensions.

whenever a repetitious process is contained within a loop, which can thus be drawn as an inner loop. It is characteristic of nested loops that the innermost loop is contained entirely within the next outer loop, and so on.

An example of a flowchart containing two nested loops is shown in Fig. 3.5. The flowchart represents an analysis for finding the sum of m vectors of n dimensions. If a_{ij} represents the jth component of the ith vector, the problem may be expressed as follows: Evaluate the set of equations appearing below and obtain values of c_j for specified values of a_{ij}.

$$a_{11} + a_{21} + \cdots + a_{m1} = c_1$$
$$a_{12} + a_{22} + \cdots + a_{m2} = c_2$$
$$\vdots$$
$$a_{1n} + a_{2n} + \cdots + a_{mn} = c_n$$

$$\sum_{i=1}^{m} a_{ij} = c_j \qquad \text{for} \qquad j = 1, 2, \ldots n$$

This problem differs from the vector summation problem discussed earlier in that the summation of m n-dimensional vectors instead of *two* such vectors is required. As was seen in the analysis of the earlier problem (Fig. 3.4), the summation of two vector components can be accomplished in two steps and a loop is introduced to perform n such summations. For the problem under consideration, the summation of m vector components is itself a repetitious process, which gives rise to a situation where a repetitive set of operations is contained within a loop. Summation of the jth components of the m vectors is shown in the flowchart in Fig. 3.5 as the inner, nested loop encompassing boxes 4, 5, and 6.

By setting the value of m equal to 2 in box 6, the inner loop of the flowchart fails to be traversed, and the analysis, in effect, reduces to that shown in Fig. 3.4. In this manner the flowchart of the 2-vector summation problem is seen to be a special case of the flowchart for the m-vector summation problem.

Further discussion of nested loops is deferred until Chapter 10, in which nests of Fortran DO statements are treated in considerable detail.

A Second Machine-Language Program for the Vector Summation Problem

We now turn to consider a second machine language program for computing the sum of two n-dimensional vectors. The program is based on the modified analysis shown in the flowchart of Fig. 3.4. This analysis differs from the original analysis of the vector summation problem, presented in Section 3.2, in that indexing and loops are introduced for the first time. This will account for the major differences between the machine language program presented in Section 3.3 and the one to be considered presently. The differences are two in number and will be enumerated here at the outset. First, the program of the present section contains a set of commands to which return is made under control of an INDEX JUMP instruction, whereas the original program does not. Second, the present program, unlike the original program, employs a technique of *address modification* to modify the set of commands appropriately each time a return is made to them. The net effect of these differences is that the second program is considerably shortened and the number of steps it employs is independent of the size of the vectors to be summed.

The heart of the second program consists of the set of commands to which return is made under control of the INDEX JUMP instruction. Assuming the same storage assignments as in the original program (see Section 3.3), and further assuming that $n - 1$ is stored in the register whose address is 00050, the set of instructions corresponding to Steps 2–5 of the flowchart in Fig. 3.4 is as follows:

$$
\begin{array}{llll}
\alpha & \text{TP} & 00500 & 32000 \\
\alpha + 1 & \text{AT} & 00600 & 00700 \\
\alpha + 2 & \text{IJ} & 00050 & \alpha + 4 \\
\alpha + 3 & \text{PS} & 00000 & 00000
\end{array}
$$

For the sake of convenience in discussing the program, symbolic labels are used in place of actual addresses of the instructions. Thus, α refers to the address of the first instruction above, $\alpha + 1$ to the address of the second instruction, and so on. The instructions at α and $\alpha + 1$, when executed, evaluate the sum of the vector components a_1 and b_1 and store it in c_1. The instruction at $\alpha + 2$ subtracts 1 from the current value of the index, which is stored in location 00050. If the resulting value of the index is 0 or positive, control is transferred to $\alpha + 4$ for the next instruction; if the value of the index is negative, control passes to $\alpha + 3$, where a PROGRAM STOP instruction is executed. Before control can be returned to address α and the sequence of instructions repeated the required number of times as specified by the flowchart, it is necessary to have modified the instructions at α and $\alpha + 1$ each time control passes to α. Modification of the instructions is necessary if the sums of *successive* values of the a_i and b_i are to be evaluated and stored in c_i. The technique of address modification is used for this purpose.

Address Modification

There are two ways to perform address modification. One method is to treat instructions as data which may be modified arithmetically. This approach is made possible by having the program stored internally in the computer. It will be considered here since it illustrates the significance of the concept of the digital computer as a *stored-program* machine. The second method, which makes use of index registers, permits the address modification to be done automatically; it is available in most modern computers.

An essential characteristic of the digital computer as a stored-program machine is that instructions and data words look alike in storage registers. This statement implies that instructions can be operated on arithmetically in the same manner as data. The two instructions located at α and $\alpha + 1$ in the foregoing program, namely

$$\text{TP} \quad 00500 \quad 32000$$

$$\text{AT} \quad 00600 \quad 00700$$

appear in storage as follows:

$$11 \quad 00500 \quad 32000$$

$$35 \quad 00600 \quad 00700$$

If they are modified by the addition of 00 00001 00000 and 00 00001 00001, respectively, they correspond to the instructions

$$\text{TP} \quad 00501 \quad 32000$$

$$\text{AT} \quad 00601 \quad 00701$$

By successively adding the above quantities to these instructions once each loop cycle, the u and v addresses of the instructions can be suitably modified to correspond to the addresses for the successive values of a_i, b_i, and c_i. This technique is called *address modification*.

Modification of the instructions at α and $\alpha + 1$ in the program corresponds to performing the operation

$$(i) + 1 \rightarrow i$$

on the subscript i in Step 4 of the flowchart in Fig. 3.4. A set of instructions for carrying out the modifications is as follows:†

$$\alpha + 4 \quad \text{RA} \quad \alpha \qquad \alpha + 7$$

$$\alpha + 5 \quad \text{RA} \quad \alpha + 1 \quad \alpha + 10$$

$$\alpha + 6 \quad \text{MJ} \quad 00000 \quad \alpha$$

$$\alpha + 7 \quad 00 \quad 00001 \quad 00000$$

$$\alpha + 10 \quad 00 \quad 00001 \quad 00001$$

†It should be kept in mind that the addresses of the instruction are designated by octal numbers; thus, $\alpha + 10$ follows $\alpha + 7$.

Since 00   00001   00000 is stored at location $\alpha + 7$, execution of RA α $\alpha + 7$ causes a 1 to be added in the rightmost digit position of the u address of the instruction stored at α, making it TP   00501   32000. Similarly, execution of the instruction at $\alpha + 5$ increments by 1 both the u and v addresses of the instruction at $\alpha + 1$. Execution of the MANUAL JUMP instruction at $\alpha + 6$ then passes control to α, after the instructions at α and $\alpha + 1$ have been suitably modified, to evaluate and store appropriately the sum of the next pair of vector components a_i and b_i. Thus a program loop is traversed as long as the value of the index stored at 00050 remains 0 or positive and execution of the INDEX JUMP instruction at $\alpha + 2$ passes control to $\alpha + 4$ for modifying instructions and finally back to α. When the index becomes negative and execution of the INDEX JUMP instruction passes control to $\alpha + 3$, the looping terminates.

The instructions at α to $\alpha + 6$, the constants at $\alpha + 7$ and $\alpha + 10$, and the constant $n - 1$ stored at 00050, together comprise a machine-language program for carrying out the analysis of the vector summation problem shown in the flowchart of Fig. 3.4. In machine coding the program would appear as in Table 3.3.

TABLE 3.3 Machine-Language Program to Sum Vectors (2)

Location	Contents		Remarks
00400	11	00500 32000	Load accumulator
00401	35	00600 00700	Perform summation
00402	41	00050 00404	Test index value. If 0 or positive, take (00404) as NI; otherwise take (00403)
00403	57	00000 00000	Stop
00404	21	00400 00407	Modify instruction at 00400
00405	21	00401 00410	Modify instruction at 00401
00406	45	00000 00400	Take (00400) as NI
00407	00	00001 00000	Constant
00410	00	00001 00001	Constant

3.5 Initializing Programs

As it stands above, the second program for the vector summation problem stops after calculation of the final c_i. Often the computational part of a program is only one aspect of the entire program. It is more realistic to view a program as consisting of input, computation, and output. In the case of the vector summation problem, a set of instructions for reading the data would normally precede the list of machine language instructions shown at the end of Section 3.4, and the PS   00000   00000 instruction at 00403 would be replaced by a MJ   0   v that transfers control to some output routine.

Assume that an input program reads the a_i into registers whose addresses are 00500, 00501, ..., that the b_i are read into registers 00600, 00601,

..., that the c_i are obtained on output from 00700, 00701, ... and that $n - 1$ is available at the start of the program in register 00050. Suppose it is desired to evaluate more than one set of a_i and b_i. A difficulty arises. As the program now stands, when one set of the a_i and b_i has been evaluated and the program loop terminates, the u and v addresses of the instructions at 00400 and 00401 will have addresses of $00500 + n - 1$, $00600 + n - 1$, and $00700 + n - 1$, and the value of the index $(n - 1)$ stored at 00050 will be destroyed by repeated subtractions. Assuming that a new $n - 1$ is read into the register whose address is 00050 for each new set of data a_i and b_i, it is still necessary to restore the addresses to their initial values of 00500, 00600, and 00700.

This task can be done by adding to the foregoing program the following instructions:

$$\alpha - 2 \quad \text{TU} \quad \alpha + 11 \quad \alpha$$
$$\alpha - 1 \quad \text{TP} \quad \alpha + 12 \quad \alpha + 1$$

and

$$\alpha + 11 \quad 00 \quad 00500 \quad 00000$$
$$\alpha + 12 \quad \text{AT} \quad 00600 \quad 00700$$

If for each new set of data a_i and b_i the computation program is entered at $\alpha - 2$ (instead of at α), the two instructions at $\alpha - 2$ and $\alpha - 1$ will always cause the u and v addresses of the instructions at 00400 and 00401 to have initial values of 00500, 00600, and 00700. In this manner the program will preset its own initial addresses so that it can be used as many times as necessary, always with the proper starting addresses.

SYMBOLIC PROGRAMMING

3.6   The Limitations of Machine-Language Programming

The instructions located in the storage unit of a digital computer consist of binary or decimal numbers. Writing a program using machine-language (numerical) instructions is an extremely tedious and exacting process. Among the major disadvantages of machine language programming are the following:

1. The programmer is prevented from using symbolic or mnemonic names to stand for actual operations and addresses where data are located. For example, the instruction to add the value of b_i to the content of the accumulator and store the result in location c_i may be expressed more conveniently in symbolic form as

$$\text{AT} \quad b_i \quad c_i$$

However, its occurrence in a machine language program must take some such form as

$$35 \qquad 00605 \qquad 00705$$

Moreover, each instruction must have its numerical operation code and numerical address parts correctly specified. Any error introduced in coding the program for the computer will result in the incorrect execution of the program.

2.   It is the programmer's responsibility to assign storage locations for every instruction and every item of data. One of the most difficult aspects of machine language programming is the fact that the exact location in storage of a particular operand often is not known at the time of writing the instruction. For example, the numerical address of the instruction to which control is transferred in a program control instruction may not be known until other matters have been decided.

3.   Since the ultimate length of a program and its data is not known as it is being written, there is a tendency to "play safe" in the assignment of storage addresses, especially in the case of temporary storage for intermediate results. This results in inefficient and wasteful allocation of storage.

4.   It is the responsibility of the programmer to assign a specific numerical location for the initial instruction of the program, and to load the program itself into the proper storage locations and direct the computer to take the first instruction from the assigned location.

5.   And finally, programs written with numerical addresses are assigned new locations in storage only with great difficulty, since many address parts of the instructions will require modification. This places a severe restriction on the revision of programs. Programs frequently make use of other programs called subroutines. In using such programs it is sometimes necessary to move them in storage to avoid storage conflicts with the main program. This usually requires minor changes to be made in the main program as well. Not only are subroutines relocatable by dint of much toil and effort, but also the programmer hesitates to introduce even minor changes in the main program.

3.7   Programming Systems

To overcome the inconveniences and difficulties inherent in machine-language programming, a major innovation occurred in programming technology with the introduction of *symbolic programming systems*.

A *programming system* is composed of two parts: (*a*) a *symbolic language* for writing programs, and (*b*) a *processor*, which translates programs so written into machine-language programs that can be executed by the computer.

The purpose of programming systems is to remove from the programmer the burden of writing programs in machine language. Programs written in a language other than machine language are called *source programs* and the language itself is called the *source language*. Translation of the source program into machine language is performed automatically by the processor. The result of the translation is a machine-language program that can be executed by the computer. It is called the *object program*, and its language is the *object language*. Hence the term "object language" always refers to some particular set of machine-language instructions. *It is important to remember that a processor is itself a machine-language program.* In fact, it is a program that runs on a particular computer and translates a source-language program into a machine-language (or object) program for that same computer.

The complexity of the processor is dependent upon the capabilities of the language. Usually the more machine-independent the language is, the more comprehensive and complex the processor must be, since there are necessarily more levels of translation that it must accomplish. However, the processor written for any particular language, no matter how complex the language, is also dependent upon the type of computer, the instruction set, and the manner in which the instructions are executed by the computer. Every machine has idiosyncrasies that affect the translation process to some extent and which, therefore, are reflected in the structure of the programming language itself. This is the principal reason that so-called machine-independent programming languages are never *truly* machine-independent. It accounts for the existence of different versions of Fortran rather than a unique Fortran language available for use on any computer.

Programming systems may be classified into two broad categories: (*a*) machine-oriented or symbolic programming systems, and (*b*) machine-independent or problem-oriented systems.

Machine-oriented systems are those whose language is designed around the machine organization of a particular computer. Problem-oriented programming systems are largely machine-independent, thus removing the necessity for the programmer to learn details about the computer itself. However, lest this last statement prove misleading, the reader should keep in mind that the programmer with a knowledge about the computer he is using is in a better position to take advantage of the particular characteristics of that computer than the programmer without such knowledge. This is true even though the language used may be machine-independent. A discussion of problem-oriented programming systems is to be found in the next main section.

3.8 Symbolic Languages

A symbolic programming language usually consists of three types of statements: *imperative* statements, *declarative* statements, and *control* statements.

Imperative statements are symbolic statements corresponding to the actual set of machine language instructions of the particular computer involved. Declarative statements define storage areas and constants in the symbolic program. And control statements control the assembly (translation) process. They do not generate any machine-language coding or data used in the execution of the object program by the computer. Rather, they supply to the processor information necessary to obtain an object program from the source program.

In using a symbolic language a programmer refers to the locations of instructions, data, and constants by symbolic names. For example, consider the problem of adding the value of the vector component b_5, stored at location 00604, to the content of the accumulator and placing the sum in location 00704 as the value of c_5. Suppose the instruction for doing this is to be stored at an address denoted symbolically as $\alpha + 12$. The machine-language statement required to perform this operation of ADD AND TRANS-MIT might be

$$35 \quad 00604 \quad 00704$$

whose address might be 00412, whereas the symbolic language statement for the same operation might be

$$AT \quad B(5) \quad C(5)$$

The symbols B(5) and C(5) represent values of variables previously defined in the program. During the translation process, the computer will assign an appropriate storage address to the instruction, convert the symbolic addresses B(5) and C(5) to actual machine addresses, and convert the mnemonic operation code for ADD AND TRANSMIT (AT) to its machine-language equivalent.

As a simple illustration of a symbolic-language program we shall consider the set of machine-language instructions for performing vector summation that appeared in Table 3.3. Assuming that an appropriate processor program exists for carrying out the translation, these instructions could have been written in the following form where symbolic names are used in the place of actual machine addresses and numerical operation codes:

ALPHA	TP	A1	ACC
	AT	B1	C1
	IJ	COUNT	ALPHA + 4

PS	0	0
RA	ALPHA	ALPHA + 1
RA	ALPHA + 1	ALPHA + 10
MJ	0	ALPHA
00	00001	00000
00	00001	00001

It would be necessary to include as part of the program certain declarative statements for defining and allocating storage areas in terms of the symbolic names used in the program. Also, a control statement would be required to instruct the processor that the program is to be stored beginning at a location whose symbolic name is ALPHA.

3.9   The Assembly Process

The term *assembler* or *assembly program* is used to apply to a processor that translates a program consisting of symbolic-language instructions into machine-language instructions. The term *compiler* is usually reserved for a processor program that translates programs written in a problem-oriented programming language into machine language. The difference between a compiler and an assembler is discussed later in this chapter in the section on "Machine-Independent Programming."

The assembler translates symbolic instructions into machine instructions. The task, which is straightforward, consists primarily of converting symbolic names of operations and addresses. The conversion is generally a one-for-one translation, meaning that one imperative statement in the symbolic language program is translated directly into one machine language instruction. For translating names of operations the only required process is one of looking in a table for each symbol and replacing it with the numerical operation code. For names of addresses the process is somewhat more complicated, but it is still essentially a matter of symbol table look-up.

It is necessary to provide the assembler with information on the manner in which the translation of the source program is to proceed. This information is contained in the declarative and control statements appearing in the source program. These statements are not translated into machine instructions but serve to direct the assembler in some way. For this reason they are sometimes referred to as *pseudo statements*. They are used for a number of purposes; among them to indicate the start and end of a program, to generate constants, and to reserve space for data and results.

The following sequence of steps is necessary in order to assemble a source program into an object program and execute it:

1. The source program is written by the programmer and coded in a symbolic language.

2. The assembler is placed in the computer.

3. The source program is entered into the computer by means of punched cards, paper tape, magnetic tape, or some other mode of input. The assembler then translates the source program statements into a machine language program, one statement at a time. The result of the translation is an object program deck and/or object program listing.

4. The assembled object program is loaded into the computer storage and executed. This last step may occur immediately following Step 3 or at a later time.

3.10   The Advantages of Symbolic Programming over Machine-Language Programming

The primary advantages of symbolic programming over machine-language programming are (a) symbolic notation may be used to represent the operation code and address part of the instruction, and (b) automatic assignment of addresses for both instructions and data are placed under the control of the computer.

These advantages help to overcome some of the limitations of machine-language programming described earlier, as follows:

1. The problem of not being able to supply operand addresses at the time each instruction is written no longer exists. The reason is that symbolic names may be used for operand addresses. Assignment of actual machine addresses is made later at assembly time by the processor.

2. Inefficient and wasteful allocation of storage space no longer occurs, since all actual storage assignments are made at assembly time when locations are set aside in sequence by the processor for all listed items.

3. Modification and revision of source programs is greatly facilitated. Subroutines are easily relocatable, and insertion of additional statements into the source program does not usually necessitate reassignment of current instruction addresses at reassembly time.

4. The use of mnemonic symbols introduces greater meaning into the coding of source programs and results in programs that are more readily understood.

Some examples of actual symbolic programming systems are SPS for the IBM 1620 computer, MAP and FAP for the IBM 7040 and 7090 computers, USE for the Univac Scientific 1105 computer and MACRO-6 for the PDP-6 computer.

MACHINE INDEPENDENT PROGRAMMING

A second major innovation in programming technology occurred with the introduction of *problem-oriented programming systems.*

We learned from the previous section that by placing the necessary burden of storage assignment on the computer and allowing the use of instructions with operation codes in mnemonic form and addresses in symbolic form, the task of writing programs is considerably facilitated. Historically, allowing programs to be coded in symbolic form rather than machine form proved to be an innovation in itself and was a first step toward freeing the programmer from the necessity of writing in machine language. Thus with the advent of symbolic programming the computer was assigned the burden of translating programs into a machine language form for entering into the storage registers of the computer. Nonetheless, while symbolic programming has reduced significantly the clerical task of the programmer, the language remains tied to the set of machine instructions of a particular computer.

Machine-independent programming represents a second step toward freeing the programmer from the necessity of writing in machine language. In this type of programming, the programs are written in a language whose structure and operations closely resemble that of the language in which the problem is formulated. A class of languages generally referred to as *problem-oriented programming languages* has been developed for this purpose. In contrast to symbolic languages, which are modified machine languages that reflect the structure and organization of particular computers, problem-oriented languages reflect the structure and organization of the language of the problem area, and are intended to be as machine independent as possible. This text is devoted to a study in detail of one such problem-oriented language.

Although problem-oriented programming languages are designed to be machine-independent, a processor is required to translate source programs written in these languages into machine language coding. Such processors are called *compilers.* Unlike the assembly process in symbolic programming, translation of source programs written in machine-independent languages is usually one-to-many; that is, many machine-language instructions are generated from a single source-language statement.

In many programming systems today, the assembler and compiler are part of a larger program which also includes *supervisory* or *monitoring* programs. These latter programs are designed to make the computer less dependent on direct supervision and operation by a human operator.

Before commencing the study of Fortran proper, which starts with the next chapter, we shall devote the remainder of this chapter to brief accounts of the several topics relating to machine-independent programming introduced above. The chapter concludes with an enumeration of the advantages of machine-independent programming.

3.11   Problem-Oriented Programming Languages

Among the major problem-oriented programming languages today are Fortran, Algol, and Cobol. Fortran and Algol (the name stands for "*ALGO*rithmic *L*anguage") are algebraic programming languages that employ a notation similar to everyday mathematical notations for solving mathematical, scientific, and engineering problems. Both languages were designed so that engineers and scientists would not be required to learn the machine language of computers to solve their problems. Cobol (from "*CO*mmon *B*usiness-*O*riented *L*anguage") is a programming language designed to provide a common set of procedures for defining and expressing business data-processing applications. The Fortran and Cobol languages are the results of extensive efforts that have occurred in recent years in the United States; the development of Algol has taken place principally in Europe. However, today both Fortran and Algol enjoy international use. Of the three languages Fortran is the most widely used; in this sense it shows the most promise of becoming a truly universal programming language. Mention should be made of the anticipated development in the United States of a new programming language called PL/1 (for "*Program Language,* version 1"), which combines features of Algol, Fortran, and Cobol.

Any problem-oriented language should provide the programmer with the capability of doing three things: (*a*) defining the constants, variables and expressions that appear in the solution of a problem; (*b*) making specifications concerning the nature of the data being used; and (*c*) stating the procedures that are to be followed in obtaining a solution using the data and expressions provided in (*a*) and (*b*).

These necessary functions for instructing a computer to solve a problem are expressed in the form of a machine-independent source program. The statements that comprise such a program can be classified into two basic types: *executable* and *nonexecutable*. These classes correspond roughly to the categories of imperative statements and the pseudo statements of a symbolic language.

Executable statements consist of three basic types: arithmetic, control, and input/output. In this respect they perform functions similar to the imperative statements of a symbolic language, with the following important exception. The executable statements of a problem-oriented language are in general more compact than their equivalent counterparts in a symbolic language. Thus, only *one* Fortran arithmetic statement, for example, is required to evaluate one of the roots of a quadratic equation given by the formula

$$y = \frac{-b + \sqrt{b^2 - 4ac}}{2a}$$

The Fortran statement expressing this formula is

$$Y = (-B + \text{SQRT}(B**2 - 4.*A*C))/(2.*A)$$

Yet a long series of instructions would be required to express the same formula in symbolic or machine language.

Nonexecutable statements do not give rise to any instructions in the object program. Instead, they provide the compiler with information about the allocation of storage space and the form in which data is to be stored internally. Typical of nonexecutable statements are the Fortran DIMENSION and FORMAT statements.

A series of sample Fortran programs will be presented to illustrate the structure of programs written in a problem-oriented language. The programs also serve to illustrate how the concepts of loops and indexing, discussed in earlier sections of this chapter, are implemented at the level of machine-independent programming.

The following two programs provide a solution to the vector summation problem whose analysis appears in the flowchart of Fig. 3.4. The two programs illustrate alternative ways of writing the analysis in Fortran. (Statement numbers to the left in these two programs correspond to numbered boxes in the flowchart.)

```
  DIMENSION A(100), B(100), C(100)
  I = 1
2 C(I) = A(I) + B(I)
  I = I + 1
  IF (I–N) 2,2,6
6 STOP
  END
```

```
  DIMENSION A(100), B(100), C(100)
  DO 2 I = 1,N
2 C(I) = A(I) + B(I)
  STOP
  END
```

The Fortran program below performs the summation of *m* vectors of *n* dimensions. The analysis for this problem appears in the flowchart of Fig.

3.5. It is an example of a Fortran program that contains a *nest* of DO statements (loops).

```
      DIMENSION A(100, 100), C(100)
      DO 5 J = 1,N
      C(J) = 0
      DO 5 I = 1,M
    5 C(J) = C(J) + A(I,J)
      STOP
      END
```

The foregoing account of problem-oriented languages is intended only as a cursory description of their central features. Its main purpose is to provide the reader at this point with a preliminary introduction to the language of Fortran. Detailed explanations of the various elements of Fortran, and the manner in which they function, will be the subject of later chapters.

3.12   Compilation

Computer programs that translate source programs written in problem-oriented languages into machine language are called *compilers*, and the translation process is known as *compilation*. The compilation process is similar in its basic function to the assembly process discussed in Section 3.9, but differs from the latter in an important respect.

The basic function of both assembly and compilation processes is the translation of source programs into machine language object programs. However, the two processes differ from one another principally with respect to the nature of the translation. Symbolic languages basically are modified machine languages that, to a large degree, reflect the structure of a computer. Problem-oriented languages, on the other hand, are machine-independent languages and reflect the structure inherent in problem areas. Source programs written in a symbolic language usually consist of a set of instructions in which symbolic names are used for the operation codes and numerical addresses. Hence, a one-for-one translation generally suffices to convert a symbolic language statement into a machine-language instruction.

In contrast, source programs written in a problem-oriented language consist of statements that reflect the structure and operations of a class of problems. Translation of these statements into machine-language almost invariably results in a one-to-many correspondence of source statements to machine instructions, since several machine-language instructions are generally required to perform the operations of a single source statement. For this reason compilation of a machine-language program from a source program written in a problem-oriented language is a more complicated process than the assembly process.

Although, in principle, problem-oriented languages may be viewed as truly machine-independent languages, in practice they never are. The actual details of computer design and organization produce obvious differences between computers, and these differences invariably become reflected in the compilers, which are written to implement the languages on different computers. This fact accounts for why different versions of a problem-oriented language exist, and it explains such possible variations in a language as, for example, the number of permissible characters in a variable name, the allowable magnitudes of integers and floating-point numbers, and other differences, which the programmer may have to learn.

3.13   Monitors

In many computer systems today the assembly and compiler programs used for translating source programs into machine language are part of a larger control program which also includes *supervisory* or *monitoring* programs. These latter programs are designed to increase the operational efficiency of the computer by reducing the amount of supervision required from a human operator in the day-to-day operation of computers. With the use of a monitor program, a number of source programs can be stacked and loaded; their actual execution will then proceed under control of the monitor, which will arrange for each to be compiled and executed with a minimum of supervision from the operator. Automatic execution of a sequence of programs is often referred to as *batch processing*, since it permits continuous operation of the computer without interruption between the execution of many independent data-processing jobs.

A typical sequence of programming jobs that would be processed under supervision and control of a monitor program might include the following:

1. A program written in symbolic language, which has to be translated and executed.

2. A program written in machine language, which is to be executed; in this case no translation is required.

3. A program consisting of a main routine written in Fortran with subroutines written in an assembly language. This program is to be compiled only; no execution is presently desired.

4. A Fortran program requiring the use of library subprograms,† which is to be compiled and executed.

If a monitor program is to supervise the proper processing of a sequence of programming tasks, such as the ones above, it is necessary that certain information pertaining to each task be available to the monitor. For this

†Subprograms are discussed in Chapter 11.

purpose it is convenient to view each programming task as consisting of three parts: (a) control information for the monitor, (b) the source program and (c) data.

A set of control cards is usually employed to inform the monitor about salient characteristics of the programming job; for example, the language in which the program is written, whether the program is to be compiled only, or compiled and executed, and so on. In the case of the programming job 1 listed above for example, control cards would inform the monitor that the program is written in a symbolic language and the program is to be executed after assembly. This information would cause the monitor to read into storage the assembly program and transfer control to it. Under control of the assembler, the source program would be read into storage and translated. If the translation were unsuccessful, due to detection of errors by the assembly processor, the user would be informed and control would be transferred back to the monitor in order to begin the processing of job 2.

If, however, assembly of the source program were successful, the object program would be stored in storage and control transferred to it. During execution of the program, the data of job 1 would be read into the computer storage under control of the program. Upon the completed execution of the program, control would be transferred back to the monitor in order to begin processing job 2.

In addition to *batch processing*, a recently developed computing technique referred to as *time sharing* has gained considerable attention. This technique permits programs to be entered into the computer from remote console stations and processed in accordance with a priority program that functions under the control of the monitor. Thus any number of users at independent, concurrently operable consoles have the capability to introduce, operate, and modify their own programs on the computer as though each were the only user. By dispensing processing time to each user when and as he requires it, the time-shared computer functions very much in the manner of a public utility.

The use of advanced monitoring techniques makes the practical business of writing programs very different from that of the earlier days of computing when only machine-language programming, or at best limited symbolic programming, was available to the user.

3.14 The Advantages of Machine-Independent Programming

In summary, machine-independent programming offers a number of advantages over machine-language and symbolic programming. Among the advantages are the following:

1. Programs are written in a language to which the programmer is

accustomed. Thus, an element of simplicity not found in symbolic or machine language programming is introduced into the programming task.

2. The programmer needs to know very little about the structure and organization of the computer, including the repertoire of machine instructions.

3. Programs written in problem-oriented languages reduce substantially the number of statements that must be written to define and solve a problem, thereby reducing the opportunity for clerical error.

4. The programmer need not concern himself with the tedious jobs of storage allocation and assignment of addresses, and may specify the details of input/output manipulation and arrangement of data format with considerable ease.

5. Extensive error diagnostics, which are included in most compilers, serve to help the programmer in locating and removing errors from the source language program and data.

This chapter concludes the introductory part of this text. The reader is encouraged to refer to it whenever the need arises in studying the later chapters on Fortran. A complete mastery of the fundamentals of Fortran programming is possible only with a thorough understanding of how the computer functions and of how basic programming concepts are implemented at the level of machine language programming.

Problems

3.1 Draw a flowchart for computing the sum of the squares of n numbers

$$S = X_1{}^2 + X_2{}^2 + \cdots + X_n{}^2$$

$$= \sum_{i=1}^{n} (X_i)^2$$

3.2 Draw a flowchart for finding the square root of a positive integer N in which the computation is based on the Newton approximation formula

$$X_{i+1} = \frac{1}{2}\left(X_i + \frac{N}{X_i}\right)$$

where X_i is the ith estimate of the square root of N. Assume an initial nonzero estimate X_1 is given for $\sqrt{N}$, and that the iteration is continued until the absolute value of the difference between N and the square of the current estimate is less than a predetermined value; that is,

$$|N - (X_i)^2| < \epsilon$$

For Problems 3.3–3.6, assume that the following machine-language instructions are available, in addition to those described in Table 3.1:

Op Code	Name	Format	Remarks
23	REPLACE SUBTRACT	RS u v	$(u) - (v) \rightarrow u$
36	SUBTRACT AND TRANSMIT	ST u v	$(AC) - (u) \rightarrow v$
71	MULTIPLY	MP u v	$(u) \times (v) \rightarrow AC$
73	DIVIDE	DV u v	$(AC) \div (u) \rightarrow v$ AC holds remainder

3.3 Write a machine-language program for the "sum of squares" problem that was flowcharted in Problem 3.1. Assume that the n numbers are stored sequentially starting at location 01000, that $n - 1$ is stored at location 00050, and the program begins at 00200.

3.4 Write a machine-language program that incorporates the analysis obtained in Problem 3.2 for finding an integer square root of a positive number N. Assume that the initial estimate X_1 for $\sqrt{N}$ is located at 01000, N is located at 00500, ε at 00600, and that the program begins at 00200.

3.5 Write a machine-language program for the m vector summation problem whose analysis is shown in the flowchart of Fig. 3.5. Assume that the program is to sum seven vectors of 100 dimensions each, and that the components of the first vector are stored sequentially beginning at location 01000, those of the second vector starting at location 02000, etc. Assume further that $m - 1$ is stored at location 00050, $n - 1$ at location 00075, and that the starting address of the program is location 00200. Assume that the arithmetic instructions perform only integer arithmetic. Discuss the difficulties arising from this limitation.

3.6 Discuss the significance of the computer as a stored-program machine for the modification of instructions in machine-language programs.

References

1. FISHER, F. P., and G. F. SWINDLE, *Computer Programming Systems*. New York: Holt, Rinehart and Winston, Inc., 1964.

2. SHERMAN, P. M., *Programming and Coding Digital Computers*. New York: John Wiley & Sons, Inc., 1963.

3. STEIN, M. L., and W. D. MUNRO, *Computer Programming: A Mixed Language Approach*. New York: Academic Press, Inc., 1964.

4

Basic Elements of Fortran

INTRODUCTION

Fortran (from the words "*FOR*mula *TRAN*slation") is the name of a programming system that consists of two parts: the Fortran language and the Fortran compiler. The principal feature of Fortran is that it enables a person with only a slight knowledge of a computer to utilize a computer for problem solving. The Fortran language greatly simplifies programming by allowing the programmer to state in a relatively simple language, closely resembling that of ordinary algebra, the steps of a procedure to be carried out for the solution of a problem. The Fortran language (hereafter called Fortran) was designed primarily for use in the scientific and engineering areas. Persons working in these disciplines often do not have the time to learn the intricacies of programming a computer in its basic machine language. However, problems arising in these disciplines are best solved (and sometimes only solvable) with a computer. Therefore, Fortran gives to the scientist the facility of communicating with and using this powerful tool.

A Fortran program consists of a sequence of statements written in the Fortran language. These statements might appear as follows:

$$A = B + C - D$$
$$X = 2.*A$$
$$Y = A + X$$

Of course, the computer cannot respond to instructions like these since it responds to numerical machine-language instructions only. Therefore, these Fortran statements must be *translated* into a corresponding set of machine-language instructions which will perform the calculations indicated by the Fortran statements.

The Fortran compiler or translator is a computer program which analyses and translates Fortran statements into the appropriate machine language instructions. It is not important that the reader understand how the Fortran compiler functions, but it is important to recognize what its function is.

The following are definitions of terminology used in this and subsequent chapters:

1. *Fortran language.* A set of statements somewhat similar to the expressions used in ordinary algebra. These statements are used by a programmer to describe the solution of a problem.

2. *Source statement.* One Fortran language statement.

3. *Source program.* A program written in the Fortran language. It is made up of a series of Fortran statements that completely describe the procedure for the solution of a problem.

4. *Fortran compiler* (also called *Fortran translator* or *Fortran processor*). A computer program that analyzes the source statements comprising the source program and translates them into the machine language instructions to which the computer responds.

5. *Object program.* The totality of machine language instructions produced by the Fortran compiler by operating on and translating the statements of the source program.

The sequence of events leading to the solution of a problem by the use of Fortran can be summarized as follows:

1. The problem is analyzed for an appropriate method of solution.

2. This method or procedure is programmed in Fortran.

3. The computer under the direction of the Fortran compiler program translates† the source program produced in Step 2 into a series of machine-language instructions to which the computer can respond.

4. The machine-language instructions (object program) are executed by the computer and the results made available for analysis.

The Fortran language has gained wide acceptance as a useful method of man-computer communication. It is the most widely used of all the various programming languages in existence today. Fortran is known as a problem-

---

†The process of translation includes an analysis of the Fortran statements to determine whether they have been correctly formed. If errors are present, they are noted and the programmer must correct them. Only then will the translation process be successfully completed. This process of locating and correcting errors is called *debugging*.

oriented language, as contrasted with machine-oriented languages. Fortran statements are problem-oriented in nature and look very much like algebraic statements. To use Fortran one need know very little about how the computer operates. On the other hand, a machine-oriented programming language is closely allied to the functioning of a particular computer. A knowledge of how the computer functions is essential when programming in a machine-oriented language. A program written in a machine-oriented language for one computer cannot (in general) be executed by another computer. However, this is not true of Fortran; a program written in Fortran can be run on any computer that has a Fortran compiler. It is the compiler, not the Fortran language, that differs from computer to computer. The ideas presented in the preceding two sentences are somewhat idealistic, since unfortunately — but factually — differences (some slight, some major) in the Fortran language as defined for different computers do exist. Fortunately, it is not usually a difficult matter to adjust to these differences.

FORTRAN ARITHMETIC

4.1 Fixed-Point and Floating-Point Arithmetic

The Fortran system provides for two types of arithmetic operations: fixed point and floating point. Fixed-point arithmetic operations (addition, subtraction, multiplication, division, and exponentiation) are performed on numbers represented in a fixed-point form; these numbers are restricted to integral values. Floating-point arithmetic operations (addition, subtraction, multiplication, division, and exponentiation) are performed on numbers represented in a floating-point form (see Section 2.10). These numbers are *not* restricted to integral values.

The primary advantage of using floating-point arithmetic is that the programmer is relieved of the critical responsibility of keeping track of the decimal point in all of the calculations. This advantage far outweighs the fact that floating-point arithmetic takes longer for the computer to perform than the corresponding operations in fixed-point arithmetic. Fixed-point arithmetic is used mainly for operations such as counting or for subscripting, where the numbers involved are restricted to integral values.

Results produced by using fixed-point arithmetic are always truncated to integral values. Thus, the calculation 5 ÷ 2 performed using fixed-point arithmetic will give a result of 2; the fractional portion of the result is always *truncated*, and no rounding occurs. Results produced by using floating-point arithmetic are not restricted to integral values, but include the fractional portion as well.

The following illustrates the results of fixed-point and floating-point calculations:

FLOATING POINT

Arithmetic Statement	Result
A = 8.31 + 6.419	A = 14.729
B = 9.0 ÷ 4.0	B = 2.25
C = 1.0 − 3.2 + 1.6	C = −0.6
D = 15.0 × 1.5	D = 22.5
E = 1.0 ÷ 3.0	E = 0.3333
F = (2.5 ÷ 2.0) × 6.21	F = 7.7625

FIXED POINT

Arithmetic Statement	Result
I = 6 × 2	I = 12
J = 8 − 2 + 6	J = 12
K = 6 ÷ 3	K = 2
L = 9 ÷ 2	L = 4†
M = (5 ÷ 2) × (10 ÷ 3)	M = 6‡
N = (5 × 10) ÷ (2 × 3)	N = 8§

Since Fortran is a programming language closely related to the language of ordinary algebra, it must provide a means for expressing certain elements basic to a mathematical language. These elements are numeric constants, variable quantities, subscripted variables, operations, and expressions.

4.2 Constants

A constant is a quantity that has a fixed value for the entire program. In the equation for determining the area of a circle, $A = 3.1416R^2$, the quantity 3.1416 is a constant; it does not change. Although different values

†The true answer is 4.5; however, the 0.5 is truncated.
‡Truncation causes this to be calculated as 2 × 3.
§The true answer is 8⅓; the ⅓ is truncated. Compare this with the previous example. Note that a reordering of the operations produces a different result.

for R may be substituted in the equation, the constant 3.1416 remains a fixed value.

Fortran provides the programmer with the flexibility of specifying constants in two forms: fixed point or floating point. The type of arithmetic calculation (fixed or floating point) to be performed on the constant determines whether it should be written in the fixed-point form or the floating-point form. If a constant is to be used in floating-point calculations only, it should be written in the floating-point form; if it is to be used in fixed-point calculations only, it should be written in the fixed-point form; and if it is to be used in both fixed-point and floating-point calculations, it must be written in both forms.

4.3   Rules for Specifying Fixed-Point Constants

Fixed-point constants are written *without* decimal points. The decimal point is always assumed to be to the right of the rightmost digit in the constant; for example, the fixed-point constant 1375 represents the number 1375.0. Fixed-point constants may consist of from one to eleven decimal digits. The constant may be positive or negative. If it is negative it must be preceded by a minus sign; if it is positive it may be written with or without a preceding plus sign.

General Form

One to eleven significant digits without a decimal point.† A minus sign must precede the constant if it is negative. If the constant is positive a preceding plus sign is optional.

Examples of Fixed-Point Constants

1401	−369812
82	−10
0	64
062	+64
+3	−1247

Examples of Fixed-Point Constants Incorrectly Written

82.   (Decimal point is not allowed)

67+   (Plus sign must precede the constant)

6−82   (Minus sign must precede the constant)

167234598132   (More than eleven decimal digits)

†The maximum number of digits varies with the version of Fortran and the particular computer used.

4.4 Rules for Specifying Floating-Point Constants

Floating-point constants may be written in either one of two forms: without exponent or with exponent.

Floating-Point Constants (without Exponents)

Floating-point constants are always written *with* a decimal point. One can immediately distinguish between a floating-point constant and a fixed-point constant by the presence or absence of the decimal point. Floating-point constants may consist of from one to nine significant decimal digits with a decimal point at the beginning, at the end, or between any two digits. The constant may be positive or negative. If the constant is negative it must be preceded by a minus sign. If the constant is positive it may be written with or without a preceding plus sign.

General Form

One to nine significant decimal digits with a decimal point at the beginning, at the end, or between any two digits.† A minus sign must precede the constant if it is negative. If the constant is positive a preceding plus sign is optional.

Examples of Floating-Point Constants (without Exponents)

187.671

0.

.00000123456789   (Note: Leading zeros are not considered to be significant digits)

−71.62

−10.

+822.107

1.

−.1

---

†The maximum number of digits varies with the version of Fortran and the particular computer used.

Examples of Floating-Point Constants (without Exponents) Incorrectly Written

      67   (Decimal point is missing)

18754321.674   (More than nine significant decimal digits)†

    75.+   (Plus sign must precede the constant)

   .1234−   (Minus sign must precede the constant)

  6.12.5.   (More than one decimal point)

Floating-Point Constants (with Exponents)

A floating-point constant as defined earlier may have appended to it an exponent representing a power of ten by which the constant is to be multiplied. The exponent is written with the letter E followed by a one-or two-digit *fixed-point constant* (positive or negative) indicating the power of ten by which the constant is to be multiplied. For example, $2.34E+3$ represents the constant 2.34×10^3 or 2340.0.

General Form

One to nine significant decimal digits with the option of omitting the decimal point in an integer number.‡ This constant is followed by the letter E and a one- or two-digit fixed-point integer (positive or negative). A minus sign must precede the constant if it is negative; a minus sign must precede the integer part of the exponent if it is negative. If the constant is positive a preceding plus sign is optional; if the exponent is positive a preceding plus sign is optional.

Examples of Floating-Point Constants (with Exponents)

1.23E+07	(1.23×10^7)
87.E+5	(87.0×10^5)
75.128E6	(75.128×10^6)
−.012E10	$(−.012 \times 10^{10})$
21.2E−11	(21.2×10^{-11})
.162E−5	$(.162 \times 10^{-5})$
+67.19E5	(67.19×10^5)
612E+02§	$(612. \times 10^2)$
38E−05§	$(38. \times 10^{-5})$

†In some Fortran systems this is considered a double-precision constant; see Chapter 16.
‡The maximum number of digits varies with the version of Fortran and the particular computer used.
§Omission of the decimal point is permissible in Fortran IV but is not allowed in Fortran II.

Examples of Floating-Point Constants (with Exponents) Incorrectly Written

9.7E1.5   (No decimal point allowed in exponent)

−181.1E125   (Three-digit exponent)

4.5   Variables

A variable is a symbolic name given to a quantity that may change in value during a program. As an example, consider the equation for determining the area of a circle $A = 3.1416R^2$. It was previously explained that 3.1416 is a constant. *R*, on the other hand, is a variable; it is the symbolic *name* given to any number representing the radius of a circle. The value of the radius may be any positive number. Therefore, the area could be evaluated for *R* = 0.5, *R* = 1.5, *R* = 15.0, etc. Fortran provides the programmer with two types of variables: fixed-point variables and floating-point variables.

4.6   Rules for Specifying Fixed-Point Variables

Fixed-point variable names may be from one to six alphameric characters in length. Alphameric characters refer to the twenty-six letters of the alphabet and the ten decimal digits. The first character of the variable name must be either I, J, K, L, M, or N. This first character is used to distinguish a fixed-point variable name from a floating-point variable name, which may not start with I, J, K, L, M, or N†. No special characters (., /, *, +, etc.) may be used in the name. Fixed-point variable names are given to quantities that are restricted to integral values. A fixed-point variable may take on any value allowed a fixed-point constant.

General Form

One to six alphabetic and/or numeric characters (no special characters), of which the first must be I, J, K, L, M, or N.‡

Examples of Fixed-Point Variables | J | K12 | NA | LD9 | LL

Examples of Fixed-Point Variables Incorrectly Written

D1   (First character must be I, J, K, L, M, or N)

MN12ABC   (Exceeds six characters)

I.1   (Special characters not allowed)

†Exceptions to this form are allowed in Fortran IV by the use of Type Declaration statements. See Chapter 14 for a discussion of these exceptions.
‡The maximum number of characters varies with the version of Fortran and the particular computer used.

4.7   Rules for Specifying Floating-Point Variables

Floating-point variable names may be from one to six alphameric characters in length. The first character of the variable name must be alphabetic and other than I, J, K, L, M, and N. No special characters may be used in the name. Floating-point variable names are given to quantities that will be used in floating-point arithmetic calculations. A floating-point variable may assume any value allowed a floating-point constant.

General Form

One to six alphabetic and/or numeric characters (no special characters) of which the first must be alphabetic and other than I, J, K, L, M, or N.†

Eamples of Floating-Point Variables | A | DELTA | R1 | OHM | W1234

Examples of Floating-Point Variables Incorrectly Written

I1   (First character must be alphabetic and other than I, J, K, L, M, or N)

A1B2C3D   (Exceeds six characters)

W(6   (Special characters not allowed)

1AX   (First character not alphabetic)

4.8   Choosing Variable Names

It is advisable, when possible, to assign names with a high mnemonic content to variable quantities. For example, if one were to assign names to three variable quantities representing current, voltage, and resistance he might choose the names AMP, VOLT, and OHMS respectively. Of course, these names assume that the variables will take on floating-point values. If fixed-point arithmetic were to be used the names assigned might have been IAMP, IVOLT, and IOHM, respectively.

Assigning variable names with a high mnemonic content makes Fortran programming easier and greatly facilitates the process of checking a program for errors.

4.9   The Relationships among Variables, Constants, and Storage Registers

Variable names and constants as previously discussed can be related to the hardware of a computer. A variable can be thought of as a symbolic name

†The maximum number of characters varies with the version of Fortran and the particular computer used.

given to a storage register in the computer. During the execution of a program the different numeric values that the variable assumes will be stored in this register. A variable, as used in a Fortran program, therefore refers to the name of a storage register whose content at any time represents the current value of the variable.

A constant as used in Fortran can also be thought of as a symbolic name for a storage register. However, the numeric value of the constant is also stored in the storage register. As an illustration, the constant 78.123 as used in Fortran can be thought of as the symbolic name of a storage register whose numeric content is 78.123 or, in the notation of Section 1.9, (78.123) = 78.123.

A constant not only causes a name to be assigned to a storage register, but also causes the value of the constant to be stored in that register. A variable merely causes a name to be assigned to a storage register.

These concepts are vital to a clear understanding of the Fortran language. As an illustration of these concepts, consider the interpretation of the following Fortran expression:

$$3.1416*R*R \tag{4.1}$$

The asterisk (*) in Fortran is the symbol for multiplication. Expression 4.1 can be interpreted as follows:

Multiply the content of the storage register whose symbolic name is 3.1416 by the content of the storage register whose symbolic name is R. This product is then to be multiplied by the content of the storage register whose symbolic name is R. Using the parenthesis notation of Section 1.9 expression 4.1 can be denoted as

$$(3.1416) \times (R) \times (R)$$

where (3.1416) = 3.1416.

4.10   Arithmetic Operations

The Fortran language provides for the following arithmetic operations: addition, subtraction, multiplication, division, and exponentiation (raising a number to a power). The symbols used by Fortran to designate these mathematical operations are as follows:

Symbol	-|	—	*	/	**
Operation	Addition	Subtraction	Multiplication	Division	Exponentiatoin

The symbols simply denote the operation to be performed; they do not designate the type of arithmetic (fixed point or floating point) to be used. This is dependent upon the quantities on which the arithmetic is to be performed. If the quantities are both floating point (e. g., A+3.) the floating-point arithmetic system will be used; if the quantities are both fixed point (e. g., I+J), the fixed-point arithmetic system will be used. Fortran, with one exception which will be noted, does not allow expressions of the form A+2, where one argument is floating point and the other fixed point.

4.11   Arithmetic Expressions

An expression in Fortran is defined as a sequence of one or more variables and/or constants joined by any of the operation symbols to indicate a quantity or series of calculations to be performed. The following are examples of some simple Fortran expressions:

A+B−C	3.
X+Y/A+2.	B**2.−4.*A*C
J*12	D

Expressions must be written according to a set of rules that specify the allowable forms an expression may take. The rules for forming arithmetic expressions will be presented with some examples illustrating the necessity for the rule as well as its use.

Consider the Fortran expression A+B*C. Is this equivalent to the algebraic expression $A + (B \times C)$ or the algebraic expression $(A + B) \times C$? Consider the Fortran expression A**B+C. Is this equivalent to the algebraic expression $A^B + C$ or the algebraic expression $A^{(B+C)}$? Clearly, a rule is necessary to specify the priority of operations.

Rule 1. The priority of operations is as follows:

a. Exponentiation   **   High

b. Multiplication and division   * /   ↑

c. Addition and subtraction   + −   Low

Thus the operation of exponentiation has the highest priority, with multiplication and division next; addition and subtraction have the lowest priority. A few examples will serve to illustrate the application of Rule 1.

Fortran Expression	A+B*C	A**B+C	I*J+2*K	A−B*C**D	I*J**M−3
Algebraic Equivalent	$A + (B \cdot C)$	$A^B + C$	$(I \cdot J) + (2 \cdot K)$	$A - (B \cdot C^D)$	$(I \cdot J^M) - 3$

The application of Rule 1 does not help in interpreting expressions of the form A*B/C*D where all the operation symbols are of the same rank in the priority table. This leads to the necessity for Rule 2.

Rule 2. When an expression contains a sequence of operation symbols that are of equal rank (have the same priority), the order of execution of the operations is from left to right.† To illustrate Rule 2 the following examples are presented:

Fortran Expression	A*B/C*D	A/B/C
Algebraic Equivalent	$\left(\dfrac{A \cdot B}{C}\right) \cdot D$ or $\dfrac{A \cdot B \cdot D}{C}$	$\left(\dfrac{A}{B}\right) \div C$ or $\dfrac{A}{B \cdot C}$

An expression of the form A**B**C, involving exponentiation, is not allowed in Fortran. It would seem that Rule 2 would apply to this expression, however, the expression is not allowed and is considered a violation of Rule 3.

Rule 3. An expression of the form A**B**C is not allowed in the Fortran language. Parentheses must be used in the expression to denote priority.

Fortran Expression	A**(B**C)	(I**J)**K
Algebraic Equivalent	$A^{(B^C)}$	$(I^J)^K$

The use of parentheses in a Fortran expression introduces Rule 4.

Rule 4. Parentheses may be used in an expression to specify the order or priority of operations just as in ordinary algebra. The following examples illustrate the application of Rule 4:

Fortran Expression	A**(B+C)	(I+2)*N	A−B/(C+2.)	I**(J/K)+4
Algebraic Equivalent	$A^{(B+C)}$	$(I + 2) \cdot N$	$A - \dfrac{B}{C + 2}$	$I^{(J/K)} + 4$

Instances often occur in which more than one set of parentheses appear in the same expression. In fact, one set of parentheses may contain a second set, etc. Rule 4.1 describes the order of priority of nested parentheses (one set of parentheses containing a second set of parentheses).

Rule 4.1. When parentheses are nested in a Fortran expression the innermost set of parentheses has priority and the operations enclosed therein are executed first. The following examples illustrate this rule:

†In some Fortran systems the operation of division takes precedence over multiplication.

Fortran Expression	Algebraic Equivalent
((A+B)*C)**D	$[(A + B)\cdot C]^D$
((B**2−4.*A*C)**.5)/(2.*A)	$\sqrt{B^2 - 4\cdot A\cdot C} \div (2\cdot A)$
A*(B−C)/((D+2.)*E)	$\dfrac{A\cdot(B - C)}{(D + 2)\cdot E}$

In the examples presented on the last few pages the discerning reader will have noted that in every case each expression contained elements (variables and/or constants) all of the same mode (floating point or fixed point). The mode of the elements determines the type of arithmetic that will be used. With a single exception, discussed in Rule 6, it is *not* possible in Fortran to perform an arithmetic operation on two numbers that are not of the same mode.

Rule 5. *All* the variables and constants in an expression must be in the same mode. They must either be all floating-point quantities or all fixed-point quantities. The following examples illustrate this rule:

Valid Fortran Expressions		Invalid Fortran Expressions containing Mixed-Mode Quantities	
B*C+2.	I*J/3	B*C+2	A−R+K
A/B−6.7	A**2.+F	I/J*6.7	I*J/D
A−R+W2	A**2+F		

The example A**2+F in the list of valid Fortran expressions above would seem to violate Rule 5, and in fact it does; however, as noted previously, there is one exception to Rule 5 that is valid. This exception occurs in the allowable forms of exponentiation.

Rule 6. The following forms of exponentiation are allowed in a Fortran expression:

$$A**B \qquad A**I \qquad I**J$$

where A and B are any floating-point expressions and I and J are any fixed-point expressions.

The second form of exponentiation is allowable even though it violates Rule 5. The reader should carefully note that in the allowable forms of exponentiation the base as well as the power may themselves be expressions containing operation symbols.

Allowable Forms of Exponentiation

A**B	D**(I+3)
A**(B+3.)	(C+2.)**(K−1)
D**(E**2.+F)	I**2
B**2.	I**(J+K)
B**2	(L+3)**(M+N/J)

Invalid Forms of Exponentiation

I**A   (Cannot raise a fixed point expression
to a floating point power)

B**(I+2.)   (Mixed mode in parentheses)

A**(B+3)   (Mixed mode in parentheses)

Rule 7. An operation symbol must not precede a plus or minus sign used to signify that a variable, constant, or expression is positive or negative. Parentheses can be used to enclose the sign and the variable or constant. The following examples illustrate Rule 7.

A*−D   (Invalid)   I/−J   (Invalid)

A*(−D)   I/(−J)

Table 4.1 is used to illustrate some of the most common errors made in writing expressions. An algebraic expression is presented with both an incorrect and correct Fortran expression for it. The errors in the incorrect Fortran expressions are explained in the commentary following the table.

TABLE 4.1   Common Errors in Writing Fortran Expressions

Algebraic Statement	Incorrect Fortran Expression	Correct Fortran Expression
a) $X \cdot Y$	XY	X*Y
b) $I(-J)$	I*−J	I*(−J)
c) A^{I+2}	A**I+2	A**(I+2)
d) I^X	I**X	A**X
e) $\sqrt{B+C}$	(B+C)**(1/2)	(B+C)**(1./2.) or (B+C)**.5
f) $(A+B)^2$	(A+B**2	(A+B)**2
g) $\dfrac{AB}{CD}$	A*B/C*D	A*B/C/D or A*B/(C*D) or A/C*B/D or (A*B)/(C*D)
h) $4 \cdot A \cdot C$	4*A*C	4.*A*C

Comments on the Incorrect Fortran Expressions of Table 4.1

a) One of the most common errors in Fortran programming is the omission of the multiplication symbol. The symbol XY in Fortran does not mean X · Y; it is a variable name.

b) This is violation of Rule 7; parentheses are required to separate the multiplication symbol and minus sign.

c) Parentheses are required to indicate the correct priority. Without the parentheses the Fortran expression is interpreted as $A^I + 2$, since exponentiation has a higher priority than addition.

d) A fixed-point quantity cannot be raised to a floating-point power in Fortran. The variable should be given a floating-point name.

e) It is allowable to raise a floating-point quantity to a fixed point power; however, in this case the exponent is evaluated as 0 not .5, since the division is carried out using fixed-point arithmetic.

f) A parenthesis has been omitted. This is a very common error in writing expressions, particularly where the expression includes more than one set of parentheses.

g) Parentheses are needed to enclose the denominator C*D. The failure to use parentheses to enclose the denominator in a division operation is a very common error.

h) Mixed-mode expressions are not allowed. A decimal point is required after the 4 to make it agree in mode (floating point) with the variables A and C.

A Note Concerning Exponentiation

It is necessary to discuss in more detail the two forms of exponentiation, A**B and A**I. If a floating-point quantity is to be raised to an integral power, either form of exponentiation may be used. Thus, A**3 and A**3. are both valid expressions for representing A^3. When a quantity is raised to a fixed-point power the operation is usually carried out in the computer by performing successive multiplications. Therefore, A**3 is evaluated as (A*A*A). When a quantity is raised to a floating-point power, the operation is carried out using logarithms. The log of the base is evaluated, multiplied by the exponent and the antilogarithm evaluated giving the desired result. For the expression A**3., the logarithm of A is evaluated and multiplied by 3, then the antilogarithm is evaluated giving the result. If the quantity to be raised to a power is negative the logarithm does not exist. In this case the Fortran system causes an error message to be printed out, indicating that an attempt has been made to take the logarithm of a negative number. Most systems will not terminate the calculations at this point, but will use the absolute value of the quantity being raised to a power to evaluate the result. If the integral exponent is odd, an incorrect result will occur. Also, if $A = 0$ an error will be indicated, since $\log_{10}(0) = -\infty$. To illustrate this, two examples are presented:

1. $(-2.)**3$ is evaluated as $(-2)(-2)(-2)$ or -8.
2. $(-2.)**3.$ is evaluated as $10^{3(\log_{10}|-2|)}$ or $+8$ and an error message is printed.

The process of evaluating a logarithm requires about 17 multiplications. Since round-off errors occur, an exact result may not be obtained. Therefore, when the exponent is known to be an integer, it should be written as a fixed-point quantity.

Problems

4.1 Why is it necessary to translate Fortran statements into machine-language instructions?

4.2 Indicate the results of the following operations performed with *fixed-point* arithmetic.

a) $6 - 7$
b) $8 + 2$
c) $9 \div 10$
d) $5 \div 4$

e) $7 \div 2$
f) $(8 \div 3)(6 \div 5)$
g) $(9 \div 3)(5 \div 6)$
h) $(17 \times 2 \div 3) + 9 + 4 \div 2$

4.3 What is a major advantage of using floating-point arithmetic?

4.4 Identify each of the following as either a permissible fixed-point constant, a permissible floating-point constant, or neither.

a) 00.1
b) .2
c) 7
d) $1-23$
e) $87E-05$

f) 9875.164
g) 12$4
h) $6.1E-.5$
i) $467+1$
j) 43.1.2

4.5 Do each of the following pairs of floating-point numbers represent the same number?

a) 3.167 $+03.167$
b) 890. $.89E+03$
c) .0057 $57.0E-05$
d) $87.21E+02$ $.008721E+05$

4.6 Which of the following are acceptable names of fixed-point variables? Of floating-point variables? Which are unacceptable names for any variable?

a) B   f) I$J
b) SYSTEMS   g) YOUYOU
c) FOR   h) X/Y
d) I7   i) 2AB
e) AB+2   j) A.B

4.7 Which of the following Fortran expressions are invalid? Indicate the reason for your answers.

a) AB+C/E   e) 2.*A/(B+C**D)
b) E**M+A*M   f) I+2*J−N**2.
c) −B−B*B   g) A+B)/C+D)
d) (A*−B+2.*C)   h) D − E/1.5 + 6.7/A/X

4.8 Write equivalent algebraic expressions for each of the following Fortran expressions:

a) A+B/C**2−D
b) A−B*C**3/D
c) A**(10**4)+B/C+D/(E+3.)
d) I/K*K1**3
e) 7.2*X**5−6.7*X**4+8.1*X*X+3.
f) X*(3.*X+X*(2.*X+X*(6.1*X+3.))+2.)+7.5

4.9 Write Fortran expressions for each of the following algebraic expressions:

a) $B + \dfrac{(C - D)}{A}$

f) $\dfrac{10^{30}A}{B(-C)}$

b) $\left(\dfrac{A \cdot 10^4}{3} + \pi R^2\right)/(A^{(BC)} - 989.9\sqrt{ABC})$

g) $\left(A + \dfrac{B}{3}\right)^{(C+D)}$

c) $\dfrac{A}{B} + \dfrac{B - C}{D} \times \dfrac{X^3}{8}$

h) $-(B + D)^2$

d) $(I^2 + K^2)^2 + 2JK + J$

i) X^{-B}

e) $\dfrac{E}{R^2 + \sqrt{\left[2\pi FL - \dfrac{1}{2\pi FC}\right]^2}}$

j) $X^3 + X^2 + 2X + X$

4.10 How does Fortran evaluate each of the following two expressions? What is the value of each of the expressions as calculated in Fortran?

a) (−2)**5.   b) (−2)**5

5

Fortran Arithmetic Statements
and Functions

The discussion up to this point has concerned the rules for writing constants, variables, and expressions. Now these basic elements of the Fortran language will be used to form the Fortran arithmetic statement.

5.1   The Arithmetic Statement

The arithmetic statement specifies how the value of a dependent variable should be calculated. The statement looks like a simple statement of equality in algebra (for example, $A = B$, $I = J + 2$). The quantity to the left of the equal sign in an arithmetic statement is usually either a floating point variable or a fixed point variable.† Constants and expressions involving operation symbols, except when appearing as subscripts, are *not* permitted to the left of the equality symbol. The right side of any arithmetic statement consists of an arithmetic expression as previously defined in Section 4.11.

The equality symbol ($=$) has a unique meaning in Fortran. It does not denote equality, but means "to compute the numerical value of the expression on the right side and assign the result to the variable whose symbolic name is on the left side." The statement $X = X + 1$. is valid in Fortran whereas in ordinary algebra the statement is meaningless.

General Form

$$a = b$$

where a is a variable (fixed point or floating point) and b is any valid arithmetic expression.

---

†For all of the allowable forms of the arithmetic statement in Fortran, see Table 17.2.

By the above definition, statements of the form A = I and J = B, where A and J are variable names, I is a fixed-point expression and B is a floating-point expression, are permissible. If the expression to the right of the equal sign is a *fixed-point* expression and the variable to the left of the equal sign is a *floating-point* variable, the expression is evaluated using *fixed-point* arithmetic, and the result is converted to the *floating-point* form and stored in the register whose name appears to the left of the equal sign. If the expression to the right of the equal sign is a *floating-point* expression and the variable to the left of the equal sign is a *fixed-point* variable, the expression is evaluated using *floating-point* arithmetic, and the result is truncated and converted to the *fixed-point* form and stored in the register whose name appears to the left of the equal sign.

The following are some examples of arithmetic statements:

$$A = B + 1.$$
$$D = A*B**3$$
$$I = (J+4)/(K-2)$$
$$L = A + B**.5$$
$$X = (-B + (B**2 - 4.*A*C)**.5)/(2.*A)$$

$$DEL = D3 + D4882$$
$$J1 = L + 2$$
$$A = I + 1$$
$$Y = Y + 1.$$

Statements of the form $Y = Y + 1.$ are important in Fortran, and a closer examination of them is in order since they differ from statements found in ordinary algebra. The expression to the right of the equal sign is evaluated. Therefore, in the above example, 1. and the content of the storage register called Y are added. The result is stored back in the register called Y replacing the original value.

Assume that the following variables have the values indicated:

$$A = 2. \quad C = 10. \quad E = -4. \quad J = 3$$
$$B = 5. \quad D = 2.5 \quad I = 2 \quad K = -2$$

The following are examples of arithmetic statements and the value assigned to the variable whose name is to the left of the equal sign, as a result of evaluating the expression to the right of the equal sign.

Fortran Statement	*Value Stored After Execution of Statement*
X = A**I + B	9.0
Y = B/C + D	3.0
M = I**J + K	6
N = 3.*D	7
T = I/J	0.0
R = E + C/D − A**J	−8.0
W = C**2 + D*E − 10.E + 02	−910.0
B = B + 2.*C	25.0

5.2   *A Partial Fortran Program*

Suppose we are to calculate $X = A^2 + B^2 - C^2$, where $A = 67.12$, $B = -112.617$, and $C = 0.0$. The Fortran statements to describe this calculation are

$$A = 67.12$$

$$B = -112.617$$

$$C = 0.0$$

$$X = A*A + B**2 - C**2$$

The first statement means to assign the value 67.12 to the variable whose name is A. The next two statements have a similar meaning. The fourth statement evaluates the expression $A^2 + B^2 - C^2$ with the previously assigned values for A, B, and C. The result is stored in the register called X.

Note that in the fourth Fortran statement two different methods of squaring a number are used. Both methods are equally acceptable. However, if either B or C had been raised to a floating point power, error messages would be printed and in some systems the program would terminate execution.

The requirements of the problem could have been met with the following single Fortran statement:

$$X - (67.12*67.12) + (-112.617)**2 - (0.0)**2$$

5.3   *Mathematical Functions*

Frequently, the method of solution of a problem requires that some mathematical function, such as logarithm, sine, or cosine, be evaluated. Most computers do not have a built-in (hardware) ability to calculate these functions; therefore, there is no one machine language instruction that will cause the required mathematical function to be evaluated. However, most of these functions can be *approximated* quite accurately by an arithmetic series involving only the basic operations of arithmetic which the computer can perform. Certain of these approximating series have been programmed and are included in Fortran for use when the corresponding function is required to be evaluated. A detailed description of how to use prewritten programs is given in Chapter 11. Now only the information necessary to use these mathematical functions will be presented. Table 5.1 lists some mathematical functions† available for use in Fortran.

†Not all the mathematical functions listed are found in every Fortran system.

TABLE 5.1   Fortran Mathematical Functions

Function	Fortran IV Name†	Operation
Natural logarithm	ALOG	$\log_e X$
Common logarithm	ALOG10	$\log_{10} X$
Natural antilogarithm (or exponential)	EXP	e^X
Arctangent	ATAN	arctan X
Arctangent	ATAN2	arctan $\dfrac{X}{Y}$
Sine	SIN	$\sin X$
Cosine	COS	$\cos X$
Hyperbolic tangent	TANH	$\tanh X$
Square root	SQRT	$\sqrt{X}$
Arc sine	ARSIN	$\arcsin X$
Arc cosine	ARCOS	$\arccos X$

†The Fortran names of the mathematical functions are not standard for all Fortran systems. The reader should consult the specifications of the Fortran system used at his installation for the proper names of these functions.

The programmer can use any of these functions in an arithmetic expression by using the Fortran name of the function in the following form:

General Form

NAME (a)

where NAME is the Fortran name of a mathematical function and a is any floating-point expression.

Fortran Statement	Algebraic Equivalent
Y = ALOG (B+C)	$Y = \log_e (B + C)$
D = EXP (X/Y**3)	$D = e^{(x/y^3)}$
F = R+X/(D**3 − 6.3) − ALOG10 (W*2.5)	$F = R + \dfrac{X}{D^3 - 6.3} - \log_{10}(W \times 2.5)$
W = ALOG (B+EXP(Z+R)+SQRT(SIN(B)))	$W = \log_e (B + e^{(Z+R)} + \sqrt{\sin B})$

It can be seen from these examples how the function names are used in arithmetic expressions. There is no limit to the number of function names that can be used in an expression or to the complexity of the expression following the function name. A function may be the argument of a function as illustrated in the last example by SQRT(SIN(B)).

The following items concerning the mathematical functions should be noted:

Function Name	Comment
ATAN	The result is given in radians in the range $\pm(\pi/2)$.
ATAN2	Two arguments are necessary for this function. The two arguments must be separated by commas and must both be enclosed in the set of parentheses following the name. Each argument may be any floating point expression. The function computes the arctangent of the first argument divided by the second argument. As an example, consider the Fortran statement:

$$Y = B + ATAN2(C*D+3.5,A)$$

The algebraic equivalent is

$$Y = B + \arctan\left(\frac{C \times D + 3.5}{A}\right)$$

The result is given in radians and lies in the quadrant dictated by the signs of the arguments.

SIN	The argument must be expressed in radians. If it is desired to compute the sine of a variable A that represents an angle in degrees, it is the responsibility of the programmer to convert degrees to radians. This could be done as follows:

$$X = SIN(A*3.141593/180.)$$

where $\pi/180$ is the conversion factor for degrees to radians.

COS	The argument must be expressed in radians.
ARSIN	The result is given in radians in the range $\pm(\pi/2)$.
ARCOS	The result is given in radians in the range $\pm(\pi/2)$.

Problems

5.1 What is the meaning of the equality symbol ($=$) as used in Fortran? How does this differ from its use in ordinary algebra?

5.2 For each of the following arithmetic statements indicate whether the computations are carried out using fixed-point arithmetic or floating-point arithmetic. Also indicate whether the result is stored in a fixed-point form or floating-point form.

a) A = B*C−D*E+X/Y**2   *c*) A = M+N/2+J

b) K = I+J−2*K   *d*) I2 = B+C−D*3.

e) B = ALOG(B+C−D)

5.3 Which of the following arithmetic statements are invalid? State the reasons for your answers.

a) A = −B   h) B = C = D

b) B+2. = A   i) A = B+ALOG10(ALOG(X**Y))

c) 3 = K   j) D = 6.+3.

d) DEL = ALOGX   k) W = (X)+(Y)

e) D = B+SQRT(I)   l) −K = I

f) XYZXYZ = −XYZXYZ   m) D = (C+I)**2

g) D = 6.*   n) X = X+1.

5.4 For each of the following arithmetic statements, indicate the result assigned to the variable whose name is to the left of the equal sign:

a) X = 5/4   f) C = 2.**3./2.

b) Y = 9/2+8/2+7   g) D = 2.**3/2.

c) I = 2**4   h) K = 2**(9/4)

d) A = 4.**(3/2)   i) J = 6./2.**3.

e) B = 4.**(3./2.)   j) L = 2.*3.5+8.3

5.5 Assume that the following variables have the values indicated:

$$A = 1. \qquad C = 10. \qquad I = 2$$
$$B = 2.5 \qquad D = 3. \qquad K = 3$$

Indicate, for each of the following arithmetic statements, the value assigned to the variable whose name is to the left of the equal sign, as a result of evaluating the expression to the right of the equal sign.

a) L = I/K   h) R = 3**K+2*(I**K)

b) M = K/I   i) S = B+ALOG10(C*C)+SQRT(B*C)

c) AX = I/K   j) T = B**I/C*(C*D)

d) DB = B/C   k) I1 = B**I/C

e) J = B/C   l) N = (C+2.*B)**I

f) X = A+B/C−D   m) A1 = I/K*K

g) Y = A+B/(C−D**I)   n) DA = (−C)**K−(−C)**I

5.6 Write Fortran statements for each of the following algebraic statements.

a) $X = \dfrac{U + V}{U - V}$

h) $V = \sin^2 X + \cos^2 Y$

b) $Y = \dfrac{N(N + 1)}{2}$

i) $B = \log_e (e^x - e^{\sqrt{x}})$

c) $Z = \dfrac{6X - 7Y}{6W - R}$

j) $C = \sqrt{\sqrt{\log_e \left(\arctan \dfrac{X}{Y}\right)}}$

d) $S = \sqrt{Y^3}$

k) $E = \log_{10} \left(-\dfrac{1}{X + Y} - \cos (X + Y)\right)$

e) $T = A + \dfrac{B}{C - D} - \dfrac{Y}{B + W/(R + S)}$

f) $A = \pi R^2$

l) $U = \dfrac{1}{6\sqrt{R^3 - S^2}}$

g) $W = \log_{10}\left(\dfrac{X - Y}{C - D}\right) + Y$

m) $X = -X$

5.7 Consider the following ten arithmetic statements as ten consecutive statements of a Fortran program. Indicate the values of the variables A, B, and C *after* each statement is executed. The initial values of the variables are 5.0, 2.0, and 1.0, respectively.

	A	B	C
Initial values	5.0	2.0	1.0
A = B+C			
B = B**A			
C = C+A**2			
A = 2.*C−A*B			
A = −A			
C = A*B/2.			
C = A*(A−B)+C			
A = A*2.+C*3.			
C = 2.*A−B**2			
C = C/(−6.)			

6

Statement Numbers and Fortran Coding

6.1   Statement Numbers

Fortran statements are normally executed in the same sequence in which they occur in the source program; that is the first statement of a program is executed, then the second statement, then the third, and so on. In the partial Fortran program of Section 5.2, repeated below, the four statements are executed in the order in which they occur:

$$A = 67.12$$

$$B = -112.617$$

$$C = 0.0$$

$$X = A*A + B**2 - C**2$$

If the third and fourth statements were interchanged, the computer would attempt to evaluate $X = A^2 + B^2 - C^2$ *before* having the desired value of 0.0 stored in C. X would therefore be evaluated using some unknown value for C. Of course, in a strict sense, a Fortran statement is never executed; rather it is the machine-language instructions generated from the Fortran statement that are executed by the computer. However, in discussions of Fortran programs and statements it is convenient to refer to the execution of a Fortran statement, although it is technically incorrect.

It is often desirable to deviate from this sequential execution of instructions. To illustrate this, consider the problem of determining the roots of the quadratic equation whose form is $AX^2 + BX + C = 0$. The roots can be calculated from the formula $(-B \pm \sqrt{B^2 - 4AC}) \div (2A)$. If $(B^2 - 4AC)$ is less than zero, the square root of $(B^2 - 4AC)$ is not a real number and the roots are complex. If $(B^2 - 4AC) \geq 0$ the roots are real. A Fortran program written to calculate the roots of a quadratic equation would first evaluate the quantity $(B^2 - 4AC)$. Depending upon the value of the result either *one* of the following two steps would occur.

1. A sequence of Fortran statements to evaluate the real roots would be executed.

2. A sequence of Fortran statements to evaluate the complex roots would be executed.

One and only one of the two *different* sets of Fortran statements would be executed. It is obvious that a method of deviating from sequential execution is necessary.

To accomplish this a method of referencing different Fortran statements must be provided. The technique used is to allow the programmer to assign statement numbers to Fortran statements.

A statement number has the form of a 1–5-digit unsigned fixed-point constant. Almost every Fortran statement may be assigned a statement number, and the numbers do not have to be assigned in numerical order The first statement of a Fortran program may be assigned the number 99, and the fifth statement of the program may be assigned the number 1. The order of execution of the statements is in no way dependent on the numeric value of a statement number. It is advisable, although not necessary, to number only those statements that will be referenced; adherence to this will facilitate interpretation and debugging (that is, correcting) of Fortran programs. Obviously, in a single program two statements should not be assigned the same statement number.

General Form

A one-to-five-digit unsigned fixed-point constant.

6.2   The Fortran Coding Form

A Fortran program consists of a sequence of Fortran statements. The programmer usually writes these statements on a standard Fortran coding form from which the statements are keypunched into cards. This form is shown in Figure 6.1. Each line is divided into seventy-two columns, which correspond to columns 1–72 of a punched card (see Section 1.8). If a Fortran statement has been assigned a statement number, the number is written in columns 1–5. It is advisable although not mandatory to "right-justify" the statement number within the five columns. For example, if a statement has been assigned the number 5 by the programmer, the 5 should be written in column 5; if a statement has been assigned the number 123, the 1 should be in column 3, the 2 in column 4, and the 3 in column 5. This concept is illustrated in Fig. 6.1.

FORTRAN CODING FORM

| Program | EXAMPLE | | | Punching Instructions | | Page 1 of 1 |
| Programmer | JOHN DOE | Date 1/10/66 | Graphic / Punch | | Card Form # * | Identification 73 80 |

STATEMENT NUMBER		FORTRAN STATEMENT
		X = A+B*C**DEL
		X = A + B * C * * DE L
		X= A+ B *C ** D E L
123		SUMM=X1+X2+X3+X4+X5+X6+X7+X8+X9+X10+X11+X12+X13+X14+X15+X16+X17+X1
		8+X19+X20
48		A=A+1.
5		B=A
C THIS		IS A COMMENT

FIGURE 6.1 Standard Fortran coding form showing sample program entries.

The Fortran statement is written in columns 7–72 inclusive. If a statement consists of more than 66 characters and is, therefore, too long for one line, it may be continued on the next line. This is indicated by writing in column 6 of the continuation line some character other than zero. The statement on line 5 of Fig. 6.1 is a continuation of the previous statement. The statement on any line that has a character other than zero or blank (a blank column) in column 6 is a continuation of the previous statement. For most Fortran systems a maximum of nine continuation cards is allowed to any one statement, giving a possible total of 660 characters for any one statement. Column 6 on the first line of any statement must contain a blank or zero.

Blank characters, except when used in column 6 or in alphameric fields of a format statement (see Section 9.14) are ignored by Fortran, and can be included in Fortran statements to improve their readability. Thus the first three statements in Fig. 6.1 are equivalent; blanks have been used in the latter two statements at the discretion of the programmer and do not alter the meaning of the statement.

Any statement with the character C written in column 1 is considered to be a comment and is not processed by the Fortran translator; however, when a Fortran program is listed (that is, the source statements are printed) the comments are also listed. Comments are written in columns 2–80, and are usually included to explain what certain parts of the program accomplish. The authors encourage the liberal use of comments throughout all programs.

Columns 73–80 are not used by Fortran, but may be used by the programmer for any code or identifying information desired. These columns are frequently used for numbering in sequence the statements of the source program. This is desirable in the event the punched cards containing the source statements should become inadvertently disarranged. If a sequence number has been punched in columns 73–80, it becomes a relatively simple matter to restore the cards to their original order.

After the Fortran statements comprising a program have been written on the Fortran coding form, the information on the coding form is used to prepare the punched cards. The information on each line of the coding form is punched into the respective columns of a card. One card is punched from one line of information on the coding form.

Problems

6.1 Which of the following statements are false?
  a) Statement numbers must be assigned sequentially.
  b) Statement numbers may be variable quantities.
  c) A statement number may consist of from one to eleven digits.
  d) It is valid to assign the same statement number to several statements in a program.
  e) Every Fortran statement must be assigned a statement number.

6.2 What does a character other than blank or zero in column 6 of a Fortran source card indicate?

6.3 What does a C in column 1 of a Fortran source card indicate?

6.4 When punching a Fortran statement, what columns are used for the statement number? The statement itself? What are columns 73–80 used for?

7

Transfer Statements

Fortran statements are executed in the same sequence in which they occur in the source program; the fact that this is not always desirable was illustrated in Section 6.1. The set of Fortran statements called transfer-type statements provides a means of deviating from the sequential execution of instructions by specifying the statement number of the statement which is to be executed next.

7.1   The GO TO Statement

General Form

GO TO n

where n is a statement number.

Examples of the GO TO *Statement* | GO TO 88 | GO TO 4 | GO TO 1934

The GO TO statement is used to specify, at some point in a program, that the next statement to be executed is not the one following as would normally be the case, rather it is the statement with statement number n. This statement may be located anywhere in the program; it may be a statement that has preceded the GO TO statement or one that follows it at some later point in the program. The coding below illustrates these two conditions.

a)
$$\text{———}$$
$$\text{———}$$
$$\text{———}$$
$$\quad A = 12.$$
$$\quad B = 6.$$
$$\quad \text{GO TO } 9$$
$$14 \quad D = A + B$$
$$\quad \text{GO TO } 3$$
$$9 \quad D = A - B$$
$$3 \quad Y = D**.5$$
$$\text{———}$$

b)
$$\text{———}$$
$$\quad C = 0.$$
$$\quad A = 12.1$$
$$9 \quad B = 6.4$$
$$10 \quad C = A + B$$
$$16 \quad A = 7.5$$
$$13 \quad \text{GO TO } 10$$
$$14 \quad A = 13.1$$
$$\quad B = 7.4$$
$$\text{———}$$

In *a*, after the GO TO 9 statement is executed, the next statement to be executed is the statement with number 9; execution then continues sequentially, with the statement whose number is 3 being executed next, and so on. Note that the statement numbered 14 is *not* executed. In *b*, after the GO TO 10 statement is executed, the next statement to be executed is the statement with number 10, followed by the statement whose number is 16, and so on. Actually, in this example the statements numbered 10, 16, and 13 will be repeatedly executed. The computer would continue to execute these statements over and over again until some physical action were taken to stop the computer.

It is important to note that in the general form of the GO TO statement, *n* designates a *statement number*. The following two statements would *not* cause the statement with statement number 9 to be executed after the GO TO statement.

$$I = 9$$
$$\text{GO TO } I$$

The GO TO statement is in an incorrect form and would be detected as an invalid statement by the Fortran compiler.

Consider the following Fortran program:

$$X = 1.$$
$$\text{SUM} - 0.$$
$$6 \quad \text{SUM} = \text{SUM} + X$$
$$X - X + 1.$$
$$\text{GO TO } 6 \qquad\qquad (\text{P7.1})\dagger$$

Theoretically, the above program will evaluate the sum of the integers

†This notation will be used as a reference to the Fortran programs presented

from 1 to infinity. Actually, the program will halt when the value in SUM exceeds the greatest allowable floating-point value. The first two statements of the program are called "initialization" statements because they assign an initial value to the variables X and SUM respectively. X is assigned an initial value of 1, and SUM an initial value of 0. The third statement SUM = SUM + X develops the sum of the integers. The next statement causes the value of X to be increased by 1. The GO TO 6 statement causes the statement with statement number 6 to be executed next. Thus, the last three statements of the program will be repeatedly executed with the value of X being increased by 1 each time and this value being added to SUM every time the statement whose number is 6 is executed. Table 7.1 shows the numeric value of the variables as the program progresses.

TABLE 7.1 Value of Variables Before and After the Statement
SUM = SUM + X is Executed

Before		After	
SUM	X	SUM	X
0	1	1	1
1	2	3	2
3	3	6	3
6	4	10	4
10	5	15	5
15	6	21	6
.	.	.	.
.	.	.	.
.	.	.	.

The second statement, SUM = 0., in the above program is required to set SUM equal to some initial value; in this example the required value was zero. The first time the statement SUM = SUM + X is executed, the content of the storage register called X, which was initialized to one, and the content of the storage register called SUM, which was initialized to zero, are added and the result stored in SUM. If the statement SUM = 0. had been omitted from the program what would the content of the storage register called SUM have been the first time the statement SUM = SUM + X was executed? There is no way of knowing. Since SUM is merely the name of a storage register which all programs could use, there is the strong possibility that some number other than zero was stored by another program in the register designated in P 7.1 as SUM. This number would be used by the program the first time the statement SUM = SUM + X was executed, leading to an incorrect result. Therefore, the variable SUM must be initialized to zero to insure that the correct results are obtained. This is a very important concept and should be clearly understood.

7.2 The IF Statement

The foregoing program is not of great practical use. A more practical problem would be to determine the sum of some consecutive finite sequence of integers; for example, to determine the sum of the integers from one to one hundred, inclusive. To alter the previous program to accomplish this would require some method of testing the value of the variable X, and only executing the statement SUM = SUM + X for values of X from one to one hundred, inclusive. A Fortran statement that provides for the evaluation of an expression and then transfers to one of several different Fortran statements based on the result is the arithmetic IF statement.

General Form

IF (a) n_1, n_2, n_3

where a is any arithmetic expression (fixed point or floating point) and n_1, n_2, and n_3 are statement numbers.

Examples of   IF (X − 100.) 7,5,9   IF (I+K − 2*J) 1,1,2
the IF *statement*   IF (B**2 − 4.*A*C) 6,4,89   IF (L) 3,4,4

The arithmetic IF statement operates as follows:

1. The expression a is evaluated.
2. Depending upon the value of a one of the following conditions occur:

   a) If the value of the expression is less than zero, the Fortran statement with statement number n_1 is executed next.

   b) If the value of the expression is zero, the Fortran statement with statement number n_2 is executed next.

   c) If the value of the expression is greater than zero, the Fortran statement with statement number n_3 is executed next.

Note that in the general form of the IF statement the expression is enclosed in parentheses and the statement numbers, of which there must always be three, are separated by commas. The Fortran statements with statement numbers n_1, n_2, n_3 may appear anywhere in the program; however, they must appear.

A program that will sum the positive integers from 1–100 is

$$X = 1.$$
$$SUM = 0.$$
8    $$SUM = SUM + X$$
$$X = X + 1.$$
IF (X − 100.) 8,8,6
6   STOP
END   (P7.2)

This program is similar to the one presented to sum the positive integers from one to infinity in several respects; however, *(a)* an IF statement has been included, and (*b*) a STOP statement and an END statement have been included.

It is not the authors' intention to describe in detail the functions of the STOP and END statements at this time. Let it be sufficient to say that to terminate a program a STOP statement should be executed, and every source program *must* have an END statement as the last statement of the program.

The IF statement has been included so that the program will terminate after the integers from one to one hundred have been summed. When the value of the expression $(X-100.)$ is less than zero, X is less than one hundred and its value must be added to SUM, therefore, statement number 8 is executed next. When the value of the expression is equal to zero, X has the value 100. It is important to note that when X has the value of 100. in the expression $(X-100.)$ it has not yet been added to SUM, and it is therefore necessary to transfer back to the statement numbered 8 again. Finally, when the value of the expression is positive X will have the value 101., and the program terminates by executing the STOP statement.

The program could also have been written as follows:

$$X = 1.$$
$$SUM = 0.$$
8 $\quad SUM = SUM + X$
$$X = X + 1.$$
IF $(X-101.)$ 8,6,6
6 $\quad$ STOP
$\quad$ END $\qquad\qquad$ (P7.3)

The expression in the IF statement has been changed to $(X-101.)$. This requires that on the zero condition (when the expression $X-101.$ has the value zero) the program terminates instead of executing the statement numbered 8 again. Both programs are correct and equally good. There is no uniquely correct way to write a Fortran program. Given one problem and ten programmers, the likely result would be ten different Fortran programs. Statements may appear in a different order, different variable names may be used, etc., etc.

A third program to compute the sum of the integers from one to 100 is

$$X = 1.$$
$$SUM = 0.$$
8 $\quad SUM = SUM + X$
$\quad$ IF $(X-100.)$ 7,6,6
7 $\quad X = X + 1.$
$\quad$ GO TO 8
6 $\quad$ STOP
$\quad$ END $\qquad\qquad$ (P7.4)

In this program the IF statement precedes the statement that increases X. Therefore, even though the expression $(X-100.)$ is used in the IF statement, the zero condition should cause the program to terminate since the value of X has *previously* been added to SUM.

A program to sum the *even* integers 2–100 inclusive might be written as follows:

$$X = 2.$$
$$SUM = 0.$$
$$8 \quad SUM = SUM + X$$
$$X = X + 2.$$
$$IF \ (X - 100.) \ 8,8,6$$
$$6 \quad STOP$$
$$END \qquad\qquad (P7.5)$$

This program is identical with P7.2 except X has been initialized to 2 instead of 1, and has been increased by 2 instead of 1.

The following program presented without commentary will determine the sum of the squares of the odd integers 1–100 inclusive.

$$X = 1.$$
$$SUM = 0.$$
$$8 \quad SUM = SUM + X*X$$
$$X = X + 2.$$
$$IF \ (X - 100.) \ 8,6,6$$
$$6 \quad STOP$$
$$END \qquad\qquad (P7.6)$$

Note that the zero condition of the IF statement *must* be provided for even though it will never be realized.

A program to determine the *product* of the integers 1–20 could be written as follows:

$$X = 1.$$
$$SUM = 1.$$
$$8 \quad SUM = SUM*X$$
$$X = X + 1.$$
$$IF \ (X - 20.) \ 8,8,6$$
$$6 \quad STOP$$
$$END \qquad\qquad (P7.7)$$

The variable SUM has been initialized to one rather than zero as in all the previous programs; this is because we are now developing a product of integers not a sum. If SUM had been initialized to zero every product would have been zero, and when the program terminated SUM would have the value zero.

7.3   The IF Statement and Inexact Numbers

Because decimal fractions cannot always be exactly represented in binary form (see Section 2.7) a word of caution is necessary when using the IF statement to determine whether a floating point expression is equal to some floating-point value. Suppose we wish to write a program to sum the following series:

$$0.1, 0.2, 0.3, \ldots 9.8, 9.9$$

The following program might be used:

$$X = .1$$
$$SUM = 0.$$
$$2 \quad SUM = SUM + X$$
$$X = X + .1$$
$$\text{IF } (X - 10.0) \ 2,6,6$$
$$6 \quad \text{STOP}$$
$$\text{END} \qquad\qquad (P7.8)$$

It may seem that the statement

$$\text{IF } (X - 10.0) \ 2,6,2$$

could have been used in place of the IF statement included in the program since the "greater than zero" condition should never occur; that is, a transfer on the "equal" condition should always occur first. However, in a binary computer the number 0.1 cannot be represented exactly. Therefore, instead of 0.1 the number used may have been equivalent to 0.10000001 or 0.09999999, both of which are very close to the true value of 0.1. Thus, X may never attain the exact value of 10.0 and the equal condition in the IF statement will never be realized. In this case the alternate IF statement proposed at the beginning of this paragraph would result in an endless loop: the IF statement would always transfer to the statement numbered 2. The IF statement shown in the program will work correctly if the value used for 0.1 is slightly on the high side. However, if the value used for 0.1 is on the low side then an extra number will be added to the sum.

This undesirable situation is easily remedied. The representation of a number in binary even though not exact is for most purposes adequate and well within the accuracy desired. Care must, however, be exercised by the programmer. In the example above the programmer could have used some number between 9.9 and 10.0 as the test value. The IF statement could have been written:

$$\text{IF } (X-9.95) \ 2,6,6$$

The situation described above does not occur when fixed-point numbers are being used, since they are always represented exactly in the computer. Also computers that represent numbers in BCD (see Section 2.9) usually represent decimal fractions exactly and, therefore, avoid the problem.

The Logical IF Statement

The logical IF statement is a very powerful transfer-type statement. However, its use requires a knowledge of the relational and logic operators that are not discussed until Section 15.6. Therefore, a detailed discussion of the logical IF statement is deferred to Chapter 15.

7.4   *The Computed GO TO Statement*

It is often desirable to have a transfer statement that will transfer control to one of many statements. The IF statement is useful if the number of possible statements to be executed next is three or less. If there are more than three possibilities, more than one IF statement must be used and it becomes somewhat cumbersome to program. The computed GO TO statement in Fortran provides for transferring to one of many statements based upon the value of some fixed-point variable.

General Form

GO TO $(n_1, n_2, \ldots n_m), i$

where $n_1, n_2, \ldots n_m$ are statement numbers and i is an unsigned nonsubscripted† fixed-point variable such that the range for the value of i is $(1 \leq i \leq m)$.

Examples of the Computed GO TO *Statement*

GO TO (1,8,7,914,211), M

GO TO (67,42), JDEL

GO TO (100,211,41,1,98,6,4), K1

†See Chapter 10 for a discussion of subscripted variables.

If the variable i has the value k at the time the computed GO TO statement is executed, then the Fortran statement with statement number n_k is exe cuted next. The value of the variable i indicates a position in the list of statement numbers. Thus, if the variable i had the value 4, the fourth statement number in the list is the number of the statement to be executed next. Table 7.2 illustrates the operation of the computed GO TO statement.

TABLE 7.2   Operation of the Computed GO TO Statement

Fortran Statement	Present Value of Variable	Number of Statement To Be Executed Next
GO TO (1,5,98,167,4), K2	K2 = 5	4
GO TO (44,28), J	J = 1	44
GO TO (51,6,7,1,46,112), M	M = 4	1
GO TO (38,67,42,11), I	I = 2	67
GO TO (2,1,67,48,10), L	L = 6	Incorrect, since there are only five statement numbers in the list.
GO TO (8,9,4), 2	2	Incorrect, since i must be a variable name.

To illustrate the use of the computed GO TO statement in a program, consider the following problem. A company with a payroll of 5000 employees decides to pay a bonus based on the employee's longevity with the company. Longevity is broken into six groups, as follows:

Group Code	1	2	3	4	5	6
Years	0–3	4–8	9–14	15–20	21–25	over 25
Bonus	$100	$200	$400	$600	$1000	$1500

Assume that a computer program has been written to calculate the pay, including bonus, for each employee; just that portion of the program concerned with the calculation of the bonus will be illustrated here. Also assume that the employees' records are processed one at a time, that the employee's group code is stored in a variable named LCODE, and that the total pay including bonus is to be stored in a variable called PAY. The portion of the program that determines the bonus might appear as follows:

———

———

———

GO TO (6,81,9,1,4,101), LCODE

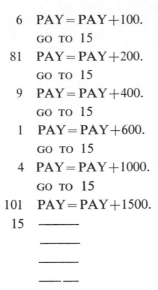

```
  6   PAY = PAY + 100.
      GO TO 15
 81   PAY = PAY + 200.
      GO TO 15
  9   PAY = PAY + 400.
      GO TO 15
  1   PAY = PAY + 600.
      GO TO 15
  4   PAY = PAY + 1000.
      GO TO 15
101   PAY = PAY + 1500.
 15   ———
      ———
      ———
      ———
```

Depending on the integer stored in LCODE, either $100, $200, $400, $600, $1000, or $1500 will be added to the employee's pay. Note the necessity for the GO TO 15 statements. These statements are necessary because an employee is to get one and only one bonus. If the GO TO 15 statements were omitted all the employees in groups 1, 2, 3, 4, or 5 would be credited with more than one bonus.

7.5   The Assigned GO TO and ASSIGN Statements

Two additional transfer-type statements, which are used in conjunction with one another, are available in some Fortran systems. These statements do not have wide usage; they accomplish the same thing as the computed GO TO statement although in a slightly different way. For these reasons the statements will be presented without practical illustrations as to their use in a program.

The Assigned GO TO Statement

General Form

GO TO i, $(n_1, n_2, \ldots n_m)$

where i is an unsigned nonsubscripted† fixed-point variable appearing in a previously executed ASSIGN statement, and $n_1, n_2, \ldots n_m$ are statement numbers.

---

†Subscripted variables are described in Chapter 10.

| *Examples of the* | GO TO J, (6,8,75,40) |
| *Assigned* GO TO *Statement* | GO TO IDENT, (94,1,13,42,80) |

The assigned GO TO statement causes the statement with the statement number equal to that value of i that was last assigned by an ASSIGN statement to be executed next. The statement numbers $n_1, n_2, \cdots n_m$ must include all the possible values that may be assigned to i.

The ASSIGN Statement

General Form

ASSIGN n TO i

where n is a statement number and i is an unsigned nonsubscripted† fixed-point variable that appears in an assigned GO TO statement.

| *Examples of the* ASSIGN *statement* | ASSIGN 75 TO J | ASSIGN 1 TO IDENT |

The ASSIGN statement assigns a value n to a variable i, so that when it is used in a subsequent assigned GO TO statement, the statement with statement number n will be executed next.

Consider the following program:

———
———
———

ASSIGN 6 TO K

———
———

8 GO TO K, (2,6,15,98,4)

———
———
———
———

6 ———

———
———
———

†Subscripted variables are described in Chapter 10.

ASSIGN 98 TO K

———
———
———
———
———
———

GO TO 8

———
———
———

98   ———

———
———
———

In this program the statement ASSIGN 6 TO K assigns the value 6 to K so that after the assigned GO TO statement is executed the next statement to be executed will be that statement with statement number 6. Execution will continue sequentially with the statement ASSIGN 98 TO K assigning the value 98 to K. When the assigned GO TO statement is executed the second time (as the result of the statement GO TO 8) the next statement to be executed will be the one with statement number 98.

Problems

7.1 Which of the following Fortran statements are invalid? State the reasons for your answers.

a) IF (X)1,2,3

b) IF (X−0.)1,1,2

c) IF (X=3.)8,7,4

d) IF (A+B/C−SQRT(W))89,60,48

e) IF (R−1.),3,2,99

f) IF (W−V+U)8,7

g) IF (DEL−1)75,94,94

h) GO TO 9998

i) GO TO I

j) GO TO K1

k) GO TO (6,94,3,1),D

l) GO TO (6,6,6,8)K

m) GO TO (7,1,1,7),ID387

n) GO TO (89,1001,2),4

o) GO TO (1,7,6,12),I+K

p) GO TO (2,A),J

7.2 Assume that the following variables have the values indicated:

A = 5.   B = 2.   C = 4.   I = 2   J = 4

After each of the following statements listed below is executed indicate the number of the statement to be executed next.

a) IF (A)5,6,7   *e)* IF (J − I*I)42,43,44

b) IF (I − 3)8,9,61   *f)* GO TO (9,82,83,67),I

c) IF (A − B − C)4,30,40   *g)* GO TO (3,2,67,1,9),J

d) IF (A − B**I)31,31,24   *h)* GO TO 9981

7.3 Indicate the values stored in the registers named x and sum for each of the following programs after the STOP statement is executed. Indicate your answers symbolically or numerically.

a)   X = 1.   *b)*   X = 1.
       SUM = 0.   8 SUM = 0.
   8 SUM = SUM + X*X   SUM = SUM + X*X
       X = X + 2.   X = X + 2.
       IF (X − 200.)8,8,7   IF (X − 99.)8,8,9
   7 STOP   9 STOP
       END   END

c)   I = 2   *d)*   B = 1.
       X = 0.   SUM = 0.
       SUM = 1.   4 A = 1.
   5 X = X + 1.   5 SUM = SUM + A*B
       SUM = SUM + X   A = A + 1.
       IF (100. − X)6,5,5   IF (A − 10.)5,5,7
   6 I = I + 2   7 B = B + 1.
       X = 0.   IF (B − 10.)4,4,2
       IF (6 − I)7,5,5   2 STOP
   7 STOP   END
       END

e)   X = 1.   *f)*   I = 1
       SUM = 0.   X = 1.
   3 IF (10. − X)8,8,7   SUM = 1.

e)   *Cont.*

   7 SUM=SUM+1./X

      X=X+1.

      GO TO 3

   8 STOP

      END

f)   *Cont.*

   8 SUM=SUM*X

      X=X+1.

      I=I+1

      GO TO (8,8,8,8,8,8,8,8,9),I

   9 STOP

      END

7.4 Write a Fortran program to sum the natural logarithms of the even integers from 100 to 200, inclusive.

7.5 Write a Fortran program to sum the factorials of the integers from one to fifteen, inclusive. The factorial of an integer N is denoted $N!$ and is given by $N! = N(N-1)(N-2)\cdots(2)(1)$.

7.6 Write a Fortran program to sum the cubes of the negative integers from -10 to -1 inclusive, that is, $[(-1)^3 + (-2)^3 + \cdots + (-10)^3]$.

7.7 Write a Fortran program to sum those integers between one and two hundred inclusive that are divisible by three or seven.

7.8 Write a Fortran program to sum the squares of the prime integers between one and two hundred inclusive.

7.9 Five numbers are stored respectively in registers named A, B, C, D, and E. Write a Fortran program to sum the positive numbers, sum the negative numbers, and count the number of zeros.

7.10 Five numbers are stored respectively in registers named A, B, C, D, and E. Compute T based on the value stored in the register LCODE as follows:

$$T = A + B + C + D + E \quad \text{if} \quad \text{LCODE} = 1$$

$$T = A - B - C - D - E \quad \text{if} \quad \text{LCODE} = 2$$

$$T = A^2 + B^2 - C^2 - D^2 \quad \text{if} \quad \text{LCODE} = 3$$

$$T = \log_{10} A + \log_e B \quad \text{if} \quad \text{LCODE} = 4$$

$$T = E^D - A \times B - C \quad \text{if} \quad \text{LCODE} = 5$$

$$T = \sqrt{A \times B} - \sqrt{C \times E} \quad \text{if} \quad \text{LCODE} = 6$$

8

Program Halt Statements

8.1 The PAUSE Statement

The PAUSE statement causes the computer to halt during execution of the object program. Depressing the start key on the computer causes the object program to resume execution with the next executable Fortran statement. The temporary halt in processing provided by the PAUSE statement may be utilized by the machine operator or programmer to analyze intermediate results before continuing the program, or perhaps to load new magnetic tapes, put more cards in the card reader or punch unit, etc. The PAUSE statement may also be used as a debugging (or error-locating) feature. By placing PAUSE statements at strategic points in a program it is possible to trace the sequence of statement execution by noting the order in which the PAUSE statements are executed. This procedure is possible because a number that may be associated with a PAUSE statement will be printed out when the statement is executed. Thus it is possible to differentiate between many PAUSE statements in a program by associating a different number with each one.

General Form

PAUSE or PAUSE *n*

where *n* is an unsigned *octal*† integer constant of from one to five digits; this constant is printed on the typewriter when the PAUSE statement is executed.

---

†Some Fortran systems permit an unsigned *decimal* integer constant.

It is important to note that when a PAUSE statement is executed, records processed by previous output statements may not have been completely written on the output device. Thus when a PAUSE statement is executed and the output of the program is examined the investigator should be aware that possibly the last few records of output may not be available to him until the next output statement is executed.

8.2   The STOP Statement

The STOP statement *terminates* the execution of the object program. This is done in one of two ways:

1. If the program is being run under the control of a monitor program, control is returned to the monitor.
2. If the program is not being run under monitor control, the computer will halt. Unlike the PAUSE statement, after a STOP statement is executed, depressing the start key will not cause the computer to resume execution of the program.

General Form

STOP

8.3   The CALL EXIT Statement

The CALL EXIT statement may be used in place of the STOP statement when programs are executed under monitor control.

General Form

CALL EXIT†

8.4   The END Statement

The END statement is used as an indication to the Fortran compiler that the end of the source program has been encountered. The END statement *must* physically be the last statement of every Fortran program. The omission of the END statement will allow the compiler to seek additional Fortran statements to process, with the consequence that an error will occur. It is of

†Strictly speaking, this is a CALL to the EXIT subprogram. See Chapter 11 for a discussion of subprograms.

importance to note that the END statement has no significance in the object program; no machine language instructions are generated from the END statement; it is used strictly as an indicator to the compiler.

General Form

END

Problems

8.1   Which of the following statements are false?

  a)   Every Fortran program must have a PAUSE statement.
  b)   Every Fortran program must have a STOP statement.
  c)   Every Fortran program must have an END statement.
  d)   Object-program execution may continue after a STOP statement is executed.
  e)   Object-program execution may continue after a PAUSE statement is executed.
  f)   The END statement does not cause any instructions to be generated in the object program.

9

Basic Input/Output Statements

If a Fortran program were written to perform designated calculations on one and only one set of data, the data could be entered in the form of constants in arithmetic expressions. Thus, if one wanted to calculate $X = A^2 + B^2 - C^2$ for $A = 16.23$, $B = 49.8$, and $C = 13.12$, the Fortran program could be written as:

$$X = 16.23**2 + 49.8**2 - 13.12**2$$

STOP

END

or

$$A = 16.23$$
$$B = 49.8$$
$$C = 13.12$$
$$X = A*A + B*B - C*C$$

STOP

END

However, if this method of entering data were followed and X were to be calculated for each of many different sets of values of A, B, and C, a new program would be required for each set of data. Obviously, this is time-consuming and inefficient. It would be desirable to have one program that would process all the different sets of data. This statement implies that the

119

data be external to the program and entered in the form of variable quantities.

Assume that 1000 cards are each punched with three numbers representing A, B, and C. A value of X for $X = A^2 + B^2 - C^2$ is to be calculated for each of the 1000 sets of data. Also assume that execution of the Fortran statement

READ (5,6) A,B,C

will cause the following to take place:

1. The information on a card is read into the storage unit.
2. The number representing a value of A is stored in a register called A.
3. The number representing a value of B is stored in a register called B.
4. The number representing a value of C is stored in a register called C.

Assume also that the Fortran statement

WRITE (6,19) X,A,B,C

will cause the values stored in registers X, A, B, and C to be printed. Under the foregoing assumptions the following program will process the 1000 sets of data and print the results:

$$I = 0$$
12   READ (5,6) A,B,C

$$X = A*A + B*B - C*C$$

WRITE (6,19) X,A,B,C

$$I = I + 1$$

IF $(I - 1000)$ 12,13,13

13   STOP

END

This program will cause the data cards to be read and processed one at a time. Each time the READ statement is executed the three numbers on the card just read are stored in A, B, and C and used to calculate a value for X. The WRITE statement causes the value of X and the values of A, B, and C from which X was calculated to be printed. The variable I is used as a counter to determine when the 1000th card has been read and the data thereon processed. The IF statement transfers control back to the READ statement if more data cards remain to be processed; if the last data card has been processed, the IF statement transfers control to the STOP statement, which terminates the program.

Input/output statements in general must provide the following items of information:

1. Which input/output device (card reader, card punch, printer, magnetic-tape unit, etc.) are the data to be read from or the results written on?
2. What data are to be transmitted and in what order? For input this means: In what registers are the data to be stored (as the values of what variables)? For output: Which data are to be written (the values of what variables)?
3. What form are the data in for input, and in what form should the results be for output? This description of the form of the data is called *Format*.

The input/output statements specify the first two of these items. A FOR-MAT statement, which describes the form of the data, is associated with each input/output statement. The input and output statements will be described first, followed by a discussion of the FORMAT statement. For all examples card input and printer output will be assumed; however, the descriptions will apply equally well to other forms of input and output, except where noted. A special section in Chapter 13 will be devoted to magnetic-tape input/output operations.

BASIC INPUT STATEMENTS

9.1 The Fortran IV READ Statement

General Form

READ (*i,n*) *list*

where *i* designates an unsigned fixed-point constant or a fixed-point variable that refers to an input device, *n* is the statement number of an associated FORMAT statement, and *list* is a sequence of one or more variable names separated by commas.

Examples of the	READ (5,10) A,B,DEL,K,C	READ (5,2) Y
READ *statement*	READ (5,14) I1,X	READ (5,7) X,I,Y,J,K2

The input device to be used is specified by *i* in the general form of the READ statement. The values for *i* and the associated input devices may vary with the installation; therefore, the specifications in use at a given installation should be consulted. For purposes of this text, Table 9.1 will be used. Note that i may be a variable, so for a given program the input device can be varied according to the value of the variable.

When the input device specified is the card reader, the READ statement always causes at least *one* new card to be read, and in accordance with the specified FORMAT statement, as many numbers as there are variable names

TABLE 9.1   **Input Device Specification**

i	Input Device
1	magnetic tape unit 1
2	magnetic tape unit 2
3	magnetic tape unit 3
4	magnetic tape unit 4
5	card reader

in the list are transmitted from the card, transformed to the appropriate mode (fixed point or floating point) and stored in the registers whose symbolic names appear in the list. The procedure is ordered, in that the first number on the card is stored in the register whose symbolic name appears first in the list, the second number is stored in the register whose symbolic name is second in the list, etc.

The general form of the READ statement just presented is the basic input statement of the Fortran IV language. Another form of the READ statement *although it applies to the card reader only*, serves as the basic input statement of the Fortran II language *and is also accepted by Fortran IV*. This form appears in the following section.

9.2   *The Fortran II READ Statement*

General Form

READ n, *list*

where n is the statement number of an associated FORMAT statement, and *list* is a sequence of one or more variable names separated by commas.

Examples of the	READ 10,A,B,DEL,K,C	READ 2,Y
Fortran II READ *statement*	READ 14,I1,X	READ 7,X,I,Y,J,K2

This READ statement always causes at least *one* new card to be read and, in accordance with the specified FORMAT statement, as many numbers as there are variable names in the list are transmitted from the card, transformed to the appropriate mode (fixed point or floating point), and stored in the registers whose symbolic names appear in the list. The procedure is ordered, in that the first number on the card is stored in the register whose symbolic name appears first in the list, the second number is stored in the register whose symbolic name is second in the list, etc.

Since this latter form of the READ statement is in more *general* usage today, it will be used in this text. The reader should recognize that the two statements

$$READ \ n, \ list$$

$$READ \ (5,n) \ list$$

operate in exactly the same way; they differ in form only.

To illustrate the functioning of the READ statement, consider the following Fortran statement:

$$READ \ 1,A,B,K1,DELTA$$

Assume that the data card read by this READ statement is punched as follows:

$$First \ number \ on \ the \ card \ - \ 13.61$$

$$Second \ number \ on \ the \ card \ = \ -8.00$$

$$Third \ number \ on \ the \ card \ = \ 25$$

$$Fourth \ number \ on \ the \ card \ = \ 167.123$$

The execution of the READ statement would cause the card to be read, and (*a*) the number 13.61 to be converted to the floating point form and stored in A, (*b*) the number -8.00 to be converted to the floating-point form and stored in B, (*c*) the number 25 to be converted to the fixed-point form and stored in K1, and (*d*) the number 167.123 to be converted to the floating-point form and stored in DELTA. Obviously, the READ statement alone does not supply enough information for all of these operations to be accomplished; for example, the number 13.61 might be punched in card columns 1–5, or maybe 15–19; the number -8.00 might be punched in card columns 6–10, or perhaps 25–29, etc. It is the FORMAT statement, to be discussed shortly, that gives this essential information. The READ statement and associated FORMAT statement are used in conjunction with one another to transform and transmit data successfully from an external source into the appropriate registers in the computer storage.

BASIC OUTPUT STATEMENTS

9.3   *The Fortran IV WRITE Statement*

General Form

WRITE (*i,n*) *list*

where *i* designates an unsigned fixed-point constant or a fixed-point variable that refers to an output device, *n* is the statement number of an associated FORMAT statement, and *list* is a sequence of one or more variable names separated by commas.

Examples of the	WRITE (6,7) A,B,I,DEL	WRITE (6,12) W,A1,OHM,ITER
WRITE *statement*	WRITE (6,10) X,X1,X2,I,J	WRITE (6,8) K

The output device to be used is specified by *i* in the general form of the WRITE statement. The values for *i* and the associated input devices may vary from installation to installation, therefore the specifications in use at a given installation should be consulted. For purposes of this text Table 9.2 will be used. Note that *i* may be a variable, and so for a given program the output device can be varied according to the value of the variable.

TABLE 9.2   Output Device Specification

i	*Output Device*
1	magnetic tape unit 1
2	magnetic tape unit 2
3	magnetic tape unit 3
4	magnetic tape unit 4
6	printer
7	card punch

When the output device specified is the printer, the WRITE statement always causes at least *one* new line to be printed; and, in accordance with the specified FORMAT statement, as many numbers as there are variable names in the list are transmitted from computer storage, transformed to the appropriate form, and printed. The procedure is ordered, in that the value stored in the register whose symbolic name appears first in the list is printed first, the value stored in the register whose symbolic name appears second in the list is printed second, etc.

When the output device specified is the card punch the WRITE statement always causes at least *one* new card to be punched; and, in accordance with the specified FORMAT statement, as many numbers as there are variable names in the list are transmitted from computer storage, transformed to the appropriate form, and punched on a card. The procedure is ordered, in that the value stored in the register whose symbolic name appears first in the list is punched first, the value stored in the register whose symbolic name appears second in the list is punched second, etc.

The general form of the WRITE statement just presented is the basic output statement of the Fortran IV language. Two other forms of the WRITE statement, although they apply uniquely to the printer and card punch, serve as the basic output statements of the Fortran II language *and are also accepted by Fortran IV*. These forms appear in the following sections.

9.4   The Fortran II PRINT Statement

General Form

PRINT *n, list*

where *n* is the statement number of an associated FORMAT statement, and *list* is a sequence of one or more variable names separated by commas.

Examples of the	PRINT 7,A,B,I,DEL	PRINT 12,W,A1,OHM,ITER
PRINT *statement*	PRINT 10,X,X1,X2,I,J	PRINT 8,K

The description of the operation of the PRINT statement is identical to that of the WRITE statement for printer output ($i = 6$) in Section 9.3. Since the PRINT statement is in more general usage today for printer output than the WRITE statement, it will be used in this text. The reader should recognize that the two statements

PRINT *n, list*

WRITE (6,*n*) *list*

operate in exactly the same way; they differ in form only.

9.5   The Fortran II PUNCH Statement

General Form

PUNCH *n, list*

where *n* is the statement number of an associated FORMAT statement, and *list* is a sequence of one or more variable names separated by commas.

Examples of the	PUNCH 7,A,B,I,DEL	PUNCH 12,W,A1,OHM,ITER
PUNCH *statement*	PUNCH 10,X,X1,X2,I,J	PUNCH 8,K

The description of the operation of the PUNCH statement is identical to that of the WRITE statement appearing in Section 9.3 for punched-card output ($i = 7$). Since the PUNCH statement is in more general usage today for card output than the WRITE statement, it will be used in this text. The reader should recognize that the two statements

PUNCH *n, list*

WRITE (7,*n*) *list*

operate in exactly the same way; they differ in form only.

To illustrate the functioning of the output statements consider the following PRINT statement,

PRINT 1,A,B,K1,DELTA

and assume that the variables named have the following values:

$$A = 13.61$$

$$B = -8.00$$

$$K1 = 25$$

$$DELTA = 167.123$$

Execution of the above PRINT statement would cause one line to be printed in accordance with the specified FORMAT statement; the number stored in A would be converted *from* the floating point form to a common decimal form and printed; the number stored in B would be converted *from* the floating point form to a common decimal form and printed; the number stored in K1 would be converted from the fixed point form and printed; and finally the number stored in DELTA would be converted from the floating-point form to a common decimal form and printed.

Obviously, the PRINT statement alone does not give enough information for all of the foregoing operations to be accomplished; for example, it might be desired to have the value of A printed in columns 1–5, or maybe in columns 10–14; perhaps it is required that the value of B be printed in columns 6–10, or in columns 25–29, etc. It is the FORMAT statement, to be discussed next, that gives this essential information. The PRINT statement and the associated FORMAT statement are used in conjunction with one another to transmit data successfully from computer storage to printed output. The same basic concepts apply also to the PUNCH statement for card output.

THE FORMAT STATEMENT

If quantities are to be transmitted correctly from the input medium to the storage and from the computer storage to the output medium, it is necessary that information, regarding what form the data is in or is to be in, be supplied to the Fortran system. Special subroutines (prewritten computer programs) are used to convert data to and from the floating-point and fixed-point forms used by Fortran. In order for this conversion to be carried out correctly the subroutines must be supplied information as to what form the data fields are in and into which forms they are to be converted. The function of the FORMAT statement is to supply this information.

General Form

n FORMAT $(S_1, S_2, \ldots S_n)$

where n is the statement number of the FORMAT statement that is referenced by an associated I/O† statement, and $S_1, S_2, \ldots S_n$ are specifications that will be described.

9.6 Format Specifications

The format specification consists of a conversion code, followed by either a single integer, or two integers separated by a decimal point, depending on the conversion code. It is used to specify what form a data field is in or to what form it is to be converted. Basically, there are three types of conversions for numeric data which are to be transmitted to and from storage. The conversion codes that are used for both input and output are as follows:

Internal Data Form	Floating point	Floating point	Fixed point
Conversion Code	F	E	I
External Data Form	Decimal	Decimal with exponent	Integer

The conversion codes are used as follows for *input* data: if the input quantity is in the decimal form (e.g., 12.8, 129.42, 6.), the F conversion code should be used in the specification for that quantity. If the input quantity is in the decimal-with-exponent form (e.g., .67E+04, 87.1E−05, 1.E−06), the

†An accepted symbol meaning "input/output."

E conversion code should be used in the specification for that quantity, and finally, if the input quantity is to be stored as an integer the I conversion code should be used in the specification for that quantity.

The conversion codes are used in a similar manner for output. If a floating-point quantity is to be written in the decimal form, the F conversion code should be used in the specification for that quantity. If a floating-point quantity is to be written in the decimal-with-exponent form, the E conversion code should be used in the specification. For fixed-point quantities, the I conversion code should be used in the specification.

9.7   Data Fields

A numeric field consists of one or more columns of data which together represent a number. Thus, if a card is punched in columns 1–6 with the *characters* − 16.39 which represent the *number* − 16.39, these columns constitute a data field, or more simply a field.

The conversion codes alone do not give sufficient information to allow for the proper conversion of input and output data. Certain additional information must be supplied to the conversion subroutines. For *input* data the subroutine must be given information as to which columns contain each input quantity. For example, in one problem the input quantity corresponding to the first variable name in the list may be punched in columns 1–10, whereas in another problem the first input quantity may be punched in columns 8–15. For *output* data the subroutine must be given the information as to how many print positions the programmer wishes to reserve for each output quantity, and how many places to the right of the decimal point should be printed for each output quantity.

To supply this information the conversion codes, when used in the specification portion of the FORMAT statement, appear in the following forms:

$$Iw \qquad Ew.d \qquad Fw.d$$

The decimal point in the E and F type specifications is required punctuation. The above complete specifications will be discussed first as used for input and then for output.

9.8   Input Specifications

I Specification: Iw

The *w* designates an integer that specifies the complete field width, including sign (if any); *w* columns are examined by the conversion routine for the input quantity. If an input quantity is positive, it is not necessary to punch the plus sign. If a sign, positive or negative, is punched it must be included in the count w. The following examples show the required specification for the input quantities appearing below:

Input Data	139	+21	−612	1	−23
Specification	I3	I3	I4	I1	I2†

†Inaccurate because of an insufficient specification. An I3 specification is required.

F Specification: Fw.d

The w designates an integer that specifies the complete field width including sign (if any) and decimal point (if any); w columns are examined by the conversion routine for the input quantity. The d designates an integer that specifies the number of places appearing to the right of the decimal point in the input field. If an input quantity is positive, it is not necessary to punch the plus sign. If a sign, positive or negative, is punched it must be included in the count w. The following examples show the required specification for the input quantities appearing below:

Input Data	13.21	+1.041	−21.1	+.00124	.6	675.192	−7.12
Specification	F5.2	F6.3	F5.1	F7.5	F2.1	F7.3	F4.2‡

‡Inaccurate because of an insufficient specification. An F5.2 specification is required.

E Specification: Ew.d

The w designates an integer that specifies the complete field width, including sign (if any), decimal point (if any), and exponent; w columns are examined by the conversion routine for the input quantity. The d designates an integer that specifies the number of places to the right of the decimal point, excluding exponent. If an input quantity or exponent is positive, it is not necessary to punch the plus sign. If a sign, positive or negative, is punched, it must be included in the count w. The following examples show the required specification for the input quantities appearing below:

Input Data	1.23E+04	87.E−06	174.21E+02	+61.12E+02	1.E−06	3.67E6
Specification	E8.2	E7.0	E10.2	E10.2	E7.0	E6.2

9.9   Illustrations of the READ and FORMAT Statements

We will now illustrate how the READ and associated FORMAT statements are used together and also the different forms in which data can be punched on a card. Consider the following READ statement and the associated FORMAT statement:

RFAD 2, A,B,C,K,DEL

2 FORMAT (F5.1, F6.2, F4.1, I3, E10.2)

The specifications in the FORMAT statement and variable names in the READ statement are in correspondence; that is, the first specification applies to the first variable in the list, the second specification applies to the second variable in the list, etc. *The conversion codes in the specifications in a FORMAT statement must have correspondence in mode with the variables in the list; if a floating-point variable name appears in the list the corresponding conversion code must be either E or F; if a fixed-point variable name appears in the list the corresponding specification must have the I conversion code.*

The specifications in the FORMAT statement describe the input quantities as they appear on the input medium; in the foregoing example, the medium is punched cards. The complete field width specified by *w* in the specifications refers to card columns and always starts with the next available column, which initially is card column 1. Thus, in the foregoing example, the first specification indicates that the number to be converted to floating point and stored in A is punched in columns 1–5; the number to be converted to floating point and stored in B is punched in the next six card columns (6–11); the number to be converted to floating point and stored in C is punched in the next four columns (12–15), etc. A typical data card might be punched in card column 1 through column 28 as follows:

$$123.7 - 12.5015.2 + 12175.25E - 02$$

As a result of reading this card according to the FORMAT statement in the above example, the variables would have the following values:

A = 123.7   B = −12.50   C = 15.2   K = 12   DEL = 1.7525

Suppose that the following sets of data were also to be read by the above READ and FORMAT statements:

	A	B	C	K	DEL
Set 1	123.7	−12.50	15.2	+12	1.7525
Set 2	−12.5	199.75	−5.0	−7	−515000.
Set 3	1.1	−3.75	.2	1	.00546

The cards might be punched as follows:

	Column 1	6	12	16	19	28
Card 1	123.7−	12.50 1	5.2+	12 1	75.25E−0 2	
Card 2	−12.5 1	99.75−	5.0 b	†−7−	51.50E+0 4	
Card 3	001.1 b	−3.75 b	0.2+	01 0	b5.46E−0 3	

†*b* represents a blank column.

The following items should be noted with respect to these cards:

1. Punching of the plus sign is optional. Four of the five numbers shown on card 1 are positive, but only one has the plus sign punched.

2. The sign indicating that a number is positive or negative must precede the number, but may be punched in any column preceding the first non-blank column of the number. It does not require a *unique* column within the field. Note that in the first number on the 2nd card the minus sign is punched in column 1, while on the first data card column 1 was used for a digit punch. In the number to be stored in K on card 2, the minus sign is punched in column 17. This is permissible, since the sign precedes the number. This number could also have been punched as −07.

3. Blank columns and zeros are both read as zeros under the numeric specifications (E, F, I). Thus, they may be used interchangeably as shown in the punching of card 3. The number to be stored in K in the third set of data could have been punched in any of the following forms: +01, +b1, b+1, 001, 0b1, bb1, b01. However, the number *could not* have been punched 0+1, because the sign does not precede the first nonblank column of the number.

4. In general, data must be right justified when punched. Considering again the number to be stored in K in the third set of data, if the 1 had been punched in column 17 and the number punched as +10 or +1b, the number stored in K would have been 10 not 1. Similarly, if the exponent for the number to be stored in DEL for the first data set had been punched as E-2, with column 28 blank or zero, the exponent would have been considered to be −20 not −2.

5. With a decimal point punched in column 4, the largest *positive* number that could be stored in A is 999.9. The largest *negative* number is −99.9, since the sign must be punched for negative quantities.

6. The reader should note that F5.1, the format specification for the number to be stored in A, applies to the number punched in columns 1–5 in *all* data cards read by the associated READ statement. Likewise, the specification F6.2 applies to the number punched in columns 6–11 in *all* the data cards read by the associated READ statement.

9.10   Output Specifications

I Specification: Iw

The w designates an integer which specifies the complete field width including sign. For output a position *should* always be included for the sign. When used as an output specification, w places are reserved for the number and sign. If the sign is positive the plus sign does not print or punch. Even though it is not printed or punched a *position should be provided for it.* (In many Fortran systems a position for the sign, if it is plus, need not be reserved, but in some systems it is required.) If the number of significant digits (including sign) in the quantity is less than the width specification, the number and sign are right justified in the output field and the leftmost spaces are filled with blanks. If the number of significant digits (including sign) in the quantity is greater than the width specification, only the *w* rightmost digits are printed, the high-order digits of the quantity are lost.

The following examples show how each of the quantities appearing below is printed according to the indicated specification:

Number in Storage	189	−10	−10	75	34	−55
Specification	I4	I3	I5	I4	I2	I2
Printed Output	b189	−10	bb−10	bb75	34† or b4‡ or **§	**§or −5‡

F Specification: Fw.d

The *w* designates an integer that specifies the complete field width, including sign, decimal point, and a minimum of one position to the left of the decimal point. When used as an output specification, *w* places are reserved for the number, sign, and decimal point. For output a decimal point is *always* punched or printed. If the sign is positive, the plus sign does not print or punch. Even though it is not printed or punched, a position should be provided for it. (In many Fortran systems a position for the sign, even if it is plus, is required, but in some systems it is optional). The *d* designates an integer that specifies the number of places to the right of the decimal point that are to be printed or punched. If the number of decimal places in the number to be written exceeds the value of *d*, the rightmost decimal positions are truncated. (In some Fortran systems, rounding occurs.) If the number of decimal positions in the quantity are less than *d*, rightmost zeros are provided. If the number of integer positions, including sign, in the number exceeds $(w - d - 1)$ (the 1 represents the position for the decimal point), the number is either automatically written in E15.8 format and an error message indicating the use of an insufficient specification is printed or asterisks are printed. If the number of integer positions including sign is less than $w - d - 1$, the sign and integer portion of the number are right justified in the $w - d - 1$ positions and the leftmost positions are filled with blanks.

†In some Fortran systems it is not required that a position be reserved for the sign when it is positive.

‡In some Fortran systems that require a position for the sign, the sign takes precedence over a digit.

§In some Fortran systems asterisks are printed when an insufficient specification is given.

The following examples show how each of the quantities appearing on the left is printed according to the indicated specification:

Number in Storage	Specification	Printed Output
89.676	F6.2	b89.68 or b89.67†
142.7	F8.3	b142.700
−89.12	F6.2	−89.12
99.12	F5.2	99.12 or b0.99120000Eb02 or *****‡
.001	F5.2	b0.00
−46.385	F10.3	bbb−46.385
.002	F7.4	b0.0020
67.21	F4.2	b0.67210000Eb02 or ****‡
67.21	F5.2	67.21 or b0.67210000Eb02 or *****‡
−67.21	F5.2	−0.67210000Eb02 or *****‡

E Specification: Ew.d

The w designates an integer that specifies the complete field width, including sign, decimal point, a minimum of one position to the left of the decimal point, and four positions for the exponent. A decimal point is *always* punched or printed. If the sign of the quantity or exponent is positive, the plus sign does not punch or print (a blank is provided); however, a position still should be reserved for it. (In many Fortran systems a position for the sign, even if it is plus, is required, but in some systems it is optional.) The d designates an integer that specifies the number of places, excluding the exponent, to the right of the decimal point that will be printed or punched. The $w - 7$ most significant digits (including sign) of the output quantity are written, where the 7 includes one position for the sign, one integer position to the left of the decimal point, one position for the decimal point, and four positions for the exponent. A significant digit is never printed to the left of the decimal point unless a scale factor is specified (see Section 13.3). If there are more than $w - 7$ significant digits in the number, the rightmost positions are truncated. (In some Fortran systems, rounding occurs.) The $w - 7$ most significant digits of the quantity are placed in the fractional portion of the number and left-justified if the number of significant digits is less than the value of d. The rightmost positions are filled with zeros. If the number of significant digits exceeds the value-

†Depending on whether the output routine rounds or merely truncates.
‡The output form depends on whether the Fortran system used requires a position for the sign and also the manner in which an insufficient specification is handled.

of d, the d most significant digits are used. To convert the output to a conventional decimal form, the decimal point must be repositioned according to the value of the exponent.

Only the d most significant digits of the number are written. The value of $w - d$ should be at least 7; if not, the system reduces the value of d accordingly.

The following examples show how each of the quantities appearing on the left is printed according to the indicated specification:

Number in Storage	Specification	Printed Output
6712.4167	E15.8	b0.67124167Eb04
−75.91255	E12.5	−0.75913Eb02 or −0.75912Eb02†
385.1	E12.5	b0.38510Eb03
384.1	E10.2	bb0.38Eb03
−.00675	E10.3	−0.675E−02
−.00675	E9.0	bb−0.E−02
18.24	E16.6	bbbb0.182400Eb02
−18.24	E16.6	bbb−0.182400Eb02
−77512.1	E11.4	−0.7751Eb05
77512.1	E11.4	b0.7751Eb05

9.11 Additional Rules for Specifying Format

The following four rules permit variation in specifying format:

Rule 1. If a decimal point is punched in an input data field and its position is different from that indicated in the format specification, the decimal point as punched takes priority over the decimal indication in the format specification. The following examples illustrate this rule:

Input Data	35.25	1755.1	.1525	−675.	98.7E+05
Specification	F5.1	F6.3	F5.0	F5.3	E8.3
Value Assigned to Input Variables	35.25	1755.1	.1525	−675.0	9870000.

With the application of Rule 1 the largest positive number that could be

†Depending on whether the system rounds or merely truncates.

stored in A in the example in Section 9.9 is 9999. and the largest negative number is -999.

Rule 2. The decimal point need not be punched for input data, since the position for the decimal point is given in the format specification. This flexibility facilitates the keypunching of data by allowing for the omission of the decimal point as shown in the following examples:

Input Data	12754	891456	-671245	$+12345E+04$
Specification	F5.1	F6.3	F7.2	E10.2
Value Assigned to Input Variables	1275.4	891.456	-6712.45	1234500.

Note that the positioning of the decimal point is indicated by the specification; thus, in the first example the specification F5.1 will cause 5 columns to be examined, and if the decimal point is not punched it will be taken to be between the fourth and fifth columns of the field.

Recording Data on Cards

At this point it is pertinent to discuss the punching of data and how this should be accomplished. In too many cases data are recorded into cards before a programmer is consulted. This means that the programmer must accept the data as punched and attempt to describe in a FORMAT statement how the data are punched. However, if too many inconsistencies exist in the punching of the data to make possible a *general* description of the data in a FORMAT statement, the data should be repunched. It is strongly recommended that no data be punched until a programmer is consulted. Adhering to this policy will save much frustration.

If many sets of data are to be processed, it is necessary to decide upon a format. An appropriate approach would be to scan all the values for one variable and determine the maximum number of integer positions and the maximum number of fractional positions required, determine whether the decimal point and sign are to be punched, and decide on the format for punching accordingly. Rules 1 and 2 above could be applied in an attempt to cope with any numbers that are outside the format specification decided upon. This situation could occur if additional data were added at a later time or if a mistake was made in scanning the data and not enough positions were provided.

After a set of data is punched into cards, a listing should be made of the cards and compared against the original listing from which the data were punched. Too often data, as punched, are not verified until after processing by the Fortran program. If errors in the data are discovered at this time they must be corrected and the program rerun resulting in wasted computer time. In the opinion of the authors unverified data should not be processed. The task of data verification becomes much simpler and more accurate if a consistent format is followed (i.e., decimal points punched in the same column, signs punched in the same column, etc.).

Rule 3. A format specification may be preceded by an unsigned fixed-point constant indicating the number of times the specification is to be repeated. Thus, the following pairs of FORMAT statements are equivalent:

$\Big\{$FORMAT (I2,2F4.1,2I3,F6.0)
FORMAT (I2,F4.1,F4.1,I3,I3,F6.0)

$\Big\{$FORMAT (3F5.2,2I4)
FORMAT (F5.2,F5.2,F5.2,I4,I4)

Rule 4. Parentheses may be included in a FORMAT statement to indicate a grouping of specifications for repetition. While more than one set of parentheses may appear in a single FORMAT statement, only limited nesting of parentheses (parentheses within parentheses) is allowed within the outer pair of parentheses.† The following pairs of FORMAT statements are equivalent:

$\Big\{$FORMAT (F5.1,2(I2,F4.0))
FORMAT (F5.1,I2,F4.0,I2,F4.0)

$\Big\{$FORMAT (2(F4.0,F3.1),I2,3(I3,I4))
FORMAT (F4.0,F3.1,F4.0,F3.1,I2,I3,I4,I3,I4,I3,I4)

Note that the statement

FORMAT (2(F4.0,3(I2,I3)))

is not allowed in all Fortran systems, since within the outermost pair of parentheses one set of parentheses contains a second set of parentheses (nesting).

9.12   The X Specification

Up to this point we have considered examples of input data in which the input quantities were punched in consecutive card columns beginning in column 1. Consider, however, the case of two input quantities where the first input quantity is punched in columns 5–10 in F6.2 format and the second input quantity is punched in columns 14–18 in F5.0 format. Assume that columns 1–4 and 11–13, inclusive, contain blanks or zeros. Obviously, the FORMAT statement

1   FORMAT (F6.2,F5.0)

---

†The reader should consult the specifications of the Fortran system at his installation for the degree of limitation.

does not apply, since the format specifications refer to consecutive columns starting with column 1. Thus, the F6.2 specification refers to columns 1–6 and the F5.0 specification refers to columns 7–11. Because of the assumption that columns 1–4 and 11–13 contain blanks or zeros, the FORMAT statement may be rewritten in either one of the following two ways to correctly describe the format of the input quantities:

1   FORMAT (F10.2,F8.0)

1   FORMAT (F13.5,F5.0)

Specifying a field width greater than required may be used to provide for leading or trailing zeros or blanks in input data. (The fractional portion of the specification must also be altered in the case of trailing zeros or blanks.) For output specifications, specifying a field width greater than necessary provides for leading blanks and may be used to provide for spacing. Thus if a fixed-point quantity is not expected to exceed five spaces including sign. a specification of I8 will provide for three leading blanks.

For input data the field width of a specification can be increased to provide for leading or trailing *blanks* and *zeros* only. In the foregoing example, if digits other than zeros or blanks were punched in columns 1–4 and 11–13, the field widths of the specification could not have been extended to cover the leading columns. Thus, if a card were punched as

b10b316.12bb21678.

and read in accordance with the FORMAT statement

1   FORMAT (F10.2, F8.0)

the first quantity would be considered to be 100,316.12 instead of the correct value of 316.12, and the second quantity would be considered to be 21,678. rather than the correct value of 1,678. Similarly the FORMAT statement

1   FORMAT (F13.5, F5.0)

would lead to incorrect values for the input quantities.

What is required is a method to provide for the skipping of columns for input. The X specification provides for this. *The general form of the X specification is wX, where w is an unsigned fixed-point constant.* When used as an input specification it provides for skipping *w* columns. The X specification can also be used for output; its use as an output specification provides for *w* blanks. Whenever the X specification is used it need not be followed by a comma.

To illustrate the X specification as it is used for input, consider the problem of reading three numbers punched in columns 3–8, 15–20, and 41–42, in F6.1, F6.3, and I2 formats respectively. The following Fortran statements could be used:

> READ 89,X,Y,K1
>
> 89   FORMAT (2X,F6.1,6X,F6.3,20X,I2)

or, alternately,

> READ 89,X,Y,K1
>
> 89   FORMAT (2XF6.1,6XF6.3,20XI2)

The authors will follow the practice of omitting the comma after the X specification.

When the wX specification is used with an output record, the number of characters specified by w are left blank. To illustrate the X specification as it is used for output, suppose that four fixed-point integers with six blanks between each one are to be printed. The following Fortran statements could be used:

> PRINT 60,I,J,K,L
>
> 60   FORMAT (I5,6XI5,6XI5,6XI5)

or, alternately:

> PRINT 60, I,J,K,L
>
> 60   FORMAT (I5,3(6XI5))

If the following two Fortran statements were used, six blanks would precede the first number as well as separate the numbers:

> PRINT 60,I,J,K,L
>
> 60   FORMAT (4(6XI5))

9.13   Multiple-Record Formats

A record is defined as the information on one card for input, or on one card or one line for output. Very often one set of input data is punched on more than one card, or for output it is desired to print more than one line or punch more than one card. Of course, separate I/O statements could be used which include in each list only those variables that would be read from one card, printed on one line, or punched on one card. Thus if we wanted to read three variables, A, B, and C, and the quantities for A and B were punched on' one card and the value for C on a second card, the following set of Fortran statements could be used.

> READ 1,A,B
>
> READ 8,C
>
> 1   FORMAT (F4.0,F6.1)
>
> 8   FORMAT (F6.2)

This method of providing for multiple records is cumbersome. It would be advantageous if the variables *A, B,* and *C* could have been included in one I/O list and have a specification in the FORMAT statement dictate the use of a second record. *The solidus (/) is used as a specification when more than one printed line or punched card is to be specified in a single* FORMAT *statement.* It is not necessary to precede or follow the solidus by a comma, although it is not incorrect to do so. Depending on the I/O statement it is used with, the solidus may cause any one of the following conditions: another card or tape record may be read, another card or tape record may be written, or another line may be printed. By use of the solidus, several one-line formats may be specified in one FORMAT statement.

The following examples illustrate how the solidus is used:

EXAMPLE 1

> READ 6,A,B,D,K

> 6 FORMAT (F6.0,3XE14.3/F4.0/3XI4)

Three cards would be read. The value for A would be taken from columns 1–6 of the first card. The value for B would be taken from columns 10–23 of the first card. The value for D would be taken from columns 1–4 of the second card, and the value of K from columns 4–7 of the third card.

EXAMPLE 2

> PRINT 41,I,A,K,B,D,E

> 41 FORMAT (2(I2,3XF6.1)/F3.0,E14.8)

Two lines would be printed. I, A, K, and B would be printed on the first line in I2, F6.1, I2, and F6.1 formats respectively; three blanks would separate I and A, and K and B. The values of D and E would be printed on a second line in F3.0 and E14.8 formats, respectively.

EXAMPLE 3

> READ 7,A,B,C

> 7 FORMAT (/F4.0/F3.0//F6.1)

Five cards would be read. The first card would be read and ignored. The READ statement causes the first card to be read; the first solidus in the FORMAT statement would cause the second card to be read. The value for A would be taken from the second card. The value for B would be taken from the third card, the fourth card would be read and ignored, the fifth card would be read and the value of C taken from it.

9.14   The H Specification for Alphameric Data

Up to this point the input and output of numeric data only have been considered. It is often desirable to write alphameric information for the purpose of report headings or to provide for other descriptive information. It may also be desirable to read alphameric information that at a later time might be printed or punched. There are two specifications for the manipulation of alphameric information: the H specification and the A specification. The H specification will be described at this time; a discussion of the more advanced A specification will be postponed until Chapter 13.

Alphameric information may be read or written, or both, by using the H specification. The general form of the H specification is *w*H, where *w* designates an unsigned fixed-point constant specifying the number of alphameric characters to be used. The specification, *followed by w alphameric characters*, may be used in a FORMAT statement to provide for alphameric information. A comma following the *w* alphameric characters may be omitted or included at the discretion of the programmer.

The effect of the *w*H specification depends on whether it is being used with an input or output statement. If it is used with an input statement, *w* characters are taken from the input record (punched card) and replace the *w* characters following the specification. If it is used with an output statement, the *w* characters following the specification (or the *w* characters that replaced them as a result of input operations) are written as part of the output record. If blanks are required in the alphameric information, they must be provided for *and* included in the count *w*. This is one case in which blanks are *not* ignored by the Fortran system.

The following are examples of the use of the H specification:

EXAMPLE 1

PRINT 1

1   FORMAT (24HFORTRANbPROBLEMbNUMBERb1)

These statements would cause the following message to be printed in columns 1–24:

FORTRAN PROBLEM NUMBER 1

Note that the output statement has no list associated with it; when this occurs with either an input or output statement, the statement number specifying the FORMAT statement should not be followed by a comma.

EXAMPLE 2

READ 4

4   FORMAT (27Hbbbbbbbbbbbbbbbbbbbbbbbbbbb)

PRINT 4

Assume the card read by the READ statement was punched as follows, starting in column 1:

DATAbFROMbTESTbSETbNUMBERb7

These 27 characters would be read and would replace the 27 blanks following the H in the FORMAT statement. The PRINT statement would cause these 27 characters to be printed. Actually, in this example the 27 characters following the H specification could have been *any* 27 characters, since they were to be replaced, but *27 characters had to be specified.*

EXAMPLE 3

READ 891

891   FORMAT (9X10H0123456789)

PRINT 891

Assume that the first card was punched with the following ten characters in columns 10–19:

A B C D E F G H I J

The PRINT statement would cause A B C D E F G H I J to be printed in columns 10–19; columns 1–9 would be blank. The 9X in the FORMAT statement provides for skipping columns 1–9 of the input card and provides for nine blanks in the output record.

Use of the H specification is not restricted to I/O statements without lists. Quite elaborate output can be obtained by using the H specification in FORMAT statements which are referenced by I/O statements with lists.

EXAMPLE 4

PRINT 7,A,B,C,I,D,K

7   FORMAT (2HA = F4.0,2X2HB = F8.2,3X3HCO = E10.2,4XI3,4HDEL = E9.1,4HNO. = I3)

The following line of output might result:

A = −62.bbB = b1675.12bbbCO = b−0.12E−08bbbbb12DEL = bb0.7Eb0 9NO = b18

TERMINATING AN INPUT/OUTPUT STATEMENT

The question of what terminates an I/O operation should be considered. Up to this point we have considered only cases where there were an equal number of elements in the list and specifications in the FORMAT statement. Many times it will be desirable to include more numeric (E, F, and I) specifications in the FORMAT statement than items in the I/O list. This situation could occur if more than one I/O statement referenced the same FORMAT statement. As an illustration consider the following statements:

READ 1,A,B,C

1 FORMAT (2XF5.1,3XF9.2,2XF5.0)

———

———

———

PRINT 1,A,D

This approach is permissible if it is required to print A and D in the same format as A and B were read. Note that in the case of the PRINT statement there are more specifications in the FORMAT statement than elements in the list. The rule that covers this situation is as follows:

Rule 1. If there are more numeric specifications in the FORMAT statement than items in the list, the additional numeric specifications are ignored and the I/O statement is terminated when the value of the last variable in the list has been printed, punched, or read.†

Thus, in the foregoing example, A and D would be printed in F5.1 and F9.2 format, respectively, and the printing operation would be terminated.

The opposite situation occurs when there are more variables in the list than there are specifications in the FORMAT statement. *However, each variable in the list must have an associated format specification.* An example of this case is the following:

READ 1,A,B,C

1 FORMAT (F6.2)

The rule that covers this situation is as follows:

Rule 2. If there are more items in the list than specifications in the FORMAT statement, the system will return to the rightmost left parenthesis in the FORMAT statement and repeat the specifications from this point on as many times as necessary.

Thus in the foregoing example the first left parenthesis is also the rightmost left parenthesis and A, B, and C would each be read under a specification of F6.2. It would seem that the output in this case would be the same as the output that would result from an original specification of 3F6.2. This is not so, however, because of the application of Rule 3, which follows.

†Any nonnumeric specifications (X,H,A) which occur *after* the numeric specification associated with the last variable of the I/O list and *before* the next numeric specification (if any) in the FORMAT statement will be acted upon. (See the output of Program 18.10.)

Rule 3. Whenever the *rightmost* parenthesis of a FORMAT statement is encountered *and* there are more items in the list, the rightmost parenthesis causes the system to reset for a new record (that is, to read another card, punch another card, or print another line) similar to the function of the solidus, and return to the rightmost left parenthesis for additional specifications.

In the same example, A, B, and C would each be read from a separate card in F6.2 format.

EXAMPLES OF
INPUT/OUTPUT AND FORMAT STATEMENTS†

The following examples serve to illustrate the functioning of the FORMAT statement. The PRINT statement is used in all the examples, but the application to the READ and PUNCH statements is similar and should present the reader with no problem. Assume the following variables have the indicated values:

$$A = 12.67 \qquad I = -12$$
$$B = .0007 \qquad J = 138$$
$$C = -7.1987 \qquad K = 2$$
$$D = 67496.1 \qquad L = -1$$
$$E = 1.75$$

In each of the following examples a PRINT statement, FORMAT statement, and lines of resulting output are shown.

EXAMPLE 1

        PRINT 1,I,J,K

    1   FORMAT (5HNO. = bI4,3XI4,2X3HI1bI3)
Output: NO. = bb − 12bbbb138bbI1bbb2

EXAMPLE 2

        PRINT 1,A,J,E

    1   FORMAT (3XF6.2,2XI4)

Output: bbbb12.67bbb138
        bbbbb1.75

EXAMPLE 3

        PRINT 1,B,C

    1   FORMAT (6HBETA = bE15.8/F8.4,E15.8)

†At many installations where the output medium is a high-speed printer, the FORMAT statement should contain provisions for the first character of an output record to be one of the allowable carriage-control characters. (See Section 13.4 for details.)

Output: BETA = bb0.70000000E − 03
         b − 7.1987

EXAMPLE 4

PRINT 1,A,E,J,I,K,L
1   FORMAT (2F8.2,I5,(I3))

Output: bbb12.67bbbb1.75bb138 − 12
         bb2
         b − 1

Note that in Example 4 the system returns to the rightmost left parenthesis (the one immediately preceding the I3) and repeats specifications from that point.

EXAMPLE 5

PRINT 1,C,I,J,K,L
1   FORMAT (E11.4,(I3,I5))

Output: − 0.7199Eb01 − 12bb138
         bb2bbb − 1

EXAMPLE 6

PRINT 1,C,I,J,K,L
1   FORMAT (E11.4,2(I3,I5))

Output: − 0.7199Eb01 − 12bb138bb2bbb − 1

Problems

9.1 Write the minimum specification by which each of the following numbers may be written.

a) − 0.3467E − 04   *d*) .078E+26
b) − 7.012   *e*) 1
c) 43678   *f*) 3.78

9.2 Indicate whether the format specifications to the left are sufficient to print the numbers to the right; a minimum of four significant digits is required. If the specification is not sufficient give the correct format specification.

	Specification	*Number*		*Specification*	*Number*
a)	F5.1	− 676.712	*e*)	F7.0	− 868.75
b)	I4	+8765	*f*)	E9.3	− 1987.
c)	E14.8	.0012365	*g*)	I5	− 4251
d)	F10.1	− 1234.567	*h*)	F6.4	32.123

9.3 Given are the following input statement and associated FORMAT statement:

READ 38,A,B,C,I,D,K

38 FORMAT (3HAAAF3.0, F6.2, 2XE10.2,I1,F1.1,1XI4)

Indicate the values stored in the registers A, B, C, I, D and K for each of the following two data cards, which are punched with data in columns 1–31, inclusive (b indicates a blank column).

a) Card 1   1234567689120Abb8.66E+1008912bb

b) Card 2   95.1.2+19.6199018166E−018140961

9.4 Given the following output statement and associated FORMAT statement:

PRINT 64,K,A,I,B,C,D,I1

64 FORMAT (I3,F6.2,/I4,3X3HYESF4.0,/1XF9.6,2XE10.2,2XI4)

Indicate the number of output cards, the form of the values on each card and their variable names. Indicate form by = sXXX.XX; indicate blank columns with a "b."

9.5 For each of the following sets of statements, indicate for each variable in the list (a) the format specification it will be read under, (b) the card columns the value is taken from, and (c) the data card its value will be taken from (that is, the first card read, the second card read, etc.).

a)   READ 1,A,B,C,D

   1   FORMAT (2F6.0)

b)   READ 2,I,J,K,L

   2   FORMAT (/I2/I3/I2,2XI3)

c)   READ 3,I,J

   3   FORMAT (3HABC,4XI7,I8)

d)   READ 4,A

   4   FORMAT (4F6.1)

e)   READ 5,A,B,I

   5   FORMAT (F8.2,/2XF2.2,3XI5)

f)   READ 6,A,B,C,D,E,F

   6   FORMAT (F6.3)

g)   READ 7,I,J,K,L,M,N,N1

   7   FORMAT (I2,I3,I4)

h)　READ 8,D,W,R,X

　　8　FORMAT (2H67F4.2,3F5.1,/)

9.6　Indicate which, if any, of the following Fortran statements are invalid. State the reason.

a)　READ 6,A,B,KKKKKK

b)　READ 60 D,X1

c)　READ N,X,Y,W

d)　READ 80,1,2

e) 7　FORMAT (2F3.1,F4.1,F5.1))

f) 8　FORMAT (2(I3,I4))

g) 9　FORMAT (2(I3,2(I4,I2)))

h) 5　FORMAT (//,3H444,2X3H444F1.0)

i) 4　FORMAT (4.1,I2)

j) 3　FORMAT (5HANSWER,F4.2)

k) 6　FORMAT (2I4,/F2.1)

9.7　Write the Fortran statements necessary to print each of the required messages on the lines indicated.

a) Line 1　　REGRESSIONbANALYSISbPROGRAM

b) Line 1　　A
　　Line 2　　B
　　Line 3　　C
　　Line 4　　D

c) Line 1　　NUMBERbbSQ.bbbCUBE

d) Line 1　　−10
　　Line 2　　−100
　　Line 3　　−1000

e) Line 1　　FORTRANbIS
　　Line 2　　MYbFAVORITE
　　Line 3　　SUBJECT

9.8　Consider the following pairs of Fortran statements; how many data cards will be read by each set of statements?

a)　READ 1,A,B,C,D,E　　*c*)　READ 1,I,J,K,L,M

　　1　FORMAT (//F2.0,F6.1)　　1　FORMAT (I2,I3/)

b)　READ 1,I,J,K,L,M,N　　*d*)　READ 1,I,J,K,L,M,N

　　1　FORMAT (I3,2(I4/I2))　　1　FORMAT (2I4//I3//I2/)

9.9 Write a Fortran program to read N numbers punched one per card in F4.1 format. These data cards are preceded by a card with the value of N punched in columns 1–3 in I3 format. Calculate the following:

a) The sum of the squares of the numbers $(\sum_{i=1}^{N} x_i^2)$.

b) The number of input values less than -12.5.

c) The largest number.

9.10 Write a Fortran program to read N data cards each punched with two numbers (A and B) in 2F5.1 format. The last data card is followed by a card with 99999 punched in columns 1–5; no data card has five 9's punched in columns 1–5. Calculate the following:

a) The average difference between the pairs of numbers:

$$\sum_{i=1}^{N} (A_i - B_i) \div N$$

b) $y = \sum_{i=1}^{N} x_i$

where $x_i = A + B$ if $(A^2 - B^2) > 0$

$x_i = A - 2B$ if $(A^2 - B^2) = 0$

$x_i = A + B - 5$ if $(A^2 - B^2) < 0$

10

Subscripted Variables and the DO Statement

ARRAYS

In many problems it is advantageous to work with quantities considered as elements of an array. An array can be defined as a group of quantities; a *one-dimensional* array is a group of quantities arranged in the form of a list, and a *two-dimensional* array is a group of quantities arranged in a matrix form — that is, by rows and columns. The individual quantities comprising an array (called its *elements*) are almost always related to one another in that they represent measurements of a like kind or are to be treated in similar ways. An array (the entire group of quantities) can be given *one* name. The individual elements of a one-dimensional array can be referenced by indicating their position in the list, and in a two-dimensional array by indicating their position by row and column. Arrays provide for a compact and flexible notation particularly useful in dealing with the solution of systems of linear equations.

The quantities shown below can be considered as the elements of a one-dimensional array. They might, for example, represent the scores on a test made by the members of a particular class:

$$90,85,67,86,93,100,72,89,77,68$$

If this array were assigned the name SCORE, the elements of the array could be referenced by appending to the name SCORE an integer enclosed in parentheses, indicating the number's position in the list. Thus SCORE (1) would refer to the first number in the list, or 90; SCORE (8) would refer to the eighth number in the list, or 89, etc.

The quantities in Table 10.1 can be considered as the elements of a two-dimensional array. The columns might represent different cities: Chicago, New York, Philadelphia, and Los Angeles, respectively. The rows might represent different brands of a product: Brand V, Brand W, Brand X, Brand Y, and Brand Z, respectively. The quantities might be a measure of the unit sales of the different brands in each of the cities.

TABLE 10.1   A Two-Dimensional Array

	Column 1	Column 2	Column 3	Column 4
Row 1	88	91	89	90.5
Row 2	67	98	75.5	78
Row 3	90	85.3	86	88
Row 4	95	94	93	94.5
Row 5	92.5	90	91.5	89

If this array were assigned the name SALES, the elements of the array could be referenced by appending to the name SALES two integers separated by a comma and enclosed in parentheses. The *first* integer would indicate the *row* in which an element appears, and the *second* integer would indicate the *column* in which it appears. It is common practice when referring to the position of an element in a two-dimensional array to refer first to the row and second to the column. Thus, SALES (1, 2) would refer to the quantity in the first row and second column, 91; SALES (3, 4) would refer to the quantity in the third row and fourth column, 88. This quantity is the amount of sales of Brand X in Los Angeles.

The ideas just expressed may be summarized as follows: A group of quantities can be considered as the elements of an array. A *single* name is assigned to the array. An element's position in an array is indicated by appending to the name of the array one or two integers called *subscripts*. A single subscript indicates an element's position in a one-dimensional array; a double subscript indicates an element's position in a two-dimensional array, the first subscript indicating the row and the second subscript the column where the element is to be found.

These ideas and comments may easily be extended by the reader to include arrays of higher dimensions.

10.1   The Representation of Arrays in Fortran

A variable name in Fortran may be used as the name of an array (one-, two-, or three-dimensional). The individual elements of the array are referenced by appending to the array name one, two, or three subscripts that indicate the element's position in the array. The variable is then referred to as a *subscripted variable*.† The subscripts must be enclosed in parentheses; and in the case of double and triple subscripts, the individual subscripts must be separated by commas.

Allowable Forms for Subscripts

A subscript may be in any of the following forms:

General Form

v

c

$v+c$ or $v-c$

$c*v$

$c*v+c'$ or $c*v-c'$

where v is a nonsubscripted fixed-point variable, and c and c' are any unsigned fixed-point constants.

Examples of Subscripted Variables

A(ID)	L3(3*J−2)
K(3)	DD(I,2)
B(I+2)	W(I,J)
C(K−3)	Z(3,4)
I(4*I1)	CORR(I+1,J)
X(2*J+1)	Y(2,K+1,3*J)

Subscripts are fixed-point quantities whose values determine which element of the array is being referred to. When a variable is used as a subscript, it is only the *value* of the variable that is of importance. For example, A(I) refers to the ith element in the one-dimensional array called A. If the variable I was previously assigned the value six, A(I) would refer to the sixth number in the array called A.

The following items of information relating to subscripts and subscripted variables should be noted:

1. A subscript must take on only positive values. If a subscript inadvertently violates this rule, the program may still be executed. No error message is printed on this condition, but the results are probably incorrect. Therefore, extreme caution should be observed.

2. A subscript may not itself be subscripted. Thus, A(I(2)) is invalid.

†All previous commentary referring to *variables* also applies to *subscripted variables* unless otherwise noted.

3. The allowable forms of subscripts previously presented are the *only* allowable forms; therefore, a subscript in the form $c+v$ is *not* allowed. The variable must appear first — that is, $v+c$.

4. A variable that represents the name of an array may not be used without subscripts in a Fortran program. The following two statements

$$B = A(I)$$
$$C = A + B$$

could not appear in the same program because the name A appears both with subscripts and without subscripts. There are three exceptions to this rule as follows:

a) The name of an array without subscripts may appear in an input/output list (see Section 10.10).

b) The name of an array without subscripts may appear as an argument when calling or defining a function subprogram or a subroutine subprogram (see Chapter 11).

c) The name of an array without subscripts may appear in a COMMON statement or EQUIVALENCE statement (see Chapter 12).

10.2   The DIMENSION Statement

Consider the following two Fortran statements from the standpoint of the compiler program:

$$A = 1.$$
$$X(I) = B(I)*C(I)$$

When the compiler encounters the statement $A = 1.$ it will reserve one storage register for the variable A and one storage register for the constant 1. provided it has not previously done so (that is, encountered A or 1. in a previous statement). When the compiler encounters the subscripted variables X, B, and C for the first time, how many storage registers should it reserve for each array? There is no way for the compiler to determine this. The statement $X(I) = B(I)*C(I)$ does not give any information as to the possible size of each array. However, the appropriate number of storage registers *must* be reserved for each array by the compiler. It is the responsibility of the programmer to supply the compiler with this information. The DIMENSION statement is used by the programmer to specify the *maximum* dimensions for each array appearing in the program.

General Form

DIMENSION $v,v,v,v, \ldots$

where v is the variable name of an array followed by its *maximum* dimensions enclosed in parentheses.

Examples of the DIMENSION *Statement*

DIMENSION A(10)

DIMENSION X(30),B(10,10),C(5),K(4,3,4)

DIMENSION DELT(15),JON(5,6)

The following rules pertaining to the use of the DIMENSION statement should be noted:

1. Every subscripted variable must appear in a DIMENSION statement *prior* to its first use in the program.

2. The dimensions given to an array in a DIMENSION statement must be *maximum* dimensions. A particular set of data may consist of fewer elements than dimensioned for, but never more. For example, if a program is written to invert a matrix, the maximum size matrix upon which the program will operate must be decided upon and specified in the DIMENSION statement. However, the program could be written so as to invert any matrix whose dimensions do not exceed those in the DIMENSION statement.

3. The dimensions of an array as specified in a DIMENSION statement must be *numeric* (fixed-point constants).† The statement

DIMENSION B1(J)

is invalid. The variable J must be replaced by a fixed-point constant.

4. A variable in a DIMENSION statement must have the same number of subscripts as it does in the program and vice versa. Thus, if a variable A appears with two subscripts [e.g., A(3,4)] in a program and a maximum of ten rows and ten columns are to be provided for, the following DIMENSION statement is required.

DIMENSION A(10,10)

This statement would cause 100 storage registers to be reserved for the array called A. Even though the statement DIMENSION A(100) would also cause 100 storage registers to be reserved for the array called A, it would be incorrect because the variable appears with two subscripts in the program but with only one subscript in the DIMENSION statement.

10.3   *Programming Examples Using Arrays*

To illustrate the advantage of treating a group of quantities as elements of an array the following two problems are presented

†For an exception, see Section 11.7.

Problem 1

Fifty cards are each punched with ten numbers in 10F6.2 format. It is required to write a Fortran program to calculate and print the cube root of each number. If the quantities are *not* treated as elements of an array, each of the ten numbers on a card *must* be given a different variable name. The program might then appear as follows:

$Y = 1./3.$

$I = 0$

3   READ 1,A,B,C,D,E,F,G,H,R,S

1   FORMAT (10F6.2)

$I = I + 1$

$X = A**Y$

PRINT 2,A,X

2   FORMAT (12HCUBE ROOT OF,2XF7.2,4H IS,2XE15.8)

$X = B**Y$

PRINT 2,B,X

$X = C**Y$

PRINT 2,C,X

.

.

.

$X = S**Y$

PRINT 2,S,X

IF $(I-50)3,4,4$

4   CALL EXIT

END   (P10.1)

Because it was necessary to assign to each number on a card a different variable name, it was necessary to use separate statements to calculate and print the cube root of each number, which resulted in a program consisting of 29 statements. Note that the statement $Y = 1./3.$ was used to avoid the necessity of writing each of the ten exponents as $(1./3.)$ which would have caused ten divisions to take place instead of one.

The following program is also a solution to the above problem. This program treats the ten numbers on a card as the elements of a one-dimensional array named A.

```
      DIMENSION A(10)
      Y = 1./3.
      I = 0
    5 READ 1,A(1),A(2),A(3),A(4),A(5),A(6),A(7),A(8),A(9),A(10)
    1 FORMAT (10F6.2)
      I = I+1
      J = 1
    3 X = A(J)**Y
      PRINT 2,A(J),X
    2 FORMAT (12HCUBE ROOT OF,2XF7.2,4H  IS,2XE15.8)
      J = J+1
      IF (J−10) 3,3,4
    4 IF (I−50) 5,6,6
    6 CALL EXIT
      END                                          (P10.2)
```

In this program the variable J is used as a subscript. The statement $X = A(J)**Y$ is used to evaluate the cube root of *each* of the ten numbers on a card, which are read as the ten elements of a one-dimensional array called A. Each successive time the statement is executed the value of J has been increased by one causing A(J) to reference the next element of the array. The same commentary also applies to the PRINT statement. P10.2 requires only fifteen statements, whereas P10.1 required 29 statements; this reflects a considerable saving in programming time. However, the reader should note that more computer time will be required to execute P10.2 than P10.1 because more statements will be executed.

Problem 2

As a second example, suppose it is required to find the largest and smallest of ten numbers punched on a card in 10F8.3 format. Assume no two numbers are equal. The following program will determine and print the largest and smallest of the ten numbers. The largest number will be stored in a register labeled B and the smallest number in a register labeled S. Initially the first number is considered to be both the largest and smallest number. Each succeeding number will then be compared to S and B and will be stored in S or B if it is smaller or larger, respectively, than the value previously stored.

DIMENSION A(10)

READ 1,A(1),A(2),A(3),A(4),A(5),A(6),A(7),A(8),A(9),A(10)

1 FORMAT (10F8.3)

   S = A(1)

   B = A(1)

   I = 2

7 IF (B − A(I))3,4,2

3 B = A(I)

   GO TO 4

2 IF (S − A(I))4,4,5

5 S = A(I)

4 I = I + 1

   IF (I − 10) 7,7,15

15 PRINT 50,S,B

50 FORMAT(15HSMALLEST NO. IS,F9.3,3X14HLARGEST NO. IS,2XF9.3)

   CALL EXIT

   END   (P10.3)

10.4 The DO Statement

The DO statement facilitates programming when operations involving arrays are required; but is not restricted to use with arrays. It can also be used advantageously in other situations, as the first few sample programs will illustrate.

General Form

$$DO \; n \; i = m_1, m_2, m_3$$

where n is a statement number, i is a nonsubscripted fixed-point variable, and m_1, m_2, m_3 are either nonsubscripted fixed-point variables or unsigned fixed-point constants.

Examples of the DO Statement

DO 8 I = 1,10,1

DO 16 I = J,K,L

DO 1 M2 = 1,L,2

DO 6 N = K,L,1

DO 7 L = 1,IFIN,IDEL

The DO statement is a statement that causes *repeated* execution of all the statements immediately following the DO up to and including the statement numbered n. The first time that these statements are executed the variable i is equal to m_1 ($i = m_1$); the next time they are executed i is increased by m_3 ($i = i + m_3$), and so on, each time with i being increased by m_3 until i exceeds m_2. When i exceeds m_2 for the first time the repeated execution of these statements stops and the statement immediately following the statement numbered n is then executed.

The following items of information pertaining to the use of the DO statement should be noted:

1. m_1 acts as an initial value for the variable i, m_3 acts as an increment for i, and m_2 as a terminal value.

2. The "range" of a DO is defined as the set of statements which are repeatedly executed — that is, all the statements immediately following the DO up to and including the statement whose number is n.

3. The integer variable i is referred to as the *index* of the DO. Throughout the range of a DO statement, the index is available for use in computation; that is, it may be used as an ordinary fixed-point variable or as a variable used in a subscript.

4. The statements in the range of a DO are normally never executed with i having a value that exceeds m_2.†

5. When m_3 has a value of one it need not be specified. Thus, the two statements:

$$\text{DO } 7 \quad I = 1,10,1$$
$$\text{DO } 7 \quad I = 1,10$$

are both correct and will function identically.

To illustrate the use of the DO statement consider the following three programs, all of which evaluate the sum of the integers from one to 100 inclusive.

```
        I = 0
        DO 1  J = 1,100,1
    1   I = I+J
        PRINT 6,I
    6   FORMAT (50HTHE SUM OF THE INTEGERS FROM 1
            TO 100 INCLUSIVE IS,2X18)
        CALL EXIT
        END                                    (P10.4)
```

†The one exception to this occurs when initially $m_1 > m_2$. In this case the statements in the range of the DO are executed once.

In P10.4 the range of the DO consists of one statement, $I=I+J$. The sum of the integers is developed in I using fixed-point arithmetic. The DO statement causes the variable J to take on the successive integer values from one to 100. The statement $I=I+J$ will be executed 100 times, each time with a different value of J. The first time J will have a value of one, the next time J will have the value of two, etc.

In P10.5 the range of the DO consists of two statements. This program is similar to P10.4 except that the sum is developed using floating point arithmetic. The statement $X=I$ is necessary for this reason; the statement SUM = SUM+I would be invalid because it violates the rule concerning the mode of an arithmetic expression.

>   SUM = 0.
>
>   DO 1 I = 1,100
>
>   X = I
>
> 1   SUM = SUM + X
>
>   PRINT 6,SUM
>
> 6   FORMAT (50HTHE SUM OF THE INTEGERS FROM 1
>   TO 100 INCLUSIVE ISF10.0)
>
>   CALL EXIT
>
>   END   (P10.5)

The following program is presented to illustrate the situation in which the index of a DO statement does not appear as a variable used explicitly in the range of the DO. In P10.6 it is used as a counter to control the number of times the statements in the range of the DO are executed. The statements SUM = SUM+X and X = X+1. are to be executed exactly one hundred times; the DO statement controls this.

>   SUM = 0.
>
>   X = 1.
>
>   DO 1 I = 1,100
>
>   SUM = SUM + X
>
> 1   X = X+1.
>
>   PRINT 6,SUM
>
> 6   FORMAT (50HTHE SUM OF THE INTEGERS FROM 1
>   TO 100 INCLUSIVE ISF10.0)
>
>   CALL EXIT
>
>   END   (P10.6)

The operation of the DO statement can be described in terms of other more familiar Fortran statements. The three statements illustrated in *b* of the programs below perform exactly the same function as the single DO statement in *a*. If the corresponding horizontal lines in the two programs represent identical statements, the two programs would be equivalent.

a) _____   *b)* _____

_____   _____

DO 8 I = J,K,L   I = J

2 _____   2 _____

_____   _____

_____   _____

8 _____   8 _____

9 _____   I = I + L

_____   IF (I − K)2,2,9

_____   9 _____

_____

Thus, P10.6 could be written without the DO statement as follows:

```
    SUM = 0.
    X = 1.
    I = 1 *
  4 SUM = SUM + X
  1 X = X + 1.
    I = I + 1 *
    IF (I − 100) 4,4,8 *
  8 PRINT 6,SUM
  6 FORMAT (50HTHE SUM OF THE INTEGERS FROM 1
    TO 100 INCLUSIVE ISF10.0)
    CALL EXIT
    END                                            (P10.7)
```

The three starred (*) statements in P10.7 together perform the function of the DO statement in P10.6.

A more important use of the DO statement is to facilitate the programming of calculations involving arrays. The following problem is presented to illustrate this point. There are 100 sets of two data cards. Each card has ten numbers punched in 10F7.3 format; the numbers represent the results of ten different tests performed on an electrical component. The numbers on the first card of each set represent the results of the tests performed on December 1, 1965; the numbers on the second card of each set represent the results of the same tests performed on the component on January 1, 1966. Each card has the component number punched in columns 75–80. It is required to write a Fortran program to calculate and print the natural logarithm of the average of the two test results for *each* of the ten tests for each of the 100 components. The following program will accomplish this.

```
      DIMENSION  A(10),B(10)
      I = 0
8     READ  2,A(1),A(2),A(3),A(4),A(5),A(6),A(7),A(8),A(9),A(10),ID
      READ  2,B(1),B(2),B(3),B(4),B(5),B(6),B(7),B(8),B(9),B(10),JD
2     FORMAT (10F7.3,4XI6)
      IF (ID − JD) 7,6,7
6     DO 61  K = 1,10,1
      X = ALOG((A(K)+B(K))/2.)
61    PRINT 1,X,K,ID
1     FORMAT (13HLOG. OF AVE. E15.8,5X9HTEST NO. I3,14H
      COMPONENT NO. I7)
      I = I+1
      IF(I − 100)8,9,9
7     PRINT 81
81    FORMAT (41HCARDS OUT OF SEQUENCE. CORRECT, HIT
      START)
      PAUSE
      GO TO 8
9     CALL EXIT
      END                                          (P10.8)
```

In the above program the variable I is used as a count and is tested to determine when the 100 sets of two data cards have been processed. After one set of data cards has been read, a check is made (that is, ID and JD are compared) to determine whether the data cards are the test results for the same component. If they are not, a message to this effect is printed and a

PAUSE statement executed. This allows the operator the opportunity to put the data cards in their proper sequence. To continue processing, the operator depresses the start key on the computer. This approach, however, is wasteful of computer time as the computer is idle while the operator is putting the cards in sequence. A more practical approach would be to have a message printed and a CALL EXIT statement executed so the computer would continue operation by processing the next program, leaving the corrections to be made in the present problem until a later time. The printed output of the above program consists of the logarithm of the average of the two results, the test number (K) and the component number (ID).

10.5 Rules for Using the DO Statement

Before we discuss the rules pertaining to DO statements the following definitions should be noted. There are two ways of transferring control out of the range of a DO. One is referred to as a *nonnormal exit* and the other as a *normal exit*. A *nonnormal exit* occurs when a transfer-type statement (e.g., IF, GO TO, etc.) *in* the range of a DO transfers control to a statement *outside* the range of the DO. A *normal exit* occurs when the statements in the range of the DO are repeatedly executed until the value of the index i exceeds m_2, and control passes to the statement immediately following the statement whose number is n. When a normal exit occurs, we say the DO has been *satisfied*.

Rule 1. When a *normal* exit occurs, the value of the index i is undefined and may not be used in computations before it is redefined (appears to the left of an equal sign or in an input list). As an illustration of this rule consider the following statements:

$$\rule{3em}{0.4pt}$$
$$\rule{3em}{0.4pt}$$
$$\rule{3em}{0.4pt}$$

$$\text{DO }18\ \ I = 1,20$$
$$18\quad \text{SUM} = \text{SUM} + X(I)$$
$$J = I$$

$$\rule{3em}{0.4pt}$$
$$\rule{3em}{0.4pt}$$
$$\rule{3em}{0.4pt}$$

When the DO is satisfied and the statement $J = I$ executed, the value of the storage register I is considered to be unavailable to the programmer. Therefore, I should be redefined before it is used.

When a *non-normal* exit occurs by transferring out of the range of a DO, the index *is* available for computation and *is* equal to the last value it attained in the DO loop. To illustrate this point, consider the following statements:

$$\overline{}$$

$$\overline{}$$

DO 16 KD = 1,N

IF (X(KD))3,16,16

16   SUM = SUM + X(KD)

$$\overline{}$$

$$\overline{}$$

3   J = KD

$$\overline{}$$

$$\overline{}$$

$$\overline{}$$

If any element of the X array is negative, control will pass out of the range of the DO to the statement whose number is 3. If the fifth element of the X array was the first negative quantity then J would have the value 5 after the statement J = KD was executed.

Rule 2. The index or the indexing parameters (m_1, m_2, m_3) may not be redefined in the range of a DO. Therefore, the index and any of the indexing parameters that are specified as variables may not appear to the left of an equal sign or in an input list in any statement in the range of the DO.

Rule 3. The last statement in the range of a DO (the statement whose number is *n*) must be an executable statement. Statements such as DIMENSION, FORMAT, and END are considered to be nonexecutable statements.

Rule 4. The last statement in the range of a DO cannot be a transfer statement. There is one exception to this rule; the last statement in the range of a DO may be a logical IF statement (see page 273 for a detailed description of this case). To illustrate a situation in which a programmer might want the last statement in the range of a DO to be a transfer statement, consider the problem of determining whether any element of a one-dimensional array is negative. The statements of a program to accomplish this might be

$$\overline{}$$

$$\overline{}$$

8   DO 90 L = 1,50

90   IF (X(L))3,90,90

$$\overline{}$$

$$\overline{}$$

3    $\overline{}$

$$\overline{}$$

$$\overline{}$$

However, these statements violate Rule 4, since the last statement in the range of a DO is a transfer statement. The reader should be able to ascertain that the foregoing statements would not function properly. The IF statement transfers to itself; therefore, if the first element of the X array were zero or positive, a nonending loop would be established; the index L would never be increased. Changing the IF statement to

$$\text{IF } (X(L))3,8,8$$

would not function properly either, because *each* time the DO statement is executed L is set equal to 1 again.

A Fortran statement called the CONTINUE statement may be used as the last statement in the range of a DO when the DO would otherwise end with a transfer-type statement. (See the next section for a detailed description of the CONTINUE statement.) This program can be correctly written as follows:

```
        ————
        ————
8    DO  90  L=1,50
     IF  (X(L))3,90,90
90   CONTINUE
        ————
        ————
3    ————
        ————
        ————
```

Rule 5. One or more DO's may be included within the range of another DO statement. This arrangement is called *nesting*. When DO's are nested, all the statements in the range of the innermost DO must also be in the range of the outer DO's. A set of DO's satisfying this rule is called a *nest* of DO's. The following diagram best serves to illustrate this rule:

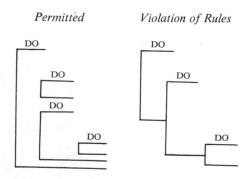

Permitted   *Violation of Rules*

One or more of the DO's in a nest of DO's may have the same statement as the last statement in their ranges. Thus, the following is permitted:

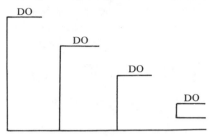

Rule 6. When DO statements are nested, the innermost DO is satisfied first. The execution of a nest of DO's proceeds from the innermost to outermost DO. Consider the following Fortran statements:

———

———

DO 6 I = 1,10

———

———

DO 7 J = 1,5

7 ———

———

———

6 ———

———

The situation illustrated here is that of a nest of DO's. When the first DO statement is executed, I is set equal to one. When the second DO statement is executed J is set equal to one. This DO is the innermost DO and is satisfied first. Thus, the statements in the range of this second DO are *repeatedly* executed with J taking on the values from one to five, inclusive. For every repeated execution of these statements, the variable I will have the value one. When this second DO is satisfied, control will eventually pass to the last statement in the range of the first DO. The index I is increased by one to two and all the statements in the range of the first DO are executed again. This includes the second DO statement. When the second DO is executed again, J is set equal to 1 and the statements in the range of this second DO are repeatedly executed until the DO is satisfied. This time, I will have the value two for every execution of the statements in the range of the DO. The procedure is repeated until the first DO is satisfied. The statements in the range of the innermost DO will have been executed fifty (10 × 5) times; all other statements in the range of the first DO will have been executed ten times.

As a second example of the execution of nested DO's, consider the following statements:

$$
\begin{array}{ll}
& \underline{\hspace{2cm}} \\
& \underline{\hspace{2cm}} \\
\text{DO} & 10 \ \ I = 1,3 \\
\text{DO} & 10 \ \ J = 1,4 \\
10 & L = I*J \\
& \underline{\hspace{2cm}} \\
& \underline{\hspace{2cm}}
\end{array}
$$

The statement whose number is 10 will be executed twelve times with the following values of I and J:

Order of Execution	1	2	3	4	5	6	7	8	9	10	11	12
Value of I	1	1	1	1	2	2	2	2	3	3	3	3
Value of J	1	2	3	4	1	2	3	4	1	2	3	4

10.6   The CONTINUE Statement

The CONTINUE statement is an executable Fortran statement that is often referred to as a dummy statement because it generates no instructions in the object program. It serves mainly as a point of reference. It provides the programmer with the means of inserting statement numbers in a program without generating any instructions. The most prevalent use of the CONTINUE statement is as the last statement in the range of a DO when the DO would otherwise end with a transfer-type statement (see page 162 for an example).

General Form

CONTINUE

INPUT/OUTPUT OF ONE-DIMENSIONAL ARRAYS

10.7   Indexing in an Input/Output List
(Implied DO Notation)

The input of one-dimensional arrays as illustrated in P10.2, P10.3, and P10.8 is somewhat cumbersome. A shorter notation may be used when it is required to specify more than one element of an array in an input or output list. This notation is called *indexing in the list* or using an *implied* DO and is somewhat the same in principle as the operation of the DO statement except the word DO and the statement number are omitted. The following three statements are equivalent, and the latter two serve to illustrate indexing in an input/output list:

    READ 1,A(1),A(2),A(3),A(4),A(5),A(6),A(7),A(8),A(9),A(10)

    READ 1,(A(I),I = 1,10,1)

    READ 1,(A(I),I = 1,10)

The following four items should be noted:

1. The operation of indexing a list is similar to the operations involving the index of the DO statement. As in the DO statement an index, an initial value, a terminal value, and an increment are specified. The index takes on the initial value and is increased by the increment until it is equal to the largest integer which does not exceed the terminal value. The following two statements are equivalent:

    READ 1,A(1),A(3),A(5),A(7)

    READ 1,(A(I),I = 1,7,2)

2. The index must be preceded by a comma.

3. The range of the indexing must be enclosed in parentheses. Consider the following statements:

    DO 8 I = 1,10

  8 X(I) = I*I

    PRINT 6, (I,X(I), I = 1,10)

  6 FORMAT (I3,2XF6.1)

The range of the indexing in the PRINT statement includes the variable I in the list. Therefore, the value of I *and* X(I) would be printed for integer values of I from one to ten, inclusive. The following output would result:

bb1bbbbb1.0

bb2bbbbb4.0

bb3bbbbb9.0

bb4bbbb16.0

bb5bbbb25.0

bb6bbbb36.0

bb7bbbb49.0

bb8bbbb64.0

bb9bbbb81.0

b10bbb100.0

If the PRINT and FORMAT statements had been

PRINT 6,I,(X(I),I = 1,10)

FORMAT (I3,(2XF6.1))

the output would have been as follows:

XXXbbbbb1.0

bbbbb4.0

bbbbb9.0

bbbb16.0

bbbb25.0

bbbb36.0

bbbb49.0

bbbb64.0

bbbb81.0

bbb100.0

Note that the first three characters on the first line of output represent the content of storage register I. Since a normal exit from the DO loop occurred, this value of I is considered to be undefined. At this point it has not been re-defined and is printed only once because the variable I is *not* included in the range of the indexing within the list.

4. When indexing occurs in a list, the list is considered to consist of all

the variables in the list as well as those specified by the implied DO. In each of the following examples, presented to illustrate this point, the two READ statements are equivalent:

READ 1,X,Y,(A(I),I = 1,4)

READ 1,X,Y,A(1),A(2),A(3),A(4)

READ 1,(A(I),B(I),I = 1,3),X

READ 1,A(1),B(1),A(2),B(2),A(3),B(3),X

READ 1,(A(I),I = 1,3),(B(I),I = 1,3),X

READ 1,A(1),A(2),A(3),B(1),B(2),B(3),X

Note in the last example that the terminating parameter N in the implied DO is read by the same READ statement in which the indexing appears. This is permissible as long as the value for the parameter is read *prior* to the indexing.

10.8 Input/Output Operations Involving Arrays

Examples of different methods for programming the input of one dimensional arrays will be presented; only the input and format statements will be illustrated. The application of these principles to the output of one-dimensional arrays is straightforward and should present no problems.

The reader should study carefully the following examples and understand the principles presented.

EXAMPLE 1

DO 6 I = 1,10

6   READ 10,A(I)

10   FORMAT (F5.1)

Each value of A(I) will be read from a separate card in F5.1 format. The input list consists of *one* element (every time the READ statement is executed, I has *one* particular value); therefore, only one number will be transformed and transmitted from each data card. The READ statement is executed *ten* times, causing ten cards to be read.

EXAMPLE 2

DO 6 I = 1,10

6   READ 10,A(I)

10   FORMAT (2F5.1)

As in Example 1, the list consists of one element; therefore, only *one* quantity will be taken from each card. The situation of having more specifications in the FORMAT statement than elements in the list prevails, the additional specifications are ignored (see page 142). As in the first example, the READ statement is executed ten times and ten data cards will be read; one quantity from each card will be transformed and stored as an element of the A array.

EXAMPLE 3

$$\text{DO } 6 \quad I = 1,10,2$$

$$6 \quad \text{READ } 10, A(I), A(I+1)$$

$$10 \quad \text{FORMAT } (2F5.1)$$

Here the list consists of two elements; notice that the index in the DO is increased by two each time. The READ statement will be executed five times, causing five data cards to be read; *two* quantities from each card will be transformed and stored as elements of the A array.

EXAMPLE 4

$$\text{DO } 6 \quad I = 1,10,2$$

$$6 \quad \text{READ } 10, A(I), A(I+1)$$

$$10 \quad \text{FORMAT } (F5.1)$$

As in Example 3, there are two elements in the list, but there is only one specification in the FORMAT statement. Since there are more elements in the list than specifications in the FORMAT statement, the system will reset for a new record (read another card) and go back to the rightmost left parenthesis for the needed specification (see page 143). The READ statement will be executed five times, however, ten cards will be read since each time the READ statement is executed the FORMAT statement causes a second card to be read. One quantity from each card will be transformed and stored as an element of the A array.

EXAMPLE 5

$$\text{DO } 6 \quad I = 1,9,2$$

$$6 \quad \text{READ } 10, A(I), A(I+1)$$

$$10 \quad \text{FORMAT } (2F5.1)$$

Assume that in this example the A array consists of *nine* elements, which are punched two elements per card. Therefore, the fifth data card contains the value of A(9). When the index I is increased to *nine*, the list of the input statement consists of two variables A(9) and A(10); therefore, *two* quantities will be taken from the last data card, transformed and stored respectively in A(9) and A(10). Whatever number is punched in columns 6–10 of the fifth data card is stored in A(10). If the foregoing statements are used to read the array, care must be exercised in writing the DIMENSION statement. The array consists of *nine* elements only; however, the DIMENSION statement *must* reserve space for *ten* elements, because a value for A(10) will be read, even though it might not be used in the program.

EXAMPLE 6

$$\text{READ } 10,(A(I),I = 1,10)$$
$$10 \quad \text{FORMAT } (F5.1)$$

The list consists of *ten* elements. Execution of the READ statement causes one card to be read. Since there is only one specification in the FORMAT statement and ten elements in the list, the specification must be *repeated* nine times, causing nine *more* cards to be read. This is identical in operation with Examples 1 and 2.

EXAMPLE 7

$$\text{READ } 10,(A(I),I = 1,10)$$
$$10 \quad \text{FORMAT } (10F5.1)$$

The READ statement causes one card to be read. Ten quantities are taken from the card, transformed, and stored as the ten elements of the A array.

EXAMPLE 8

$$\text{RAED } 10,(A(I),I = 1,10)$$
$$10 \quad \text{FORMAT } (2F5.1)$$

Five data cards will be read.

EXAMPLE 9

$$\text{READ } 10,(A(I),I = 1,9)$$
$$10 \quad \text{FORMAT } (2F5.1)$$

Five data cards will be read. When the fifth data card is read there is only one element A(9) remaining in the list to be processed. Therefore, just one quantity is transformed from the fifth card and the difficulty noted in Example 5 is avoided.

TWO-DIMENSIONAL ARRAYS

Very often it is advantageous to work with data in the form of two-dimensional arrays or matrices. The solution to many mathematical-type problems is facilitated by working with matrices and performing the operations of addition, subtraction, multiplication, inversion, etc., on them. It is not the purpose of this text to explain the operations of matrix algebra; however, examples of the manipulation of two-dimensional arrays will be presented, some of which demonstrate the programming of these matrix operations.

In Fortran a variable may be used as the name of a two-dimensional array. The individual elements of the array are referenced by appending to the variable name two subscripts separated by commas and enclosed in parentheses. The *first* subscript will always refer to the *row* the element is in and the *second* subscript will always refer to the *column* the element is in. To illustrate the programming of two-dimensional arrays, consider the two sets of data in Tables 10.2 and 10.3, which relate to the sales of five different brands of a product in four major cities for the years 1964 and 1965. The columns represent the four cities and the rows the five brands. The quantities are total sales in thousands of units of the different brands in each of the cities. (These sets are extensions of the data presented in Table 10.1.)

TABLE 10.2   Data for the Year 1964

	Chicago	New York	Philadelphia	Los Angeles
Brand V	88	91	89	90.5
Brand W	67	98	75.5	78
Brand X	90	85.3	86	88
Brand Y	95	94	93	94.5
Brand Z	92.5	90	91.5	89

TABLE 10.3   Data for the Year 1965

	Chicago	New York	Philadelphia	Los Angeles
Brand V	92	90	100	95
Brand W	65	95	89	80
Brand X	89	86	84	90
Brand Y	100	102	92	92
Brand Z	90	95	101	100

Let D64 be the name of the array of quantities representing the data for the year 1964, and let D65 be the name of the array of quantities representing the data for the year 1965. Therefore, D64(2,3) is 75.5, the amount of Brand W sold in Philadelphia in 1964; and D65(4,2) is 102, the amount of Brand Y sold in New York in 1965.

All of the following examples will pertain to the above data. In all of the examples *it is assumed that the data has been read into the storage registers.* A detailed discussion of the input and output of two-dimensional arrays is presented in Section 10.9.

EXAMPLE 1

Determine the total amount of Brand V sold in the four cities in 1964. The following Fortran statements will cause this amount to be stored in the variable X.

$$\text{DIMENSION}\ \ D64(5,4), D65(5,4)$$

$$\overline{}$$

$$\overline{}$$

$$X = 0.$$

$$\text{DO}\ 1\ \ I = 1,4$$

$$1\quad X = X + D64(1,I)$$

$$\overline{}$$

$$\overline{}$$

$$\overline{}$$

The variable I will take on the integer values from one to four inclusive causing the elements $D64(1,1)$, $D64(1,2)$, $D64(1,3)$, and $D64(1,4)$ respectively to be added to X. Note that the first subscript remains constant since the elements across the first row are being summed.

EXAMPLE 2

Determine the total amount of Brand V sold in the four cities for the years 1964 *and* 1965. The following Fortran statements will cause this amount to be stored in the variable X.

$$\text{DIMENSION}\ \ D64(5,4), D65(5,4)$$

$$\overline{}$$

$$\overline{}$$

$$X = 0.$$

$$\text{DO}\ 1\ \ J = 1,4$$

$$1\quad X = X + D64(1,J) + D65(1,J)$$

$$\overline{}$$

$$\overline{}$$

$$\overline{}$$

EXAMPLE 3

Determine the total amount of the five different brands sold in New York in 1964. The following Fortran statements will cause this amount to be stored in the variable X.

DIMENSION D64(5,4),D65(5,4)

———
———

$X = 0.$
DO 2 J = 1,5
2   $X = X + D64(J,2)$

———
———
———

In this example it is required to sum all the elements in the second column of the D64 array; therefore, the row subscript will vary, whereas the column subscript remains constant.

EXAMPLE 4

Determine the total amounts of Brands V, W, X, Y, and Z sold in the four cities in the year 1964. Store these results in a one-dimensional array called X; that is, X(1) will be the amount of Brand V sold, X(2) will be the amount of Brand W sold, etc. The following Fortran statements will do this.

DIMENSION D64(5,4),D65(5,4),X(5)

———

DO 1 I = 1,5
$X(I) = 0.$
DO 1 J = 1,4
1   $X(I) = X(I) + D64(I,J)$

———
———
———

For the solution of this problem it is necessary to develop the *sum of the quantities in each row* of the D64 array. Therefore, it is necessary to vary *both* the row and column subscripts. This is best accomplished by using nested DO statements. The innermost DO is satisfied first (see Rule 6 on page 163); therefore for *each* value of I, J will take on the integer values from one to four inclusive. D64(1,1), D64(1,2), D64(1,3), and D64(1,4) will each be added to X(1); D64(2,1) D64(2,2), D64(2,3) and D64(2,4) will each be added to X(2); etc. Note that X is included in the DIMENSION statement since it is the name of an array; and also note that the elements of the X array are set to zero *before* the elements of the D64 array are added.

EXAMPLE 5

Determine the amounts of each of the five brands sold in each of the four cities for the years 1964 and 1965 combined. Store the results in a two-dimensional array called D6465. It is desired to form a new array consisting of elements formed by adding corresponding elements of the D64 array and the D65 array. This is an example of matrix addition.

DIMENSION D64(5,4),D65(5,4),D6465(5,4)

    ―――

    ―――

    DO 10 K = 1,5

    DO 10 L = 1,4

  10   D6465(K,L) = D64(K,L) + D65(K,L)

    ―――

    ―――

    ―――

Note that it is not necessary to set the elements of the D6465 array to zero. This is because a *progressive* sum is *not* being developed.

10.9 Input/Output of Two-Dimensional Arrays

When the elements of a two-dimensional array are being pre pared (listed) for keypunching, they may be listed by rows or by columns. Thus, we say that a matrix is punched by rows or columns depending on the order in which the elements are punched. Consider the two-dimensional array for the year 1964 presented in Table 10.2. The elements of the array could be punched in either one of the two following ways:

88,91,89,90.5,67,98,75.5,78,90,85.3, . . .

88,67,90,95,92.5,91,98,85.3,94,90,89,75.5, . . .

The first is an example of the elements of the array being punched by rows; the second, by columns. To determine whether the elements of an array are punched by columns or rows it is necessary to know only the order in which the elements are punched, not how many elements are punched on each data card.

Examples of different methods for programming the input of two-dimensional arrays will be presented, but only the input and FORMAT statements will be given. The application of these principles to the output of two-dimensional arrays is straightforward and should present no problem to the reader.

EXAMPLE 1

$$\text{DO } 1 \quad I = 1,5$$
$$\text{DO } 1 \quad J = 1,4$$
$$1 \quad \text{READ } 2,A(I,J)$$
$$2 \quad \text{FORMAT } (F5.1)$$

These statements will read in the elements of an array called A. The elements are punched by rows (notice the column subscript is varying the fastest), one element to a card. The READ statement will be executed twenty (5 × 4) times, causing twenty cards to be read. Since there is only one element in the list, one number will be taken from each card, transformed, and stored.

EXAMPLE 2

$$\text{DO } 1 \quad J = 1,4$$
$$\text{DO } 1 \quad I = 1,5$$
$$1 \quad \text{READ } 2,A(I,J)$$
$$2 \quad \text{FORMAT } (F5.1)$$

The comments on Example 1 also apply here with the exception that in this example the elements are punched by columns (the row subscript is varying the fastest). The reader should recognize that the following statements are *not* equivalent to the preceding set of statements:

$$\text{DO } 1 \quad I = 1,5$$
$$\text{DO } 1 \quad J = 1,4$$
$$1 \quad \text{READ } 2,A(J,I)$$
$$2 \quad \text{FORMAT } (F5.1)$$

These statements also read the elements of a two-dimensional array by columns; however, in this case the dimensions of the array are *four* rows and *five* columns, whereas the statements at the beginning of Example 2 read in the elements of an array consisting of *five* rows and *four* columns.

EXAMPLE 3

$$\text{DO } 1 \quad I = 1,6$$
$$\text{DO } 1 \quad J = 1,6,2$$
$$1 \quad \text{READ } 2,A(I,J),A(I,J+1)$$
$$2 \quad \text{FORMAT } (2F5.1)$$

These statements will read in the elements of an array consisting of six rows and six columns, punched by rows, two elements per card.

EXAMPLE 4

DO 1 I = 1,6

DO 1 J = 1,5,2

1   READ 2,A(I, J),A(I, J+1)

2   FORMAT (2F5.1)

These statements will read in the elements of an array consisting of six rows and *five* columns, punched by rows, two elements per card. When J has the value 5, the list consists of two elements, A(I, 5) and A(I, 6); therefore, *two* quantities will be taken from this data card, transformed, and stored. Whatever number is punched in columns 6–10 of these data cards will be stored in A(I, 6). Therefore, the *first* element of *each* row of the array should be punched as the first number of a new card. The data should be punched as follows:

CARD 1	A(1,1),A(1,2)
CARD 2	A(1,3),A(1,4)
CARD 3	A(1,5)
CARD 4	A(2,1),A(2,2)
CARD 5	A(2,3),A(2,4)
CARD 6	A(2,5)
CARD 7	A(3,1),A(3,2)

.
.
.

The data should *not* be punched in the following form:

CARD 1	A(1,1),A(1,2)
CARD 2	A(1,3),A(1,4)
CARD 3	A(1,5),A(2,1)
CARD 4	A(2,2),A(2,3)
CARD 5	A(2,4),A(2,5)
CARD 6	A(3,1),A(3,2)

.
.
.

If the above input statements are used, care must be exercised in writing the DIMENSION statement; even though the array to be operated on consists of six rows and five columns, space must be reserved for a six-by-six array, because values for the sixth column of the array will be read even though they might not be used in the program.

EXAMPLE 5

DO 1 I = 1,10

DO 1 J = 1,10,2

1   READ 2,A(I,J),A(I,J+1)

2   FORMAT (F5.1)

One hundred data cards will be read. One number will be taken from each data card, transformed, and stored. This example illustrates the situation in which there are more elements in the list than specifications in the FORMAT statement.

EXAMPLE 6

DO 1 I = 1,5

1   READ 2,A(I,1),A(I,2),A(I,3),A(I,4),A(I,5)

2   FORMAT (5F5.1)

Five cards will be read. The elements of the array are punched by rows five elements to a card. Note that one data card contains all the elements of a row.

EXAMPLE 7

DO 1 I = 1,5

1   READ 2,(A(I,J),J = 1,5)

2   FORMAT (5F5.1)

The commentary of Example 6 also applies to Example 7. The sets of statements presented in the two examples are equivalent.

EXAMPLE 8

READ 2,((A(I,J),J = 1,5),I = 1,5)

2   FORMAT (F5.1)

Both subscripts are indexed in the list; the range of the index I includes the range of the index J as indicated by the parentheses. The operation is similar to that of a nest of DO's. The *list* consists of all the elements of the array and is equivalent to the following:

A(1,1),A(1,2),A(1,3),A(1,4),A(1,5),A(2,1),A(2,2),A(2,3),A(2,4),A(2,5), etc.

It is the FORMAT statement in this case that determines how many numbers are taken from each data card. The elements of the array are punched by rows one per card.

EXAMPLE 9

$$\text{READ } 2,((A(I,J),J=1,5),I=1,5)$$

2   FORMAT (2F5.1)

Thirteen cards will be read. The elements of the array are punched by rows, two per card, as follows:

CARD 1	A(1,1),A(1,2)
CARD 2	A(1,3),A(1,4)
CARD 3	A(1,5),A(2,1)
CARD 4	A(2,2),A(2,3)
CARD 5	A(2,4),A(2,5)
CARD 6	A(3,1),A(3,2)

.
.
.

Contrast this example with Example 4.

EXAMPLE 10

$$\text{READ } 2,((A(I,J),I=1,5),J=1,5)$$

2   FORMAT (2F5.1)

The elements of the array are punched by *columns*, two per card.

EXAMPLE 11

Often when it is required to read the elements of a large array, many of the elements are zero. In these cases it would be desirable to read in only the nonzero elements. Thus, each element to be read must be accompanied by its row and column designation, since the elements are not entered consecutively. If the elements of an array are entered in this manner, all the elements of the array should be set to zero before the nonzero elements are read. The following program will accomplish this.

```
      DIMENSION X(10,50)
      DO 6 I=1,10
      DO 6 J=1,50
6     X(I,J)=0.
2     READ 1,I,J,X(I,J),K
1     FORMAT (2I2,2XF8.2,65XI1)
      IF (K−1)2,8,8
8     ─────
```

Three-Dimensional Arrays

Although no examples involving three-dimensional arrays will be presented in this text, the commentary and principles as applied to one- and two-dimensional arrays are easily extended to cover three-dimensional arrays.

10.10 Input/Output of Arrays without Subscripts†

When the input or output of an entire array (the array as dimensioned) is to be provided for, a special notation may be used in the list of the input or output statement. The name of the array *without* subscripts can be used in the list. Then the *entire* array *as dimensioned* will be read or written. If the array is two or three dimensional, it will be read or written *columnwise* that is, with the first of the subscripts varying most rapidly and the last varying least rapidly. Thus, if the name of a two-dimensional array appears without subscripts in an output list, the elements of the array will be written by columns in accordance with the specified FORMAT statement. If the name of a two-dimensional array appears in an input list, the elements of the array will be read by columns (therefore, they must be punched by columns) in accordance with the specified FORMAT statement.

EXAMPLE 1

DIMENSION A(10)

READ 5,A

5   FORMAT (F5.1)

Ten cards will be read with one number from each card being transformed and stored as an element of the array A.

EXAMPLE 2

DIMENSION A(10,10)

READ 5,A

5   FORMAT (F5.1)

One hundred cards will be read, with one number from each card being transformed and stored as an element of the A array. The elements must be punched by columns.

10.11 Additional Information on Input/Output of Arrays

In many of the examples concerning the input/output of arrays previously presented, the exact number of elements to be read or written was specified

†This section applies only to some Fortran systems.

by a constant or constants in DO statements or an implied DO. Most often, however, a program is written to process any size array up to some maximum as specified in a DIMENSION statement. Any particular set of data comprising an array may be of any size up to the maximum; it is, therefore, not possible to specify the number of elements to be read by a constant in the program. Usually the size of the array is read as data along with the elements of the array, and the input/output statements in the program are written to handle variable-size arrays. The following examples illustrate this principle.

EXAMPLE 1

> DIMENSION A(100)
>
> READ 1,N
>
> 1 FORMAT (I3)
>
> DO 2 I = 1,N
>
> 2 READ 3,A(I)
>
> 3 FORMAT (F5.1)

EXAMPLE 2

> DIMENSION K(50)
>
> READ 1,M
>
> 1 FORMAT (I2)
>
> READ 3,(K(I),I = 1,M)
>
> 3 FORMAT (2F5.1)

EXAMPLE 3

> DIMENSION A(90)
>
> READ 1,N,(A(I),I = 1,N)
>
> 1 FORMAT (I3/(2F5.1))

The value for the variable representing the size of the one-dimensional array is read in the same list as the elements of the array. This is permissible; notice that a value is stored in N *before* the variable is used as a parameter in the implied DO. According to the FORMAT statement, a data card with the value of N in I3 format will precede the elements of the array punched two per card.

EXAMPLE 4

DIMENSION X(10,10)

READ 1,M,N

1 FORMAT (2I2)

DO 2 I = 1,M

2 READ 8,(X(I,J),J = 1, N)

8 FORMAT (4F5.1)

The elements of the array are punched by rows, four elements per card. The first element of each row is always punched as the first element of a card. The data might be punched as follows:

CARD 1   0405

CARD 2   X(1,1),X(1,2),X(1,3),X(1,4)

CARD 3   X(1,5)

CARD 4   X(2,1),X(2,2),X(2,3),X(2,4)

CARD 5   X(2,5)
.
.
.

EXAMPLE 5

DIMENSION X(10,10)

READ 1,M,N,((X(I,J),J = 1,N),I = 1,M)

1 FORMAT (2I2/(3F5.1))

10.12 Matrix Multiplication

The following program will perform matrix multiplication for matrices of a maximum size of 15 by 15. Assume that the elements of the matrices are punched by rows three elements per card.

Given a matrix A with N rows and L columns, and a matrix B with L rows and M columns, the resultant product matrix C will have N rows and M columns. Matrix multiplication is not commutative; in general $AB \neq BA$. For matrix multiplication of the form $AB = C$, the number of rows in the B matrix must equal the number of columns in the A matrix or the multiplication cannot take place. To compute any element C_{ij} of the product matrix, select the ith row of the A matrix and the jth column of the B matrix and sum the products of their corresponding elements. The general formula for this computation is

$$C_{ij} = \sum_{k=1}^{l} A_{ik}B_{kj}$$

```
      DIMENSION  A(15,15),B(15,15),C(15,15)
      READ 1,N,L
      READ 2,((A(I,J),J=1,L),I=1,N)
      READ 1,L1,M
      READ 2,((B(I,J),J=1,M),I=1,L1)
   1  FORMAT (2I2)
   2  FORMAT (3F5.1)
      IF (L−L1)10,11,10
  11  DO 6 I=1,N
      DO 6 J=1,M
      C(I,J)=0.
      DO 6 K=1,L
   6  C(I,J)=C(I,J)+A(I,K)*B(K,J)
      PRINT 90
  90  FORMAT (8HA MATRIX//)
      DO 20 I=1,N
  20  PRINT 7,(I,J,A(I,J),J=1,L)
      PRINT 91
  91  FORMAT (//8HB MATRIX//)
      DO 21 I=1,L1
  21  PRINT 7,(I,J,B(I,J),J=1,M)
      PRINT 92
  92  FORMAT (//14HPRODUCT MATRIX//)
      DO 19 I=1,N
  19  PRINT 7,(I,J,C(I,J),J=1,M)
   7  FORMAT (5(I3,2XI3,2XF10.2))
  10  PRINT 99
  99  FORMAT (30HMATRIX MULT. CANNOT TAKE PLACE)
      CALL EXIT
      END
```

Problems

10.1 Identify the following subscripts as being in a correct form or incorrect form.

a) X(I)

b) X(3.)

c) X(I+J)

d) X(L+2)

e) X(A)

f) X(3+M)

g) X(M5+19)

h) X(NM*3)

i) X(3*K)

j) X(6*N17+41)

k) X(I+7,K(2))

l) X(3,I*J+1)

m) X(MIN,MAX)

n) X(5*M6+4*N,1)

o) X(L,A+1)

p) X(1,1,N)

q) X(K12345,K12346,K12347)

r) X(M,M,M)

s) X(137,105,1)

t) X(IJ,I+4,J+2)

10.2 Identify the following DO statements as being in a correct form or incorrect form.

a) DO 8 I=J,K,L

b) DO N K6=5,N,2

c) DO 1 I=1,10

d) DO 692 3=1,K

e) DO 9 N124=1,3,K

f) DO 9 K=1,9.5

g) DO 18 K=I,K+2

h) DO 2 L=5,2

i) DO 7 A=1,N4A2,2

j) DO 2 K=J,6

10.3 Identify the following DIMENSION statements as being in a correct form or incorrect form.

a) DIMENSION A(5,35),B(11),K(36+5)

b) DIMENSION L(35,6,10),A(N,N),DEL(8,5.)

c) DIMENSION X(10,1,10),Y(L,2),Z(Y1,L+6)

d) DIMENSION X(4,3),I(5),Y(4,5),X(10)

e) DIMENSION I16(5),X(2,0,5),B(N)

10.4 Consider each pair of statements below as appearing in the same program. For each pair of statements indicate whether any inconsistencies exist.

a) DIMENSION X(5,5), L(10), A(15,10)

$$Y = X + 65./A(I,J)$$

b) W = N(3) + I4*6

   D = W**4

c) DEL = A(I,5)/X**8

   ST = DEL*XY−A(8)

d) DIMENSION T(10,10), K(15), A(3,4,2)

   T(I,4) = 2.*T(2,4) + A(I,5,1)*3.14

e) DO 8 I = 1,10

   DO 8 I = 1,5

10.5 Write the statements necessary to read the elements of a two-dimensional array X of maximum size 25 × 25. Only nonzero elements are
read. The elements are punched one per card in columns 10–19 in
F10.3 format. In columns 1–2 and columns 3–4 on each card are
punched the row and column, respectively, of the element. The last
data item is followed by a card which has a 99 punched in columns 1–2.

10.6 Write a Fortran program to read a matrix A of dimensions M × N
(M ≤ 10, N ≤ 10). Each data card will contain one row of the
matrix. On the card each element is punched consecutively in F6.1
format. The data cards containing the matrix elements are preceded by a card which has the number of rows and the number
of columns of the matrix punched in columns 1–2, and 3–4 respectively in 2I2 format. Calculate the sum of the elements (a_{ii}) on the
main diagonal of the matrix, the sum of the elements in the last row
and the sum of the elements in the last column. Print the three sums.

10.7 With an input matrix as described in Problem 10.6, write a Fortran
program to calculate and print the following:

a) The product of the elements on the main diagonal (Πa_{ii}).

b) The sum of the negative elements of the matrix.

10.8 Write a Fortran program to read a card punched with forty numbers
in 40I2 format. Determine and keep a count of the following:

a) The number of odd numbers.

b) The number of even numbers.

c) The number of zeros.

Print the three results with appropriate alphabetic headings.

10.9 N numbers are punched three per card in 3F4.1 format. These data
cards are preceded by a card with the value of N punched in columns

1–3 in I3 format. Write a Fortran program to calculate the following:

a) The sum of the differences between adjacent numbers,

$$\sum_{i=1}^{N-1}(a_i - a_{i+1})$$

b) The sum of the positive numbers.

c) The sum of the two smallest positive numbers.

d) The number of numbers between zero and ten inclusive.

10.10 Consider the following Fortran programs; how many data cards have been read by each program when the CALL EXIT statement is executed?

a)
```
    DIMENSION A(20)
    DO 6 I = 1,10
6   READ 1,A(I)
1   FORMAT (2F5.0)
    CALL EXIT
    END
```

d)
```
    DIMENSION A(20)
    READ 1,(A(I),I = 1,20)
1   FORMAT (10F5.0,/5F5.0)
    CALL EXIT
    END
```

b)
```
    DIMENSION A(20)
    DO 6 I = 1,10,2
6   READ 1,A(I),A(I+1)
1   FORMAT (F5.0)
    CALL EXIT
    END
```

e)
```
    DIMENSION A(20)
    READ 1,(A(I),I = 1,20)
1   FORMAT (4F5.0)
    CALL EXIT
    END
```

c)
```
    DIMENSION A(20)
    READ 1,(A(I),I = 1,20)
1   FORMAT (2F5.0)
    CALL EXIT
    END
```

f)
```
    DIMENSION A(20)
    READ 1,(A(I),I = 1,20)
1   FORMAT (/10F5.0,
        /5F5.0,/5F5.0)
    CALL EXIT
    END
```

g)   DIMENSION A(20),B(20)

    DO 1 I = 1,2

    READ 2,(A(J),J = 1,20)

    IF(I − 1)3,4,3

4   DO 5 K = 1,10

5   B(K) = A(K)

    GO TO 1

3   DO 6 K = 11,20

6   B(K) = A(K)

1   CONTINUE

2   FORMAT(5F5.0)

    CALL EXIT

    END

h)   DIMENSION A(20)

    READ 1,(A(I),I − 1,9)

1   FORMAT (2F5.0)

    CALL EXIT

    END

i)   DIMENSION A(20,20)

    READ 1,((A(I,J),I = 1,10),J = 1,7)

1   FORMAT (3F9.2/F5.0)

    CALL EXIT

    END

j)   DIMENSION A(20,10)

    DO 6 K = 1 ,9

6   READ 1,(A(J,K),J = 1,9)

1   FORMAT (4E10.2)

    CALL EXIT

    END

11

Subroutines

A subroutine is a sequence of instructions that performs some desired operation whose result is incorporated into a main program. As an example, consider how the square root of a number is evaluated by a computer. Computers, in general, do not have a built-in (hardware) ability to perform the operation of evaluating the square root of a number. However, many mathematical functions including square root may be approximated to a high degree of accuracy by evaluating a finite number of terms of some infinite arithmetic series. Therefore, a program could be written to evaluate the finite number of terms of the series used for approximating square root, thereby obtaining an approximation to the square root of the number. This program could then be incorporated into all other programs where square root calculations are required. This ability to use prewritten routines is included in Fortran. The mathematical functions described in Chapter 5 are of this type.

A prewritten subroutine may be incorporated into a program in one of two ways. It may be incorporated into the object program each time it is referred to in the source program. Thus, if a Fortran source program required the calculation of a square root at ten different points, the prewritten routine would be included in the object program at *each* of the ten different points. A subroutine incorporated into the object program in this way is called an *open subroutine*. If a subroutine contains a large number of instructions and is used many times, the concept of an open subroutine does not lend itself to the efficient utilization of storage, inasmuch as sequences of identical instructions will appear many times in one program.

186

Under these conditions, it would be more efficient to include the subroutine only once in the object program regardless of how many times it is referred to. A subroutine incorporated into the object program in this way is called a *closed subroutine*. At each point where a closed subroutine is referred to, the object program will contain instructions to (*a*) provide the subroutine with the arguments, (*b*) cause the subroutine to be executed, and (*c*) cause the object program to continue execution at the appropriate point after the subroutine has been executed.

The concept of a subroutine may be extended beyond the use of *prewritten* or library routines. Frequently, a program at different points requires that identical sets of calculations be made on different data. The writing of a program of this type is simplified if the set of calculations is written *by the programmer* only *once*, and is then referenced each time it is required. The effect would be the same as though the set of calculations were written completely at each point of reference. Fortran, in addition to providing the programmer with the use of prewritten subroutines, also allows him to define and write his own subroutines.

Fortran provides for two classes of subroutines: function subroutines, and subroutine subprograms†. Function subroutines differ from subroutine subprograms in that they always return a *single* result to the calling program, whereas a subroutine subprogram may return more than one value to the calling program.

FUNCTION SUBROUTINES

There are four types of function subroutines:

1. *Library functions*, which are prewritten *closed* subroutines that exist in a program library. These library programs may be in the form of a card deck, magnetic tape, etc.

2. *Built-in functions*, which are prewritten *open* subroutines which are included by the compiler in the object program every time they are referenced.

3. *Arithmetic statement functions*, which are subroutines defined by a programmer with a *single* Fortran arithmetic statement in the source program.

4. *Function subprograms*, which are *closed* subroutines that may be incorporated into the program library or may be used directly by the main program. Function subprograms differ from the other functions

---

†A subprogram is a subroutine consisting of a series of Fortran statements that are compiled independently of the Fortran program.

in that they are written in Fortran and consist of more than one Fortran statement. In fact, they are compiled as separate Fortran programs.

11.1 Library Functions

Library functions are described in Chapter 5. Table 11.1 lists the standard
library functions. Not all of these functions are available in every Fortran
system.

The following items of information should be noted with regard to
library functions:

1. The function is called (referenced) by using its name in an arithmetic
   expression.

TABLE 11.1 Standard Library Functions

Name	Function	Number of Arguments	Mode of Argument	Mode of Result
EXP	e^X	1	Floating	Floating
ALOG	$\log_e X$	1	Floating	Floating
ALOG10	$\log_{10} X$	1	Floating	Floating
ATAN	arctan X	1	Floating	Floating
ATAN2	arctan (X/Y)	2	Floating	Floating
SIN	sin X	1	Floating	Floating
COS	cos X	1	Floating	Floating
TANH	tanh X	1	Floating	Floating
SQRT	$\sqrt{X}$	1	Floating	Floating
ARSIN	arcsin X	1	Floating	Floating
ARCOS	arccos X	1	Floating	Floating
TAN	tan X	1	Floating	Floating
COTAN	cotan X	1	Floating	Floating
SINH	sinh X	1	Floating	Floating
COSH	cosh X	1	Floating	Floating
GAMMA	gamma X	1	Floating	Floating
ALGAMA	loggamma X	1	Floating	Floating

2. The argument is any floating-point expression. It must be enclosed
   in parentheses immediately following the function name. Note that
   the function ATAN2 has two arguments; they must be separated by
   commas.
3. Library functions are single-valued functions; they return only one
   result to the main program. The result is in the floating-point mode.
4. Library functions may be used by any Fortran program.

11.2 Built-in Functions

Built-in functions are prewritten subroutines that are included by the processor in the object program every time the function is referred to. The complete list of built-in functions is given in Table 11.2.

TABLE 11.2   List of Built-in Functions for Fortran IV†

Function Definition	Function Name	Number of Arguments	Function Type	Argument Type
Absolute value of	ABS	1	Real	Real
the argument	IABS	1	Integer	Integer
	DABS	1	Double-precision	Double-precision
Truncation, sign of	AINT	1	Real	Real
argument times absolute	INT	1	Integer	Real
value of the largest	IDINT	1	Integer	Double-precision
integer in argument				
Remaindering,	AMOD	2	Real	Real
Arg 1 — [Arg 1/Arg 2] * Arg 2,	MOD	2	Integer	Integer
where [X] indicates the				
integral part of X				
Choosing the largest	AMAX0	≥ 2	Real	Integer
value of the set of	AMAX1	≥ 2	Real	Real
arguments	MAX0	≥ 2	Integer	Integer
	MAX1	≥ 2	Integer	Real
	DMAX1	≥ 2	Double-precision	Double-precision
Choosing the	AMIN0	≥ 2	Real	Integer
smallest value of the	AMIN1	≥ 2	Real	Real
set of arguments	MIN0	≥ 2	Integer	Integer
	MIN1	≥ 2	Integer	Real
	DMIN1	≥ 2	Double-precision	Double-precision
Floating an integer	FLOAT	1	Real	Integer
Same as INT	IFIX	1	Integer	Real
Transfer of sign,	SIGN	2	Real	Real
the sign of Arg 2	ISIGN	2	Integer	Integer
times Arg 1	DSIGN	2	Double-precision	Double-precision
Positive difference,	DIM	2	Real	Real
Arg 1 — Min (Arg 1, Arg 2)	IDIM	2	Integer	Integer
Obtaining the most significant	SNGL	1	Real	Double-precision
part of a double-precision				
argument				
Obtaining the real part of a	REAL	1	Real	Complex
complex argument				
Obtaining the imaginary part	AIMAG	1	Real	Complex
of a complex argument				
Expressing a single-precision	DBLE	1	Double-precision	Real
argument in double-precision				
form				
Expressing two real arguments	CMPLX	2	Complex	Real
in complex form				
C = Arg 1 + iArg 2				
Obtaining the conjugate of a	CONJG	1	Complex	Complex
complex argument; for				
Arg = X + iY, C = X − iY				

†Table 11.2 makes reference to double precision and complex quantities. These are described in Chapters 16 and 17. Not all of these functions are available in every Fortran system.

For many of these functions there is more than one name, depending on the mode of the argument and/or result. These functions are called in the same way as library functions — that is, by including in an arithmetic expression the function name followed by its arguments enclosed in parentheses.

Examples Using Built-in Functions

X = B+C/FLOAT(J*2)

IF(ABS(X*X−Y)−.001)1,2,3

K = JD−IABS(I)

DEL = 2.*AMAX1(A(1),A(2),A(3),A(4),A(5),B)

A = 2.*AMAX0(K(1),K(2),K(3),K(4),K(5))

W = Y+Z+SQRT(ABS(B+C))

X1 = ABS(SQRT(C)−D)

The following items of information should be noted with regard to built-in functions:

1. The function is called by using its name in an arithmetic expression.
2. The argument is any floating-point expression or any fixed-point expression, depending upon the particular function used. The argument must be enclosed in parentheses immediately following the function name.
3. Built-in functions are single-valued functions; they produce only one value. The result may be in either the floating-point or the fixed-point mode, depending upon the particular function used.
4. Built-in functions may be used by any Fortran program.

11.3 Arithmetic Statement Functions

Often a programmer will find some relatively simple set of calculations *recurring* throughout his program. These calculations would involve the *same sequence of identical operations*, although the variables used might differ for each set. If the set of calculations recurs frequently enough, it would be desirable for the programmer to be able to define a subroutine that would carry out the required calculations. The programmer could then call the subroutine to perform the calculations whenever they were required. The arithmetic statement function may be used for this purpose if the set of calculations can be described by a single Fortran arithmetic statement.

The programmer uses the arithmetic statement function to *define* the set of calculations required. Dummy arguments are used for this purpose. The subroutine is called in the same way as library and built-in functions — that is, by using its name in an arithmetic expression. The name is followed by parentheses enclosing the *actual* arguments that will be used in place of the dummy arguments when the calculations are performed. Unlike the library and built-in functions, which all Fortran programs may use, the arithmetic statement function applies only to the program in which it occurs.

General Form

$$a(x_1, x_2, \ldots x_n) = b$$

where a is the symbolic name of the function, $x_1, x_2, \ldots x_n$ are the dummy arguments (they must be distinct, nonsubscripted variables), and b is an arithmetic expression that does not contain any subscripted variables.

Examples of the Arithmetic Statement Function

DISK(A,B,C) = B**2 − 4.*A*C

SUMS(X,Y,Z) = X*X − Y*Y − Z*Z

FIND(DEL,W1,W2) = (W2 − W1)/DEL

DO(A,X,J) = A*X**(J+2)

AVESQ(A1,B1,C1) = SQRT((A1+B1+C1)/3.)

JCALC(I,K) = (I − 3*M)**4 + K

IROUT(A,B) = A**2+B**2

FOFX(X) = (4.5*X**3 − 3.*X**2+C)/(Z*X+3.)

The arithmetic statement function *serves only to define the set of calculations; it does not cause any computation to occur.* The computation will occur only when the function is called in another Fortran statement. Because the variables used as arguments are only dummy variables, the same names may be used elsewhere in the program. The names used for the dummy variables are unimportant, except as they specify a fixed-point or floating-point variable.

The arithmetic statement function is called or used by writing its name in an arithmetic expression. The name must be followed by parentheses enclosing the actual arguments. *These actual arguments will be substituted for the dummy arguments when the function is being computed.* The computations defined by the arithmetic statement function will be performed using the *actual* arguments. If there is more than one argument, they must be separated by commas. The actual arguments may be in the form of *any* arithmetic expression. It may include subscripted variables and even other functions.

To illustrate the use of the arithmetic statement function, suppose in a particular program it is necessary to find the sum of a finite number of terms of a geometrical progression. Suppose that this calculation is required at many different points of the program for different progressions. The sum of n terms of a geometrical progression is given by

$$s = (r^n - 1)f/(r - 1)$$

where r is the ratio, n is the number of terms, and f is the first term.

An arithmetic statement function can be used to define this calculation as follows:

$$\text{SUMPRO(R,N,F)} = (R**N-1.)*F/(R-1.)$$

Now suppose at a particular point in the program it is necessary to compute this function for $r = 0.25$; the number of terms n is stored in a variable NT; and the first term f is given by the value of the expression $(X-Y)$. The sum is to be stored in S. The following statement will accomplish this:

$$S = \text{SUMPRO(.25,NT,X}-Y)$$

When the function SUMPRO is evaluated, .25 will be substituted for R, the value of NT for N, and the value of $X-Y$ for F.

Suppose that at another point in the program it is necessary to use this function again for $r = A1/DEL, n = K(I)$, and $f = \text{SQRT(R)}$. The result is to be added to DEL and stored in S1. The following statement will accomplish this:

$$S1 = \text{SUMPRO(A1/DEL,K(I),SQRT(R))} + DEL$$

Notice that the variable R is used in an actual argument and it also appeared in the defining statement as an argument. This is allowable as the arguments in the defining statement are simply dummy arguments which are used to define the calculations.

The following rules pertaining to the use of arithmetic statement functions must be observed:

1. All arithmetic statement function definitions must *precede* the first use of the function name either in the program or in another arithmetic statement function definition.

2. The name of an arithmetic statement function is assigned in the same way as the names of variables. If the function is to be used in a floating-point expression the name must be assigned according to the rules for naming floating-point variables. If the function is to be used in a fixed-point ex-

pression, the name must be assigned according to the rules for naming fixed-point variables.

3. The actual arguments in the calling statement must agree with the dummy arguments in the definition statement in number, mode, and order. The same number of arguments must appear in the calling statement as appear in the definition statement as dummy arguments. The actual arguments must agree in mode (fixed point or floating point) with the corresponding dummy arguments; that is, if the first dummy argument is floating point, the first actual argument must be floating point, etc. The actual arguments are substituted for the *corresponding* dummy arguments. The first dummy argument is replaced by the first actual argument, the second dummy argument is replaced by the second actual argument, etc.

Suppose the following arithmetic statement functions are defined in a Fortran program:

$$SUMPRO(R,N,F) = (R**N - 1.)*F/(R - 1.)$$
$$ROOT(A,B,C) = (-B + (B*B - 4.*A*C)**.5)/(2.*A)$$
$$POLY(A,X,Y) = A*X**3 - B*Y + CON + ALOG(A)$$
$$M(I,J) = I**J*J$$
$$LK(M1,K) = M1**3 + M(K,L)$$

Table 11.3 shows how these functions might be used in a program and the calculations that would result.

TABLE 11.3   Program Use of Arithmetic Statement Functions

Fortran Statement	Equivalent Algebraic Expression
R = DEL − SUMPRO(.6,I,A+B)	$DEL - [(.6^I - 1) \times (A+B) \div (.6-1)]$
TW = ALOG10(ROOT(15.,D,C))	$\log_{10} \dfrac{(-D + \sqrt{D^2 - 4(15)(C)})}{(2)(15)}$
V = POLY(D,EXP(R+D),CAP**2)	$D \times (e^{R+D})^3 - B \times CAP^2 + CON + \log_e D$
I1 = M(K(2),M1)	$(K_2)^{M1} \times M1$
IAM = J**2 − LK(N,I)	$J^2 - N^3 - I^L(L)$

The following items of information should be noted with regard to arithmetic statement functions.

1. The arithmetic statement function is a *closed* subroutine which is called by using its name in an arithmetic expression.

2. It is a single-valued function. The result may be in either the floating-point or fixed-point mode, depending upon the *name* of the function.

3. The arithmetic statement function may only be used in the program in which it is defined.

11.4   Function Subprograms

The arithmetic statement function restricts the programmer to using only *one arithmetic statement* when defining the subroutine. Often the programmer wishes to incorporate a *series* of Fortran statements as a subroutine. The function subprogram allows the programmer to do this. A function subprogram differs from the arithmetic statement function in another important respect: the function subprogram is a completely *independent* Fortran program, which is compiled independently of the main program which uses it. The variable names used in the subprogram are completely independent of the names used in the main program and other subprograms. Dummy arguments are used when defining the subroutine, and the actual arguments are specified when the subroutine is called. When the subprogram is executed, the actual arguments are substituted for the dummy arguments. This procedure is similar to that used with the arithmetic statement function. The function subprogram is a single-valued function.

A function subprogram is called (used) in the same way as the arithmetic statement function, that is, by writing its name in an arithmetic expression. Unlike the arithmetic statement function, the function subprogram can be used by any Fortran program and can even be added to the library functions. The *mechanics* of these procedures will not be discussed in this text.

A function subprogram is defined by describing the computations to be performed with a series of Fortran statements. These Fortran statements are considered to be a program; therefore, they must be followed by an END statement, and must contain DIMENSION statements if any arrays are specified. Any Fortran statement may appear within a function subprogram except a FUNCTION statement (see below) or SUBROUTINE† statement. The *name* of the function subprogram is used to return the computed result to the calling program. Therefore, the name of a function subprogram must appear in the subprogram either as a variable to the left of the equal sign in an arithmetic statement or as a variable in an input list. The function subprogram *must* be immediately preceded by a FUNCTION statement, which serves to identify the program following as a function subprogram.

The FUNCTION Statement

General Form

FUNCTION *name* $(x_1, x_2, \ldots x_n)$

where *name* is the symbolic name of the function. $x_1, x_2, \ldots x_n$ (where $n \geq 1$) are the dummy arguments. They must be either nonsubscripted variable names, names of arrays (without subscripts), or names of subroutine subprograms, function subprograms, or library functions.

---

†The SUBROUTINE statement is discussed in the next section.

Examples of the FUNCTION *Statement*

FUNCTION DET(N,M,X)

FUNCTION LOOP(I,ITER)

The name of a function subprogram is assigned in the same manner as the names of variables. If the function is to be used in a floating-point expression, the name must be assigned according to the rules for naming floating-point variables. If the function is to be used in a fixed-point expression, the name must be assigned according to the rules for naming fixed-point variables. Even though subscripted variables are not allowed as *dummy arguments*, they may appear in the function subprogram.

The function subprogram is called by writing its name in an arithmetic expression. The name must be followed by parentheses enclosing the actual arguments. The actual arguments are separated by commas and may be any arithmetic expressions. They must agree with the dummy arguments in number, mode, and order. *It must be carefully noted that if any of the dummy arguments appear to the left of an equal sign or in an input list in the subprogram, then the corresponding actual argument as specified by the main program will be altered.* (Some Fortran systems do not allow such occurrences of dummy arguments in the subprogram.)

The RETURN Statement

When the name of a function subprogram is encountered in a source program, a transfer to the machine language instructions generated from the function subprogram is set up in the object program. When the subprogram has been executed, a transfer back to the program that called the subprogram is made. Therefore, the subprogram must include a statement that, when executed, indicates that the subprogram has completed its computations and a transfer back to the calling program should occur. The RETURN statement is used for this purpose.

General Form

RETURN

The RETURN statement is used in subprograms to indicate that the execution of the subprogram has been completed and a return to the calling program should be effected.

To illustrate the use of the function subprogram suppose it is necessary at many points in a program to evaluate in floating point the factorial of different fixed point variables. The factorial of an integer N, denoted $N!$, is given by

$$N! = N \times (N - 1) \times (N - 2) \times \cdots \times 2 \times 1$$

The following subprogram could be used to evaluate the factorial of an integer expression which is specified as an argument:

```
       FUNCTION FACT(K)
       X1 = K
       FACT = 1.
    8  FACT = FACT*X1
       X1 = X1 − 1.
       IF(X1 − 1.)7,7,8
    7  RETURN
       END
```

The main program that uses the above subprogram might appear as follows:

```
       DIMENSION KN(50)
       ‾‾‾‾
       ‾‾‾‾
       ‾‾‾‾
       Y = A+FACT(KN(2))
       ‾‾‾‾
       ‾‾‾‾
       ‾‾‾‾
       M = FACT(I)
       ‾‾‾‾
       ‾‾‾‾
       ‾‾‾‾
       DEL = FACT(N)/(FACT(NR)*FACT(N − NR))
       ‾‾‾‾
       ‾‾‾‾
       ‾‾‾‾
       EVAL = FACT(36)
       ‾‾‾‾
       ‾‾‾‾
       ‾‾‾‾
       END
```

The illustrated statements in this program will, respectively, produce the following results:

1. The sum of A and the factorial of the number stored in KN(2) will be computed and stored in Y.

2. The factorial of the quantity stored in I will be evaluated and stored in M.

3. $\dfrac{N!}{NR! \times (N-NR)!}$ will be computed and stored in DEL.

4. The factorial of 36 will be computed and stored in EVAL.

As a second illustration of the function subprogram, suppose it is necessary at many points of a program to determine the largest element in absolute value in a particular row of a two-dimensional array. Assume the maximum dimensions are fifty rows and fifty columns. A function subprogram could be used with the arguments being the name of the array, the row in which the largest element of absolute value is to be determined and, finally, the number of columns in the array.

The subprogram could be written as follows:

```
        FUNCTION ABSEL (X,NR,NC)
        DIMENSION X(50,50)
        ABSEL=ABS(X(NR,1))
        DO 2 I=1,NC
        IF (ABSEL-ABS(X(NR,I)))5,2,2
      5 ABSEL=ABS(X(NR,I))
      2 CONTINUE
        RETURN
        END
```

The main program that uses this subprogram might appear as follows:

```
        DIMENSION A(50,50),B(50,50),C(50,50)
        READ 1,IRA,ICA,((A(I,J),J=1,ICA),I=1,IRA)
        READ 1,IRB,ICB,((B(I,J),J=1,ICB),I=1,IRB)
        READ 1,IRC,ICC,((C(I,J),J=1,ICC),I=1,IRC)
      1 FORMAT (2I2,/(5F8.2))
        ─────
        ─────

        ─────
        D=ABSEL(A,2,ICA)
        ─────
        ─────
        ─────
```

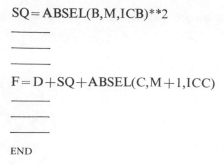

$$SQ = ABSEL(B,M,ICB)**2$$

$$F = D + SQ + ABSEL(C,M+1,ICC)$$

END

In this program the function subprogram is used respectively to:

1. Find the largest element in absolute value in the second row of the A array and store it in D.

2. Find the largest element in absolute value in the mth row of the B array, square it and store the square in SQ.

3. Find the largest element in absolute value in the $(m+1)$st row of the C array, add it to the sum of (1) and (2) and store the result in F.

When array names appear as dummy arguments in a function subprogram they must be dimensioned in the same subprogram. The corresponding array names appearing as actual arguments in the main program must be dimensioned in the main program. *The dimensions must be the same in both cases.* An array used as a dummy argument could *not* be dimensioned for 25 rows and 25 columns and the corresponding array used as the actual argument be dimensioned for 50 rows and 50 columns. If these conditions did occur the computations in the subprogram would not be carried out correctly.

SUBROUTINE SUBPROGRAMS

The function subprogram, though extremely useful, has one serious limitation: it is a single-valued function and, therefore, can be used to return only a single result to the calling program. It is often desirable to have a subprogram that is capable of computing *several* values and returning all of them to the main program. As an example, a subprogram to perform matrix multiplication may be required. The subprogram would be used to compute a product matrix that consists of more than one element; all the elements of this product matrix must then be made available to the calling program.

The subroutine subprogram is a closed subroutine, which is quite similar to the function subprogram in that it also is a completely independent program; however, the subroutine subprogram is a multivalued function. Unlike the function subprogram, it is capable of returning many values to the calling program. This is accomplished by using the dummy arguments to return values to the calling program.

A subroutine subprogram is defined by describing the computations to be performed with a series of Fortran statements. These Fortran statements are considered to be a program; therefore, they must be followed by an END statement, and must contain DIMENSION statements if any arrays are specified. Any Fortran statement except the FUNCTION statement and the SUBROUTINE statement may be used within a subroutine subprogram. As in the function subprogram a RETURN statement is used to return control to the calling program. The subroutine subprogram *must* be immediately preceded by a SUBROUTINE statement, which serves to identify the program following as a subroutine subprogram.

The SUBROUTINE Statement

General Form

SUBROUTINE *name* $(a,b,c, . . .)$

where *name* is the symbolic name of the subroutine subprogram. $a,b,c, . . .$ are the dummy arguments. They must be either nonsubscripted variable names, names of arrays (without subscripts), or names of subroutine subprograms, function subprograms, or library functions.

---

*Ex*amples of the SUBROUTINE *Statement*

SUBROUTINE MATPLY(N,M,A,I,J,B,C)

SUBROUTINE QUADRT(A,B,C,X1,X2)

The arguments specified by the SUBROUTINE statement are dummy arguments, since they will be replaced by the corresponding actual arguments specified in the calling statement. The actual arguments must agree in number, mode, and order with the dummy arguments. One or more of these arguments may be used to return results to the calling program. For example, the subroutine subprogram defined by the statement

SUBROUTINE QUADRT(A,B,C,X1,X2)

may be written to compute two values from the arguments A, B, and C; these values might then be stored in the arguments X1 and X2.

The CALL Statement

Obviously, because the subroutine subprogram can return more than one value to the calling program it cannot be called in the same way the function subprogram is called. Recall that the function subprogram uses its name, which has to be defined in the subprogram, to return a value to the calling program. The subroutine subprogram is called by using a CALL statement in the calling program.

General Form

CALL *name* (*a,b,c*, . . .)

where *name* is the symbolic name of a subroutine subprogram.   *a,b,c*, . . . are the actual arguments to be substituted for the dummy arguments in the subprogram. These arguments may be in the form of any arithmetic expression.

The name of a subroutine subprogram can be assigned according to the rules for assigning a fixed-point or floating-point variable name. The mode of the name is of no concern since it does not appear in an arithmetic expression.

As an example of the use of the subroutine subprogram suppose it is required to write a subprogram that will evaluate both real roots of a quadratic equation. A quadratic equation is of the form $ax^2 + bx + c = 0$, and the two real roots are given by

$$\frac{-b \pm \sqrt{b^2 - 4ac}}{2a}$$

If the equation has no real roots but complex roots — that is, $(b^2 - 4ac) < 0$ — an indication to the calling program is to be made. The following subprogram will accomplish this task.

SUBROUTINE QUADRT(A,B,C,I,X1,X2)

D = B*B − 4.*A*C

IF(D)3,8,8

8   I = 0

X1 = (− B+SQRT(D))/(2.*A)

X2 = (− B − SQRT(D))/(2.*A)

RETURN

3   I = 1

RETURN

END

The dummy variable I is used to indicate if the roots of the quadratic equation are real or complex. If the roots are real, I is assigned the value zero; if the roots are complex, I is assigned the value one. Note that the subprogram as written makes use of *two* RETURN statements.

The following examples illustrate the use of the foregoing subprogram:

EXAMPLE 1

———

———

CALL QUADRT (5.,E+F,SQRT(D),KIND,RTONE,RTTWO)

IF(KIND)6,7,6

7   Y = RTONE+RTTWO

GO TO 8

6   Y = 0.

8   ———

These statements will cause the roots of the equation $5X^2 + (E+F)X + \sqrt{D} = 0$ to be determined. If the roots are real they will be evaluated and Y (in the calling program) will contain the value of the sum of the roots. If the roots are complex, Y will be assigned the value zero.

EXAMPLE 2

———

———

CALL QUADRT(A(1),A(2),A(3),L,F,G)

IF (L)8,6,8

8   CALL COMPRT(A(1),A(2),A(3),F1,G1)

6   ———

These statements will cause the roots of the quadratic equation $a_1x^2 + a_2x + a_3 = 0$ to be determined. If the roots are complex, the subprogram COMPRT is called; this might be a subprogram that calculates the complex roots of a quadratic equation. If the roots are real, they are evaluated and stored in the variables F and G.

Table 11.4 serves to summarize the characteristics of the various types of Fortran subroutines.

TABLE 11.4   Fortran Subroutines

Type	Definition	Name	Method of Calling	Method of Return to Calling Program
Library Functions Closed single-valued	Predefined	Predefined names	Function name is used in an arithmetic expression	Automatic
Built-in Functions Open single-valued	Predefined	Predefined names	Function name is used in an arithmetic expression	Automatic
Arithmetic Statement Function Closed single-valued	Defined by pro-grammer with one arithmetic expression	Name assigned by programmer. Mode of name must cor-respond to mode of expression in which the name is used	Function name is used in an arithmetic expression	Automatic
Function Subpro-gram Closed single-valued	Defined by pro-grammer as complete, independent Fortran program	Name assigned by programmer. Mode of name must cor-respond to mode of expression in which the name is used	Function name is used in an arithmetic expression	A RETURN statement must be executed
Subroutine Subpro-gram Closed multi-valued	Defined by pro-grammer as complete, independent Fortran program	Name assigned by programmer	A CALL statement is used	A RETURN statement must be executed

11.5   Variable Return from a Subroutine Subprogram

Normally when a RETURN statement is executed the statement immediately following the CALL statement in the calling program is executed next. This is not always desirable; it would be advantageous to be able to return to any statement in the calling program not just the one following the CALL state-ment. Some Fortran systems allow for this in the following way.

Any argument in the CALL statement may be a statement number pre-

ceded by an ampersand (&). The corresponding dummy argument in the SUB-
ROUTINE statement is an asterisk (*). The RETURN statement can be written
in the form

RETURN i

where i is an integer designating the ith asterisk in the dummy argument
list. If the RETURN i statement is executed in the subprogram the statement
in the calling program whose number was substituted for the ith asterisk is executed next.

EXAMPLE

Calling Program	*Subprogram*
———	SUBROUTINE GO (A,W,*,*)
———	———
———	———
CALL GO (DEL,Y,&10,&7)	———
8 S = A	IF (K) 17,18,19
———	17 RETURN
———	18 RETURN 1
———	19 RETURN 2
10 S = −A	END
———	
———	
———	
7 S = A*A	
———	
———	
———	

The CALL statement causes execution of the subroutine subprogram.
Statement number 10 of the calling program corresponds to the first asterisk
and statement number 7 of the calling program corresponds to the second
asterisk. Depending on the value of K in the subprogram either statement
17 or 18 or 19 is executed. If the statement numbered 17 is executed the next
statement executed will be the statement numbered 8 in the main program.
This is a normal return. If the statement numbered 18, RETURN 1, is executed
the next statement to be executed is the statement numbered 10 in the calling program since the statement number 10 corresponds to the first asterisk. If the statement numbered 19, RETURN 2, is executed, the next statement to be executed is the statement numbered 7 in the calling program,
since the statement number 7 corresponds to the second asterisk.

11.6 Variable Entry to Function and Subroutine Subprograms

Normally when a subroutine or function subprogram is called, the first statement to be executed is the first executable statement following the FUNCTION or SUBROUTINE statement. It is sometimes desirable to be able to enter a subprogram at different points. Some Fortran IV systems allow for this in the following way.

The various entry points to be provided for in a subprogram are defined by an ENTRY statement, which is included in the subprogram.

The ENTRY Statement

General Form

ENTRY *name* (*a,b,c, . . .*)

where *name* is the name of an entry point, and *a,b,c,* . . . are dummy arguments.

Examples of ENTRY Statements

ENTRY GO (DEL,PHI,K)

ENTRY TW1(X,Y)

ENTRY R1(J,A,TW,RH,I2)

The ENTRY statement is used to define an entry point in a subprogram. An ENTRY statement is required for each entry point desired except the normal entry point, which is the first executable statement following the FUNCTION or SUBROUTINE statement. If an entry other than the normal entry is desired, the name of the desired entry point is used in the calling statement.

EXAMPLE

Calling Program	Subprogram
DIMENSION R(10),S(10)	SUBROUTINE FIND (A,B,D,I,K)
———	DIMENSION A(10)
———	X = D+B
———	———
———	———

1 CALL FIND (R,B,V,M1,M2)   ———
   ———   ———
   ———   ———
   ——— $Y = X/3.5$
   ———
2 CALL P2(S,DEC,J)   ENTRY P1(A,B,D,I,K)
   ——— $W = I + K$
   ———
   ———   ———
   ———
3 CALL DEL(S,Y,N1,N2)   ENTRY P2(A,D,K)
   ———   ———
   ———   ———
   ———   ENTRY DEL(A,B,I,K)
   ———   ———
4 CALL P1(R,B,V,M1,M2)   ———
   ———   ———
   ———   RETURN
   ———   END
   ———
   ———

   END

Execution of the statement numbered 1 will transfer control to the statement $X = D + B$. This is the normal entry to the subprogram. Execution of the statement numbered 2 will transfer control to the first executable statement following the statement ENTRY P2(A, D, K) of the subprogram. Execution of the statements numbered 3 and 4 will transfer control to the first executable statement following the ENTRY DEL and ENTRY P1 statements respectively.

The ENTRY statement does not affect the sequence of statement execution in the subprogram. In that sense it is similar to the FORMAT and DIMENSION statements, which are in a sense "passed over" during statement execution. To illustrate this point: after the statement $Y - X/3.5$ is executed, the statement $W = I + K$ is executed.

Note that the number, order, and type of the dummy arguments in the SUBROUTINE or FUNCTION statement and the ENTRY statements within the subprogram need not agree with each other. However, the number, order, and type of variables in the calling statement must correspond to the dummy arguments in the SUBROUTINE, FUNCTION, or ENTRY statement referenced. As in the foregoing example, when the various entry points have different argument lists, care must be taken to insure that all the arguments required have been defined. If the first executable statement after the ENTRY P2 statement were $J = I + K$, and entry to the subprogram was made at P2, the variable I might be undefined, since it did not appear in the argument list.

Unlike variable return which applies only to subroutine subprograms, the variable entry feature applies to both subroutine and function subprograms.

11.7 Variable Dimensions

A subprogram may be used with any programs requiring it. Consider a subprogram to transpose a matrix; it may be used with any program requiring a matrix transposition routine. Either the object deck produced from the subprogram or the Fortran subprogram itself may be used. One difficulty arises, however, in that the dimensions of the subscripted variables in the subprogram and the corresponding variables in the calling program might not agree. In this case, one would have to change the DIMENSION statements in the subprogram to conform to the calling program and recompile the subprogram. This procedure is inefficient. Fortran IV allows the dimensions of a subscripted variable in a subprogram to be specified in the DIMENSION statement as *variable* quantities, which are specified as dummy arguments in the list. The actual dimensions are then transmitted by the calling program.

EXAMPLE

Calling Program	*Subprogram*
DIMENSION X(50,75)	SUBROUTINE INV (A,J,K)
———	DIMENSION A(J,K)
———	———
———	———
———	———
CALL INV(X,50,75)	———
———	RETURN
———	END
———	
———	
END	

Problems

11.1 Describe the difference between an *open* subroutine and a *closed* subroutine.

11.2 Each of the following statements contains a call to one of the library or built-in functions. Indicate which of the following statements are incorrect.

    a) X = A/D − DEL*FLOAT(K)

    b) Y = ALOG10(N)

    c) A(K) = S+SQRT(B/C+W) − ABS(T2)

    d) CALL EXP(X)

    e) W = Z+EXP(8.)+ALOG(K+3)

11.3 Why is the mode (fixed point or floating point) of the name of a subroutine subprogram unimportant?

11.4 In each of the following pairs of statements the first is an arithmetic statement function and the second an arithmetic statement in which the function is called. Indicate whether each pair of statements is consistent.

    a) F(A,B,N) − A*B**N

        W = ALOG(S+T)+F(D(1),B3)

    b) DEL(X,Y,K,Z) = W+X**K − Y*Z/X

        T(4) = B+A − DEL(B,L,J,B+4.)

    c) Q(A,X,M) = X**M+A**3 − A**X

        S = EXP(C+D) − Q(3./C*F,A +ALOG(W),C)

    d) T(S(1),K) = (S(1)*FLOAT(K))**K

        D = X+T(T,2)

11.5 Write a subroutine subprogram to sum all the elements of a matrix· The arguments will consist of the matrix name, its dimensions, and the variable used for the sum. Give an example of a CALL statement which might be used to call the subprogram.

11.6 Describe the method by which each of the following subroutines is called:

    a) Library functions

    b) Built-in functions

    c) Arithmetic statement functions

    d) Function subprograms

    e) Subroutine subprograms

12

The EQUIVALENCE and COMMON Statements

The EQUIVALENCE and COMMON statements are used to provide the programmer with control over the allocation of storage by the compiler. In many programs the allocation of storage is critical because of the limited capacity of the storage unit. The statements EQUIVALENCE and COMMON allow the programmer to utilize the storage unit in a most efficient manner.

THE EQUIVALENCE STATEMENT

The EQUIVALENCE statement is used when it is desired to have two or more variables in the same program share the *same* storage register, thereby conserving storage usage. The EQUIVALENCE statement permits the programmer to assign different variable names to the same storage register. Of course, the values of the variables assigned to the same storage register must not be needed by the program at the same time, since no matter how many names a register may have, it can contain only one value at a time. There may be several reasons that a programmer would desire to assign more than one name to the same storage register:

1. When writing a program, the programmer may inadvertently change variable names. For example, he may begin his program by using the name RES for a register storing a value of electrical resistance; at a later point in the program the programmer may inadvertently begin using the name OHM for this same value of resistance. The programmer can use an EQUIVALENCE statement to cause both names to refer to the same register, thereby saving

the troublesome task of changing the program to use one name or the other exclusively.

2. In a lengthy program the storage capacity of the computer may be exceeded. If a programmer is attempting to utilize a minimum of storage, he may wish to assign the same storage register to several variables no two of which are needed at the same time in the program. The EQUIVALENCE statement may be used to do this. Of course, the programmer can effectively accomplish the same thing by using the same variable name to represent different quantities no two of which are needed at the same time. However, there are advantages to using variable names which have a high mnemonic relationship with the quantities they represent. The use of the EQUIVALENCE statement to conserve storage in this way is most useful when arrays are equivalenced to share the same storage area. This is only possible, however, when the values of the elements of the different equivalenced arrays are not required simultaneously.

General Form

EQUIVALENCE $(a_1,a_2, \ldots a_n),(b_1,b_2, \ldots b_k) \ldots$

where $a_1,a_2, \ldots a_n,(n \geq 2)$ are variable names (subscripted or nonsubscripted), all of which will refer to the same storage register, and $b_1,b_2, \ldots b_k(k \geq 2)$ are variable names (subscripted or nonsubscripted), all of which will refer to the same storage register.

Examples of the EQUIVALENCE Statement

EQUIVALENCE (A,B,W), (C,DEL)

EQUIVALENCE (L,J2), (E,F,G), (A(1), R(1))

Each pair of parentheses (excluding parentheses that enclose subscripts) in an EQUIVALENCE statement contains the names of variables that refer to the same storage register.

EXAMPLE
EQUIVALENCE $(X,Y,Z),(C,B),(I,J),(A,K)$

The variable names X, Y, and Z will all refer to the same storage register. The variable names C and B will both refer to the same storage register (not the same storage register that X, Y, and Z refer to). The variable names I and J will both refer to the same storage register. Finally, the variable names A and K will both refer to the same storage register. It should be noted that not all systems allow a fixed-point variable and a floating-point variable to be equivalenced. The programmer should consult the Fortran manual for the specific computer he is programming for a ruling on this point.

The ordering of the variables within a pair of parentheses does not affect the assignment of storage registers. Thus, the following two statements are equivalent:

EQUIVALENCE (A,B,W)

EQUIVALENCE (B,W,A)

12.1   Equivalencing Arrays

An array name with or without subscripts may appear in the list of an EQUIVALENCE statement. If the name appears with subscripts (integer constants only) the number of subscripts must be the same as the number of dimensions of the variable.† If the name of an array appears without subscripts the first element of the array — that is, $A(1)$, $A(1,1)$, $A(1,1,1)$ — is implied.

When an element of an array appears in the list of an EQUIVALENCE statement, the remaining elements of the array are located accordingly. Consider the following statements:

DIMENSION A(10)

EQUIVALENCE (A(1),C)

The variable names $A(1)$ and C would refer to the same storage register; $A(2)$ would refer to the adjacent register; $A(3)$ to the register adjacent to that; etc. Therefore, by specifying one element of an array in an EQUIVALENCE statement, the remaining elements are located also. It is incorrect to have two or more elements of the same array appear in EQUIVALENCE statements in the same program, since specifying one element of the array also locates all the other elements.

EXAMPLE 1

DIMENSION A(6),B(4)

EQUIVALENCE (A,B(2),C),(K,D)

Storage assignment would be as follows:

Registers:										
Names:	B(1)	A(1)	A(2)	A(3)	A(4)	A(5)	A(6)	...	K
		B(2)	B(3)	B(4)					D
		C							

---

†Some Fortran systems allow and some require the use of a single subscript in an EQUIVALENCE list even though the array is of two or three dimensions. In this case the subscript, call it j, refers to the jth element of the array as stored. Arrays are stored columnwise (see Examples 4 and 5).

Note that by equivalencing A and B(2), the following pairs of elements are automatically equivalenced: A(2), B(3); and A(3), B(4).

EXAMPLE 2

DIMENSION A(5,3),B(6)

EQUIVALENCE (A(1,1),B(1))

Storage assignment would be as follows:

A(1,1)	A(2,1)	A(3,1)	A(4,1)	A(5,1)	A(1,2)	A(2,2)		
B(1)	B(2)	B(3)	B(4)	B(5)	B(6)			

. . .

This EQUIVALENCE statement could also have been written in any of the following forms with the same results:

EQUIVALENCE (B(1),A(1,1))

EQUIVALENCE (A,B)   EQUIVALENCE (B,A)

EQUIVALENCE (A,B(1))   EQUIVALENCE (B(1),A)

EQUIVALENCE (A(1,1),B)   EQUIVALENCE (B,A(1,1))

EQUIVALENCE (A(2,1),B(2))   EQUIVALENCE (B(2),A(2,1))

and so on.

EXAMPLE 3

DIMENSION A(25,25),X(25,25),Y(25,25),Z(25,25)

EQUIVALENCE (A(1,1),X,Y,Z(1,1))

The corresponding elements of the four arrays A, X, Y, and Z would share the same 625 storage registers.

EXAMPLE 4

DIMENSION A(10,10)

EQUIVALENCE (A(25),B)

A(25) refers to the 25th element of the A array as stored. The elements are stored as follows:

a_{11} a_{21} a_{31} . . . $a_{10,1}$ a_{12} a_{22} a_{32} . . . $a_{10,2}$ a_{13} a_{23} a_{33} a_{43} a_{53} . . . $a_{10,3}$ . . . $a_{10,10}$

The element in the EQUIVALENCE statement A(25) refers to the actual element a_{53}, thus A(5, 3) and B are equivalenced and share the same storage register.

EXAMPLE 5

DIMENSION M(2,3,4),L(7,8)

EQUIVALENCE (M(6),L(10))

The elements $M(2,3,1)$ and $L(3,2)$ are equivalenced. The M array is stored as follows:

m_{111} m_{211} m_{121} m_{221} m_{131} m_{231} m_{112} m_{212} m_{122} m_{222} m_{132} m_{232} m_{113} m_{213}
m_{123} m_{223} m_{133} m_{233} m_{114} m_{214} m_{124} m_{224} m_{134} m_{234}

THE COMMON STATEMENT

The EQUIVALENCE statement provides for the sharing of storage registers by variables *within* a single program or subprogram. It is often desirable to have variables and/or arrays which are specified in a calling program and variables and/or arrays specified in a subprogram share the same location (s). Thus, it may be desirable to have the 10×10 array A of one program and the 10×10 array B of a second program use the same storage registers. The results of one program which might be the elements of the matrix A could be left in storage and used directly for further computation by a second program which would be written to operate upon the matrix B. If the matrices A and B use the same storage registers, the second program is actually operating upon the results of the first program. Of course, the first program could be written to punch the elements of the matrix A into cards and the second program to read these elements as the matrix B; however, this approach requires more effort and card handling.

The concept of a common storage area shared between programs can be used to transmit arguments between a program and its subprogram. In the function and subroutine subprograms previously described the arguments were transmitted explicitly; that is, they were listed in the calling statement. By having the corresponding arguments (actual and dummy) in the main program and subprogram occupy the same storage locations, the arguments are implicitly specified. The details of the implicit transmission of arguments are illustrated in Section 12.3

Variables including array names are assigned areas in a section of storage called *common storage*† if they are listed in the COMMON statement. Variables appearing in a COMMON statement are assigned storage registers in specific storage areas completely separate from storage used for program instructions, data, constants, and variables not appearing in a COMMON statement. The first register of the area of storage called common is the same for each of several programs which are linked‡ together. It is most important to note that common storage is assigned separately for *each* program;

---

†It should be noted that common storage is not a separate physical storage unit. When a common storage area is used, a section of the main computer storage is reserved by the compiler for this purpose.
‡That is, run as a single job as with a program and its subprograms.

thus, the common storage area specified by a subprogram is not a continuation of the common area of the calling program. Therefore, if a calling program specifies that variables A, B, and C are to be placed in common storage in that order, and in a subprogram variables X and Y are placed in common storage in that order, the variable A in the calling program and the variable X in the subprogram will refer to the same location. Similarly, B and Y will refer to the same location. Note well that if a variable X is used in the calling program it will not refer to the same location as X in the subprogram unless it is equivalenced to A.

General Form

COMMON *a,b,c,d,e,* . . .

where *a,b,c,d,e,* . . . are variable or array names.

Examples of the COMMON *Statement*

COMMON DEL,X,I7,A

COMMON C,DOC

COMMON M,N,FREQ,OHM,X1,X2

The variables appearing in the COMMON statement are assigned locations in common storage. The locations are assigned in the sequence in which the variables are listed in the COMMON statement(s) beginning with the first COMMON statement of the program.

EXAMPLE 1

COMMON X,Y,Z,I

The variables X, Y, Z, and I would be assigned to the first four registers of common storage.

EXAMPLE 2

COMMON A,B,D

COMMON I,K,BETA

The variables A, B, D, I, K, BETA would be assigned to the first six registers of common storage respectively.

EXAMPLE 3

DIMENSION X(10,10),A(5)

COMMON I,M,A,X,DEL

The first two registers of common storage would be reserved for I and M; the next five registers would be reserved for the one-dimensional array A; the next 100 registers, for the two-dimensional array X; and the next register, for the variable DEL.

EXAMPLE 4

DIMENSION PROD(10,10),VECTOR(5)

COMMON K,L,VECTOR,PROD,SEQ

If the statements in Example 3 are in a calling program and the statements above are in the subprogram being called, the following pairs of variables and/or arrays would share the same storage locations: I and K; M and L; the one-dimensional arrays A and VECTOR; the two-dimensional arrays X and PROD; and the variables DEL and SEQ.

12.2   Specifying Dimensions in a COMMON Statement

The names of arrays with their maximum subscripts may appear in a COMMON statement. If this information concerning dimensions is included in the COMMON statement the variable *must not* appear in a DIMENSION statement.

EXAMPLE 1

COMMON I,M,A(5),X(10,10),DEL

The information about dimensions is given in the COMMON statement; therefore, the variables A and X must not also appear in a DIMENSION statement. The statement above is equivalent to the two statements of Example 3 in Section 12.1.

EXAMPLE 2

DIMENSION B(10)

COMMON X,B(10),A

These statements are incorrect, since B appears with its dimensions in both a DIMENSION statement and a COMMON statement. Either eliminate the DIMENSION statement or remove the subscript from B in the COMMON statement.

12.3   Transmitting Arguments Implicitly between a Calling Program and a Subprogram

Arguments may be transmitted implicitly by having the corresponding arguments in the two programs occupy the same storage location. This can be done by having them occupy corresponding positions in the COMMON statements of the two programs.

EXAMPLE

Consider the following programs and subprograms. The subprogram is written to add two matrices, X and Y, and store the sum matrix in Z. The variables M and N contain the number of rows and columns respectively of the matrices being added.

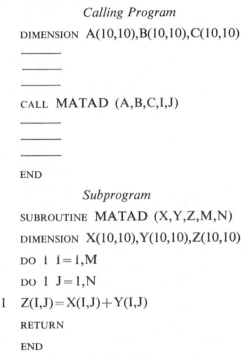

Calling Program

DIMENSION A(10,10),B(10,10),C(10,10)

_____

_____

_____

CALL MATAD (A,B,C,I,J)

_____

_____

_____

END

Subprogram

SUBROUTINE MATAD (X,Y,Z,M,N)

DIMENSION X(10,10),Y(10,10),Z(10,10)

DO 1 I=1,M

DO 1 J=1,N

1   Z(I,J)=X(I,J)+Y(I,J)

RETURN

END

The actual arguments are explicitly stated in the calling program. Thus A replaces the dummy argument X, B the dummy argument Y, etc. Consider now the following example, which makes use of the COMMON statement to make the explicit transmission of the arguments unnecessary.

Calling Program

COMMON A(10,10),B(10,10),C(10,10),I,J

_____

_____

_____

CALL MATAD

_____

_____

_____

END

Subprogram

SUBROUTINE MATAD

COMMON X(10,10),Y(10,10),Z(10,10),M,N

DO 1 I=1,M

DO 1 J=1,N

1   Z(I,J)=X(I,J)+Y(I,J)

RETURN

END

The COMMON statements would cause the variables and arrays A, B, C, I, and J of the calling program to share the same locations as X, Y, Z, M, and N respectively of the subprogram. Thus when the subprogram operates on the matrix X it is operating on the matrix A of the calling program, etc. The explicit transmission of arguments requires the execution of machine language instructions to transmit the arguments or their addresses to the subprogram. Transmitting arguments implicitly does not require any instructions since no information is actually transmitted; the result is a saving of computer time and storage space. The reader will notice that it is possible, by use of the COMMON statement, to write a subroutine subprogram without any arguments. The same principles of the implicit transmission of arguments by the use of common storage can also be applied to the function subprogram; however, the FUNCTION statement must have at least *one* argument.

12.4   *Dummy Variable Names in a COMMON Statement*

In order to force correspondence in storage locations between two variables that otherwise will occupy different relative positions in common storage, dummy variable names may be inserted to force this correspondence.

EXAMPLE 1

COMMON B,C,K,W

Given the above statement, if in a subprogram it is desired to have a variable A share the same location as B and a variable VED share the same location as W the following statement could be used:

COMMON A,Z9,V,VED

where Z9 and V are any variable names inserted in the COMMON statement to force correspondence between W and VED.

EXAMPLE 2

COMMON B,C,A(5),GO,K

If it is desired to have correspondence between B and Y; C and D; G(1) and A(1); G(2) and A(2); G(3) and A(3); and K and I, the following statement could be used:

COMMON Y,D,G(3),XYZ(3),I

The array XYZ(3) was inserted to force correspondence between K and I.

12.5   *Interaction between*
EQUIVALENCE and COMMON Statements

The following rules apply to the use of variables appearing in COMMON and EQUIVALENCE statements within the same program:

1. Variables in common storage may not be made equivalent to each other.

2. Variables not listed in a COMMON statement may be made equivalent to variables in common storage. The equivalenced variable will then also be located in common storage. Variables brought into common storage in this way may increase the size of common storage in a forward direction only.

EXAMPLE 1

DIMENSION X(4)

COMMON A,B,C

EQUIVALENCE (DEL,A),(X,C)

The layout of common storage is as follows:

A or DEL

B

C or X(1)

X(2)

X(3)

X(4)

EXAMPLE 2

DIMENSION X(4)

COMMON A,B,C

EQUIVALENCE (DEL,A),(X(4),C)

The layout of storage would be:

X(1)

A or X(2) or DEL

B or X(3)

C or X(4)

Since the size of common storage is increased in a reverse direction the above statements are invalid.

EXAMPLE 3

DIMENSION E(3)

COMMON A,B,C(3),D

EQUIVALENCE (B,E)

The layout of storage would be:

A

B or E(1)

C(1) or E(2)

C(2) or E(3)

C(3)

D

12.6   Labeled Common Storage

The programmer may find it desirable to be able to set up separate areas of common storage, each area being treated as a unique common storage. The programmer may do this by specifying separate blocks of common storage, each block being identified by a unique name specified by the programmer. For a program and its subprograms, blocks of common storage with the same name will occupy the same space. The name assigned by the programmer to a block of common storage is from one to six alphameric characters, the first of which must be alphabetic. The name appears in the COMMON statement and is preceded and followed by a slash (for example, /BL/). The variables to be placed in that block of common storage are listed after the name. The name assigned to a common block must not be used for any other purpose in the program. Common storage areas that are assigned names are known as "Labeled Common." A common storage area that is not assigned a name (there can be only one such area in a program) is known as "Blank Common." Blank Common is indicated by either omitting the block name if it appears at the beginning of the COMMON statement, or by preceding the variables to be placed in the Blank Common storage by *two* consecutive slashes. All previous examples of the use of the COMMON statement have used Blank Common.

EXAMPLE 1

COMMON X,Y/A1/W,Z/A2/DEL,I,K

This statement causes the variables X and Y to be placed in Blank Common. The variables W and Z are placed in a Labeled Common area with the name A1. The variables DEL, I, and K are assigned locations in the common block of storage called A2.

EXAMPLE 2

COMMON /I/DESK/ABLE/X,Y//A

The variable DESK is assigned a location in the common block of storage called I. The variables X and Y are assigned locations in the common block of storage called ABLE. The variable A is assigned a location in Blank Common.

EXAMPLE 3

DIMENSION A(5),B(3)

COMMON A,K/CA1/B

The one-dimensional array A and the variable K are assigned locations in Blank Common. The one-dimensional array B is assigned locations in the common block of storage called CA1.

EXAMPLE 4

COMMON A(5),K/CA1/B(3)

This statement is equivalent to the two statements of Example 3.

EXAMPLE 5

COMMON A1,B(3),X/K/I,W/Y1/D(2),T,K1

COMMON /Y2/S,T6/K/Z(2,2)//Y

COMMON D1(3)/Y1/P,L/K/G1,G2

Four blocks of common storage are reserved. The following list indicates the block names and the variables assigned to each block in the order they appear in the block:

Name	Variables
	A1,B(1),B(2),B(3),X,Y,D1(1),D1(2),D1(3)
K	I,W,Z(1,1),Z(2,1),Z(1,2),Z(2,2),G1,G2
Y1	D(1),D(2),T,K1,P,L
Y2	S,T6

Use of the Labeled COMMON Statement

The use of labeled common storage areas is most effective when some common data areas are to be shared by a calling program and its subprograms, and other common areas are required for subsets of the programs.

Consider a calling program X with four subprograms A, B, C, and D. Suppose the following common storage areas are required:

1. The programs X, A, B, C, and D are to have a common storage area.

2. The programs X, B, and C are to have a common storage area different from (1).

3. The subprograms C and D are to have a common storage area different from (1) and (2).

This could be accomplished by using blank common storage; however, it would be cumbersome to do so. Dummy variables would be required in some of the COMMON statements to cause the proper positioning of variables within the list. If any additions or deletions were made to common storage in any of the programs, all of the COMMON statements would probably require changing.

By using labeled COMMON statements to define common storage areas that are functionally independent of other common storage areas, the difficulties mentioned above can be avoided. For example, a blank common area could be used for the storage area required in (1), a labeled common area could be used for the storage area required in (2), and a different labeled common area could be used for the storage area required in (3).

Problems

12.1   Indicate which of the following statements are valid:

$a)$ EQUIVALENCE (A,T,S(3)),(K,L)

$b)$ EQUIVALENCE (B,3,DEL),(M,D)

$c)$ EQUIVALENCE (A(10,10),B(5,5)),(L,M),(X,Y)

$d)$ EQUIVALENCE (B(1),X(1),W),(X(5),K,Y)

$e)$ COMMON A,B,X(10,10),K,L

$f)$ COMMON C1,C2,DEK,3.

$g)$ COMMON (Y(6,6),Z,W),(K,D,E)

$h)$ COMMON A2,D,/NAM/F,G,H

$i)$ COMMON A,B,C/GO/,L,N

$j)$ COMMON X,Y,Z//I,K/ST

12.2   Explain why it is not necessary to specify any arguments when defining a subroutine subprogram.

12.3   When the technique of implicit transmission of arguments is used, why is it necessary to specify at least one argument when defining a function subprogram?

13

Advanced Input/Output
Statements

This chapter contains additional input/output specifications of a more advanced nature in the sense that they are ordinarily not required for the solution of a majority of problems. However, this fact should not suggest to the reader that these specifications are unimportant. The use of these advanced techniques will facilitate input/output programming and give the programmer the means with which to generalize many of his programs.

FORMAT SPECIFICATIONS

13.1 The A Specification

The A specification is used to read or write alphameric information that is to be processed. This processing may take the form of moving the data from one place in storage to another or performing arithmetic operations upon the data, perhaps for the purpose of sorting it in alphabetic order. The reader will recall that the H specification (see Section 9.14) is also used for the input/output of alphameric information. However, data read under the H specification can only be written by referencing the same FORMAT statement under which the data was read. This is quite limiting as it is quite probable that a different format would be required for output. A second limitation is that data read under the H specification cannot be processed; that is, no operation may be performed on it.

Reading alphameric information under the A specification allows the programmer to assign a variable name to this information; therefore, it may be treated as any variable quantity. The name assigned by the programmer may be either that of a fixed point variable or a floating point variable. However, if the variable is to be used in an arithmetic or logical expression the name assigned must conform to the mode of the expression.

The general form of the A specification is

$$Aw$$

where w designates an integer specifying the number of characters of information to be processed. As with the E, F, and I specifications, the A specification may be preceded by an integer specifying how many times the specification is to be repeated.

The A Specification for Input

When the A specification is used for input the next w characters on the input record are stored in the register whose name appears in the input list. The input data are stored as *characters* not as fixed or floating point numbers. We will assume that a storage register can store a maximum of six alphameric characters.† If $w > 6$, only the six rightmost characters of the input field are stored. If $w < 6$, the w characters are stored left-justified in the storage register. The $6 - w$ rightmost characters in the storage register are set to blanks.

In each of the following examples it is assumed that the data card read is punched in columns 1–15 as follows:

$$IDEN12167.2CORR$$

EXAMPLE 1

READ 1,A

1   FORMAT (A6)

The storage register A will contain the following characters:

$$(A)=I \; D \; E \; N \; 1 \; 2$$

EXAMPLE 2

READ 11,X,K

11   FORMAT (6XF5.1,A4)

The number 167.2 will be stored in the register called X. The storage register K will contain the following characters:

$$(K)=C \; O \; R \; R \; b \; b$$

Note that the four input characters are left justified and the two rightmost positions are filled with blanks.

---

†The maximum number of characters which can be stored in a register varies with the type of computer. Therefore, the reader should consult the specifications of the computer he is working with.

EXAMPLE 3

READ 7,D

7 FORMAT (A8)

The storage register D will contain the following characters:

(D) = E N 1 2 1 6

Note that only the six rightmost characters are used.

EXAMPLE 4

DIMENSION J(7)

READ 1,(J(I),I = 1,7)

1 FORMAT (7A2)

The J array will appear as follows:

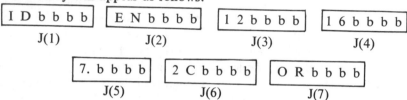

EXAMPLE 5

Assume a data card is punched as follows starting in column 1:

(1XF8.2,5F4.1,I4,3XF8.5)

and is read by the following program:

DIMENSION FMT(4)

READ 6,(FMT(J),J = 1,4)

6 FORMAT (4A6)

The FMT array would appear as follows:

(1 X F 8 .	2 , 5 F 4 .	1 , I 4 , 3	X F 8 . 5)
FMT(1)	FMT(2)	FMT(3)	FMT(4)

This example illustrates the ability to read a FORMAT statement at object time. A more detailed discussion appears later in this chapter.

The A Specification for Output

When the A specification is used for output the w leftmost characters of the storage register whose name appears in the output list are written. If $w \geq 6$ the six characters in the register are preceded by $w - 6$ blanks. If $w < 6$ the w leftmost characters in the storage register are written.

For the examples below, assume the following storage-register content:

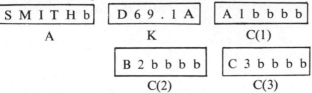

EXAMPLE 1

      PRINT 8,A

  8 FORMAT (1X8HNAMEbISb,A6)

The output would be bNAMEbISbSMITHb.

EXAMPLE 2

      PRINT 62,K

  62 FORMAT (A3)

The output would be D69.

EXAMPLE 3

      PRINT 1,K

  1 FORMAT (A8)

The output would be bbD69.1A.

EXAMPLE 4

      PRINT 1,(C(I),I = 1,3)

  1 FORMAT (3A1)

The output would be ABC.

EXAMPLE 5

      PRINT 12,(C(I),I = 1,3)

  12 FORMAT (3(A2,1X))

The output would be A1bB2bC3b.

Sample Problem

Suppose a warehouse stocks 10,000 different parts. Each part is identified by a six-digit code made up of both numeric and alphabetic characters. As an example, a code number may be A67BC4. Assume each of these codes is stored in a one-dimensional array called NAME. Each code is stored as six characters in the storage register. Assume also that there is an array called

INV which contains the quantity in stock of each part in the corresponding position of the array called NAME. Thus, INV (603) contains the quantity in stock of the part whose code is stored in NAME (603).

Three hundred order cards are each punched with a part code in columns 1–6 and a number in columns 7–10 that represents the number of items ordered. It is required to write a program to read the data cards and locate the quantity in stock for each part. If there is a sufficient quantity in stock to fill the order, the number in stock should be reduced by the quantity ordered. If there is not a sufficient quantity in stock to fill the order a message to this effect is to be printed.

The following program assumes the initial values of the arrays NAME and INV have been read.†

```
    DIMENSION NAME (10000),INV(10000)
    DO 90 I = 1,300
    READ 1,NCODE,NUM
 1  FORMAT (A6,I4)
    DO 6 J = 1,10000
    IF (NCODE−NAME(J))6,8,6
 6  CONTINUE
    PRINT 33,NCODE,I
33  FORMAT (1X13HINVALID CODE ,A6,3X9HCARD NO. ,I4)
    GO TO 90
 8  IF (NUM−INV(J))80,80,95
80  INV(J) = INV(J)−NUM
    PRINT 31,NCODE,NUM,INV(J)
31  FORMAT (1XA6,3X5HSEND I5,10X14HNO. IN STOCK I6)
    GO TO 90
95  PRINT 32,NCODE,NUM,INV(J)
32  FORMAT (1X15H**OUT OF STOCK ,A6,2X8HORDERED I5,
    3XI6,9H IN STOCK)
90  CONTINUE
    CALL EXIT
    END
```

†In a problem of this type the elements of the NAME and INV arrays would probably be read from magnetic tape or disk storage.

13.2   The O Specification†

The O specification is used when it is desired to read or write octal information (see Section 2.4). The general form of the O specification is

Ow

where w is an integer designating the number of characters to be processed.

The O Specification for Input

When used as an input specification the next w characters of octal informations (the digits 0, 1,...7) are stored in the register whose name appears in the input list. Each octal digit is converted to three binary digits. We shall assume that a storage register can store a maximum of 12 octal digits. If $w > 12$, only the twelve rightmost digits are stored. The leftmost $w - 12$ digits are ignored. If $w < 12$, the w digits are right-justified in the register and the register is filled on the left with zeros.

In each of the following examples it is assumed that the data card is punched as follows, starting in column 1:

67100523445321

EXAMPLE 1

READ 1,K

1   FORMAT (O12)

After these statements have been executed the storage register assigned to K will appear as follows:

(K) = 110 | 111 | 001 | 000 | 000 | 101 | 010 | 011 | 100 | 100 | 101 | 011
     6 | 7 | 1 | 0 | 0 | 5 | 2 | 3 | 4 | 4 | 5 | 3

The vertical lines are used to show the conversion of the octal characters.

EXAMPLE 2

READ 1,A

1   FORMAT (O3)

After these statements have been executed the storage register assigned to A will appear as follows:

(A) = 000000000000000000000000000110111001

EXAMPLE 3

READ 11,W

11   FORMAT (O14)

†The O specification is not available in all Fortran systems.

After these statements have been executed the storage register assigned to W will appear as follows:

$$(W) = 001000000101010011100100101011010001$$

The O Specification for Output

When used as an output specification the w rightmost octal characters in the register whose name appears in the output list are written. If $w > 12$, the twelve characters are written preceded by $w - 12$ blanks. If $w < 12$, the w rightmost characters in the register are written.

EXAMPLE

PRINT 6,W

6   FORMAT (O7)

Assume the register W is as follows:

$$(W) = 001000000101010011100100101011010001$$

The output would be

3445321

13.3   Scale   Factors

The E, F, and D† specifications may be preceded by a scale factor which is in the form

nP

where n designates an integer constant between -8 and $+8$ inclusive. The scale factor is used differently for input and output.

The Scale Factor for Input

For input the scale factor can only be used with the F specification. The scale factor is interpreted as follows:

$$(10^{-SCALE\ FACTOR}) \times (INPUT\ QUANTITY) = QUANTITY\ STORED$$

EXAMPLE 1

READ 1,A

1   FORMAT (2PF5.1)

If the card is punched with 145.1 in columns 1–5, the number stored in the register A is 1.451 (145.1 $\times$ 10^{-2}).

EXAMPLE 2

READ 6,B,C

6   FORMAT ($-$3P2F5.2)

†See Section 16.4 for a discussion of the D specification.

If the data card is punched with 14.12–5.25 in columns 1–10, the number stored in the variable B is 14120.0 (that is, $14.12 \times 10^{-(-3)}$), and the number stored in C is -5250.0 (that is, $-5.25 \times 10^{-(-3)}$).

The Scale Factor for Output

When used for output the scale factor can be used with E, F, and D specifications. The scale factor is interpreted as follows:

$$(10^{+\text{SCALE FACTOR}}) \times (\text{INTERNAL QUANTITY}) = \text{OUTPUT QUANTITY}$$

EXAMPLE 1

<pre>   PRINT 1,K,A,B,C
      1   FORMAT (I3,F10.3,E15.8,E17.8)</pre>

Assume the foregoing statements give the following line of output:

$-13bb1672.154b0.12345678Eb03bbb0.12345678Eb03$

Now consider the following statements:

<pre>   PRINT 1,K,A,B,C
      1   FORMAT (I3,1PF10.3,-3PE15.8,2PE17.8)</pre>

If the storage registers K, A, and B contained the same values as above the output would be

$-13b16721.540b0.12345678Eb00bb12.34567800Eb01$

When a positive scale factor is used with an E or D specification, it increases the mantissa and decreases the exponent. Thus no change occurs in the value of the number; it is simply written in a different form (with non-zero digits to the left of the decimal point). This contrasts with the use of the scale factor with the F specification, where the number itself is changed. Once a scale factor is given for a D, E, or F specification it will also apply to all D, E, and F specifications following the scale factor within the same FORMAT statement unless another scale factor is given. A subsequent scale factor in the form of 0P can be given to terminate the effect of a scale factor.

EXAMPLE 2

<pre>   PRINT 1,A,B,C,D
      1   FORMAT (1XF6.2,2PF8.1,E15.8,F4.1)</pre>

The scale factor 2P will apply to the specifications E15.8 and F4.1 as well as the F8.1 specification.

EXAMPLE 3

<pre>   PRINT 11,A,B,C,D
      11 FORMAT (1XF6.2,2PF8.1,0PE15.8,F4.1)</pre>

The scale factor 2P will apply only to the F8.1 specification since the 0P scale factor follows it immediately.

13.4 Printer Carriage Control

Very often when results are written they are either printed directly or perhaps written on magnetic tape and at a later time the information on the tape is printed. Most printers are so designed that they can be controlled with regard to vertical spacing. The *first character* of every output record (line) is considered to be a control character controlling the vertical spacing on the printer. The control characters and their effect on the printer are listed as follows:

Character	blank	0	1
Effect (before printing)	single space	double space	skip to next page

Thus, it is possible to program for report-type output. When *the printer* is being used as the final output device the *first character of every line of output must be one of the above control characters. It is the responsibility of the programmer to provide for these control characters to be written as part of the output record.* He may do this by using the X or H specification. The control character itself will not be printed.

EXAMPLE 1

        PRINT 1,A,B,C,D

   1 FORMAT (1XF6.2,3XF8.1,3XF6.2,3XF10.4)

The 1X specification will cause the printer to single space before printing.

EXAMPLE 2

        PRINT 4,A,B

   4 FORMAT (1H02F10.2)

The 1H0 specification will cause the printer to double space before printing.

EXAMPLE 3

        PRINT 1

   1 FORMAT (19H1THIS IS A NEW PAGE)

The 1 following the H, since it is the first output character, is regarded as a control character and will cause the printer to skip to the next page before printing.

The following items should be noted:

1. If a character other than 1, 0, or blank appears as the first character of an output record to be printed, it is difficult to predict what will happen. Quite often the printer will start passing paper at a rapid rate and only quick manual action will prevent a great waste of paper. In this event the output will usually be sufficiently disarranged to require corrections in the FORMAT statements.

2. If output is to be on a typewriter or cards which are to be listed on a low-speed printer, Section 13.4 does not apply.

3. The slash is not a valid control character. As a specification it will cause the printer to skip to another line, but when this new line is printed it must have a control character.

13.5   FORMAT Statements Read as Data

The necessity of including FORMAT statements within a program is a very inflexible feature of Fortran. A particular program will correctly accept data only if it is in the form specified in the FORMAT statement. Many programs are in wide use at many computer installations. It is quite restrictive to expect each user of a program to have his data in the form specified by the program's author. Perhaps the author wrote his program to accept data in a format of 8F6.2, and a user has data punched in the form of F8.1, 5F6.4, 2E14.8. For the program to be of use the user must change the FORMAT statement and have the Fortran program recompiled. This, of course, is a time-consuming and inefficient process. It would result in as many programs as forms of data. What is desirable would be to have the format of the data read as part of the data itself and not specified as part of the program. Some Fortran systems allow this to be done as follows:

A nonsubscripted variable name may be used in place of the statement number of a FORMAT statement in an input/output statement. Thus, the following are valid input/output statements:

$$\text{READ } (5, \text{FORM})(A(I), I-1, 10)$$

$$\text{WRITE } (6, \text{OUT})X, Y, X2, Y2, \text{IDEN}$$

It remains for the variables FORM and OUT to be defined. These variables will not take on numeric values but will store the actual characters of the FORMAT statement, which will be read under the A specification as part of the data. The following will accomplish this:

$$\text{DIMENSION } \text{FORM}(12), \text{OUT}(12)$$

$$\text{READ } (5,6)(\text{FORM}(I), I=1, 12), (\text{OUT}(I), I=1, 12)$$

$$6 \quad \text{FORMAT } (12A6/12A6)$$

The first two data cards which supply the format information might be punched as follows *starting in column 1:*

$$(F6,2,2XF4.1,8(1XF6.3))$$

$$(1XF10.4,2XF10.4,6XF8.2,2XF8.2,10XI4)$$

These are identical with regular FORMAT statements except the word FORMAT is omitted and they are punched starting with the left parentheses in column 1. The *characters* of the two FORMAT statements are read under the A specification and stored in the one-dimensional arrays FORM and OUT respectively. When the I/O statements using the names FORM and OUT in place of statement numbers are executed the format specifications used will be those previously read into the FORM and OUT arrays.

The length of the FORMAT statement read into storage need not be restricted to 72 characters. The FORMAT statement may require several cards; in this case the dimensions of the array into which the characters are read must be adjusted.

EXAMPLE 1

DIMENSION VAR(12),A(99,99)

READ (5,99)(VAR(J),J = 1,12)

99 FORMAT (12A6)

READ (5,98)M,N

98 FORMAT (2I2)

READ (5,VAR)((A(I,J),J = 1,N),I = 1,M)

The two-dimensional array A is read according to the FORMAT statement read by the first READ statement.

EXAMPLE 2

DIMENSION A(26),MAT(25,25)

READ (5,16)(A(I),I = 1,26)

16 FORMAT (13A6)

READ (5,A)M,N,((MAT(I,J),J = 1,N),I = 1,M)

The variables M and N and the array MAT are read according to the FORMAT statement that was read and stored in the A array. The first two data cards are considered to contain the FORMAT statement punched in columns 1–78 of each. This provides for a maximum of 156 characters. If the FORMAT statement contains fewer characters, the remaining columns are left blank. If the FORMAT statement can be punched on one card a second card must be provided as the first *two* data cards will always be read and considered to provide the format information.

MAGNETIC TAPE INPUT/OUTPUT

The manner in which information is represented on magnetic tape was illustrated in Section 1.8. Frequently, magnetic tape serves as the primary input medium for a computer system. One advantage of using magnetic tape is the speed with which characters are transmitted from tape to computer storage and vice versa. Characters may be transmitted at rates of from 20,000 to 100,000 characters per second depending upon the model tape unit used. This character transmission rate far exceeds that of card input and many other input/output devices, and results in a more efficient utilization of the computer.

A group of characters consecutively recorded on tape is called a *record* (also called a *physical record*). A record may contain any number of characters within the storage capacity of the computer. Consecutive records may be written on tape in which case they are separated by a section of blank tape called a record gap. Records may be grouped together to form files. Consecutive files may be written on tape in which case they are separated by a longer section of blank tape or by a special character called a tape mark. Figure 13.1 illustrates these concepts.

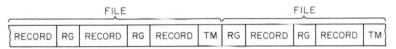

FIGURE 13.1 Records and files on magnetic tape. RG = record gap. TM = tape mark.

To relate the above definitions to the basic tape operations of reading and writing it should be noted that a read operation will cause at least one tape record to be read, and a write operation will cause at least one record to be written. The term "at least" is used in the description above because the specifications (such as the solidus) in the associated FORMAT statement may cause additional records to be read or written. In general, all the data to be read or written by a single program is put on tape as a file — that is, a series of records followed by a tape mark.

The magnetic tape unit, under control of the computer, reads and writes information from or on magnetic tape. The reel of tape is mounted on the upper left of the unit; the reel to the right is the take-up reel. The tape ordinarily moves from left to right, but may be backspaced. Reading and writing of the tape is accomplished by the READ/WRITE head which for reading senses the information on the tape as it passes over the head; for writing information is recorded on the tape as it passes over the READ/WRITE head.

The magnetic tape unit has an address selector switch that can be set to any digit 0–9 inclusive. By changing the setting of the selector switch the operator can effectively alter the address of the tape unit.

Tapes are usually read or written in a forward direction only. However, some magnetic tape units have the facility to read or write tapes in either a forward or reverse direction. Although a tape may be read or written in a forward direction only, a tape may be backspaced and this information read at a later time or new information written. A BACKSPACE command (described later in this chapter) causes the tape to move in a reverse direction to the beginning of the current record.

When information is written on tape it completely replaces any information recorded on that section of the tape that is being written on. To prevent the accidental erasing of information, some tapes have a file protection device which may be used. Such tape reels have a circular groove around its center into which a removable plastic ring fits. If the plastic ring is removed, it is impossible to execute a write operation on that reel of tape; only a read operation may occur. The plastic ring must be inserted in the tape reel for writing to take place. Thus, master tape files which are to serve as input only will have the plastic ring removed.

Information is usually not recorded directly on magnetic tape. If magnetic tape input is to be used, the data are keypunched onto cards and then a card-to-tape operation is performed in which the data on a card are read into the computer and then written on magnetic tape. The tape is then used as input to the program. This process may not seem very time-saving since the computer is used to perform the card-to-tape operation and then again to read the data from tape. However, the card-to-tape operation is usually carried out on a small low-cost computer, whereas the program utilizing the data is run on a costlier high-speed computer that uses the tape as input. This procedure results in a saving of time on the higher-cost computer. Similarly, results can be written on magnetic tape much faster than they can be printed. The tape can later be taken to a smaller computer and listed, resulting in a saving of computer time and cost.

13.6   Magnetic-Tape Input

The most frequent use of magnetic-tape input occurs when the cards on which data are punched are copied onto tape. Each tape record then consists of the information on a card. These tape records are sometimes called *card images* since they are identical with the card records.

The general form of the READ statement for tape input is the Fortran IV READ statement shown in Section 9.1 and repeated here:

General Form

READ (i,n) *list*

where i designates an unsigned fixed-point constant or a fixed-point variable that refers to an input device, n is the statement number of an associated FORMAT statement, and *list* is a sequence of one or more variable names separated by commas.

The programmer should consult with the personnel of his computer center as to what tape units should be used for input and therefore for the value of i to be used in this general form.

When i designates a magnetic tape unit, execution of the READ statement causes at least one new tape record to be read (more than one record may be read as the result of the format specifications), and in accordance with the specified FORMAT statement as many quantities as there are variable names in the list are transmitted from the tape record(s), transformed to the appropriate mode, and stored in the registers whose symbolic names appear in the list.

The associated FORMAT statement is written as described in Chapter 9 for card input. The input medium is changed when using tape instead of cards; however, the data is described in the same manner. The occurrence of the solidus in the format specification, when used with tape input, causes the system to read the next tape record.

13.7 Magnetic-Tape Output

The most significant use of magnetic-tape output is to write final results on tape instead of directly on the printer or cards. The information on the tape is usually printed at a later time, using a low-cost computer; this results in a more efficient computer operation.

The general form of the WRITE statement for tape output is the Fortran IV WRITE statement shown in Section 9.3 and repeated here:

General Form

WRITE (i,n) *list*

where i designates an unsigned fixed-point constant or a fixed-point variable that refers to an output device, n is the statement number of an associated FORMAT statement, and *list* is a sequence of one or more variable names separated by commas.

The programmer should consult with the personnel of his computer center as to what tape units should be used for output and therefore for the value of i to be used in the above general form.

When *i* designates a magnetic-tape unit, execution of the WRITE statement causes at least one new tape record to be written, and in accordance with the specified FORMAT statement as many quantities as there are variable names in the list are transmitted from computer storage, transformed to the appropriate form and written on tape.

The associated FORMAT statement is written as described in Chapter 9 for printer or card output. The output medium is changed when using tape instead of the printer; however, the data is described in the same manner. The occurrence of the solidus in the format specification, when used with tape output, causes the system to terminate the present record and begin a new one. Two consecutive slashes in a FORMAT statement result in a blank tape record which, when printed, results in a blank line.

It must be carefully noted that when tape output is used and the information on the tape is to be *printed*, the programmer must provide for the carriage control characters to be the first character of every tape record.

13.8   Input/Output of Binary Information

It frequently occurs that the storage unit of a computer is not large enough to store the program, the data, and the intermediate and final results simultaneously. It might become necessary after calculating some intermediate results to write the results on an output device and later to read them in when required by the program. Thus, the output medium is being used as an intermediate storage device, freeing storage registers for other use. If the methods of input/output described in the preceding section and in Chapter 9 were used, each intermediate result would be converted according to format specifications to some output form and then converted back again when the results are read. Usually it is not necessary to examine intermediate results; therefore, the conversion to and from a readable form is unnecessary and inefficient. Fortran IV provides an output statement whereby data is written in the same form as it is stored (in binary). *No conversion takes place.* Fortran IV also provides an input statement to read information which was written in the binary form. These two statements are described as follows:

The Binary WRITE Statement

General Form

WRITE (*i*) *list*

where *i* designates an unsigned fixed-point constant or a fixed-point variable that refers to an output device, and *list* is a sequence of one or more variable names separated by commas.

Examples of the Binary WRITE *Statement*

WRITE (4)((X(I,J),I = 1 ,N),J = 1,M)

WRITE (2) A,B,(K(L),L = 1,10),((MAT(I,J),I = 1,N),J = 1,N1)

The binary WRITE statement, when used for tape output, causes one Fortran tape record† to be written. The record consists of the values (in binary) of the variables in the list in the order in which the variables appear in the list. No conversion takes place. If the WRITE statement is used for card output, as many cards as necessary are punched until all the variables in the list have been punched.

Data which have been written with a binary WRITE statement can only be read into storage by the following Fortran statement:

The Binary READ Statement

General Form

READ (*i*) *list*

where *i* designates an unsigned fixed-point constant or a fixed-point variable that refers to an input device, and *list* is a sequence of variable names separated by commas.

Examples of the Binary READ *Statement*

READ (4) A,B,(X(I),I = 1,50)

READ (3) ((M(I,J),I = 1,N),J = 1,N1)

The binary READ statement results in the reading of one Fortran tape record or a group of cards. The quantities on the tape or card(s) are stored without conversion in the registers whose names appear in the list. The operation is ordered in that the first quantity on tape is stored in the register whose name appears first in the list, etc. If the record being read contains more words than variables in the list, the additional words are ignored in the sense that they are not transmitted to the storage unit of the computer; however, the tape unit is positioned at the *end* of the record. If the record being read contains fewer words than variables in the list, only the words in the record are transmitted to storage. A second record is not read.

†A Fortran tape record is the sequence of values written by one Fortran output statement. It may consist of several physical tape records.

EXAMPLE 1

WRITE (4) A,B,C,(X(I),I = 1,10)
.
.
.

BACKSPACE 4

READ (4) A,B,C,(X(J),J = 1,10)
.
.
.

The contents of the registers A, B, C, X(1), X(2), . . . , X(10) are written without conversion on tape unit 4. The tape is later backspaced† and the values previously written are read and stored without conversion in the registers A, B, C, X(1), X(2), . . . ,X(10) respectively.

EXAMPLE 2

WRITE (1)((A(I,J),I = 1,50),J = 1,50)
.
.
.

BACKSPACE 1

READ (1)((X(K,L),K = 1,50),L = 1,50)

The elements of the array A are written on tape unit number one and later read and stored as the elements of the array X.

13.9   Auxiliary Magnetic Tape Instructions

The following three instructions are used with magnetic tape input-output operations:

General Form

END FILE *i*

REWIND *i*

BACKSPACE *i*

where *i* designates an unsigned fixed-point constant or fixed-point variable that refers to a magnetic-tape unit.

Examples of Auxiliary Tape Instructions | END FILE 2 | REWIND 4 | BACKSPACE 3

†See Section 13.9 for an account of the BACKSPACE statement.

The END FILE statement when designating a tape used for output causes a tape mark to be written on the tape. The tape is *not* rewound.

The REWIND statement when designating a tape used for output causes a tape mark to be written on the tape. The tape designated in the REWIND statement, whether it is a tape used for input or output, is rewound to the beginning of the tape.

The BACKSPACE statement usually causes the magnetic tape designated to be backspaced one physical record. However, if the *last* record written on the tape is a binary record — that is, written by a WRITE (*i*) *list* statement — the tape is backspaced one Fortran tape record or, in other words, to the beginning of the record written by the WRITE (*i*) *list* statement. This may in fact cause backspacing over several physical records.

Problems

13.1 For each of the following sets of output statements describe the output record, assuming the variables have the following values:

$$A = 127.18$$

$$B = 012345673621 \text{ (octal characters)}$$

$$C = 1681.21$$

$$T = +1.1002$$

$$K = A671B9 \text{ (characters)}$$

$$I = -28$$

$$J = CORREL \text{ (characters)}$$

a)   PRINT 6,A,I,K,J,B

    6   FORMAT (1H03XF12.4,4XI4,3X2A3,O11)

b)   PRINT 7,C,T,K,J

    7   FORMAT (4XF10.0,2XF8.5,2XA6,A10)

c)   PRINT 9,B,K,J,T

    9   FORMAT (1XO8,2(1XA2),2XF3.0)

d)   PRINT 1,A,B,J,I,K

    1   FORMAT (1H1F10.3,1XO12,2X8HWORD IS A6,5XI10/1XA2)

13.2 Write a Fortran program to read a single alphabetic character from column 5 of a card. Starting with the letter A, print the letters of the alphabet up to and including the letter read from the card.

13.3 Write a Fortran program to read the three binary numbers listed below into registers I, J, K:

1) 1101110110100001011000100011110111101
2) 101001010001001110110100110110000101
3) 111011100101001100010110110001101011

The numbers are to be punched one per card. Convert the numbers to octal form and read them, using the O specification.

13.4 Fifty cards are each punched with a five-character code in columns 1–5. The code can contain numeric, alphabetic, or special characters. These fifty cards are followed by twenty-five cards, each punched with a five-character code in columns 6–10. Write a Fortran program to determine how many of the codes on the second set of data cards also appear on the first set of data cards.

13.5 Indicate what will be stored when each data item below is read according to the specification indicated. Assume that the data is punched starting in column 1 and that an appropriate READ statement is given.

	Format Specification	Data
a)	1XA7	ABCD12345
b)	O4	12345670
c)	1X1PF4.1	16782451
d)	1X−1PF5.2	812.47192
e)	A1	6ABCD
f)	O15	0123456770123456
g)	O3,A2	672148
h)	2PF6.1	123.4568
i)	−3PF7.2	−123.1289
j)	A6	12A$,64(

13.6 Describe the advantages and disadvantages of using magnetic tape as an input/output media.

13.7 Under what circumstances would the binary read and write instructions be used?

14

Type Declaration Statements, DATA, and BLOCK DATA Statements

Fortran permits the use of different types of variables (real, integer, double precision, etc.) in computational problems. The Type Declaration statement allows the programmer to specify the types of variables used in the program. This enables the programmer to override the alphabetic naming convention of variables described in Chapter 4. The DATA and BLOCK DATA statements allow the programmer to set variables to an initial value, these values being placed in the object program at compilation time.

14.1 Type Declaration Statements

It is necessary when working with double-precision, logical, and complex variables† to designate these variables as such. The Type Declaration statement is used for this purpose. Since each complex quantity and each double-precision quantity requires two storage registers the compiler must be given this information so that the proper storage can be allocated. It is also possible to use a Type Declaration statement to override the alphabetic naming convention of variables described in Sections 4.6 and 4.7. Thus, a variable may be designated as either a fixed- or floating-point variable regardless of the first character of the variable name. The Type Declaration statements, of which there are six, have the following form:

†The use of these variables in Fortran is discussed in later chapters.

General Form

INTEGER $a_1, a_2, \ldots a_n$

REAL $a_1, a_2, \ldots a_n$

DOUBLE PRECISION $a_1, a_2, \ldots a_n$

LOGICAL $a_1, a_2, \ldots a_n$

COMPLEX $a_1, a_2, \ldots a_n$

EXTERNAL $b_1, b_2, \ldots b_n$

where $a_1, a_2, \ldots a_n$ are subscripted or nonsubscripted fixed- or floating-point variables and $b_1, b_2, \ldots b_n$ are nonsubscripted fixed or floating-point variables.

Examples of Type Declaration Statements

INTEGER K,DEL,B,ARAY(15,5)

REAL I4,OHM,N(12),J

DOUBLE PRECISION A,L,B4,T(5)

LOGICAL L3,C,F(5,5)

COMPLEX D1,CD,B1,K,G(10,20)

EXTERNAL MULT,COS,ALOG,CALC

The following rules apply to the use of the Type Declaration statements:

1. INTEGER specifies that the variables listed are integer (fixed point) regardless of the first letter of their names.

2. REAL specifies that the variables listed are real (floating point) regardless of the first letter of their names.

3. DOUBLE PRECISION specifies that the variables listed are double-precision variables.

4. LOGICAL specifies that the variables listed are logical variables. They may assume only the values TRUE or FALSE.

5. COMPLEX specifies that the variables listed are complex variables.

6. EXTERNAL specifies that the names listed are subprogram names to be used as arguments in a call to a subroutine or function subprogram. Any argument in a function or subroutine calling statement which is

itself a subprogram name must appear in an EXTERNAL type declaration. The variable names listed in the EXTERNAL statement may not be subscripted.

7. An array name appearing in a Type Declaration statement may have its dimensions specified in the Type statement. If a variable has its dimensions specified in a Type statement then it must not have its dimensions specified in a DIMENSION or COMMON statement.

8. If a variable appears in a Type Declaration statement, the type declaration must precede the first appearance of the variable in an executable statement.

9. Once the type of a variable is specified, it may not be changed in the program.

10. A variable may appear in only one Type Declaration statement with the exception that if a variable name appears in an EXTERNAL type declaration, it may also appear in *one* of the other Type Declaration statements.

EXAMPLE 1

INTEGER A,L,X3(10)

The variables A and L and the array X3 are all designated as integer (fixed point) quantities. X3 must not appear in a DIMENSION statement and can only be used in a COMMON statement without its subscripts.

EXAMPLE 2

REAL N,K1,B,M(10,5)

The variables N, K1, B, and the array M are all designated as floating-point (real) quantities. M must not appear in a DIMENSION statement and can only be used in a COMMON statement without its subscripts.

EXAMPLE 3

DOUBLE PRECISION TWO,W6A,A(10),G

The variables TWO, W6A, G, and the array A are all designated as double-precision quantities. The quantity A must not appear in a DIMENSION statement and can only be used in a COMMON statement without its subscripts

EXAMPLE 4

LOGICAL S,T,L,M

The variables S, T, L, and M are designated as logical variables. Each of these variables may take on either the value true or false.

EXAMPLE 5

COMPLEX C,C1,X,Y

The variables C, C1, X, and Y are designated as complex variables.

EXAMPLE 6

EXTERNAL ALOG,SUMMAT

ALOG and SUMMAT are subprogram names to be used as arguments in a subroutine or function call.

EXAMPLE 7

REAL MATAD

EXTERNAL MATAD

These two statements indicate that the name of a subprogram MATAD appears as an argument in a calling statement and the name MATAD is a floating-point subprogram name.

EXAMPLE 8

REAL A

——————

——————

——————

——————

——————

INTEGER A

——————

——————

——————

These statements violate Rule 9, which states that once the type of a variable is specified it may not be changed within the same program.

14.2 Type Declaration for a Function Subprogram

The type of a function subprogram name may be declared by preceding the word FUNCTION in the defining statement by one of the following words: INTEGER, REAL, DOUBLE PRECISION, LOGICAL, or COMPLEX. The type of function is as specified and overrides the alphabetic naming convention. The FUNCTION statement may thus take any of the following forms:

FUNCTION name $(a_1,a_2, \ldots a_n)$

REAL FUNCTION name $(a_1,a_2, \ldots a_n)$

INTEGER FUNCTION name $(a_1,a_2, \ldots a_n)$

DOUBLE PRECISION FUNCTION name $(a_1, a_2, \ldots a_n)$

LOGICAL FUNCTION name $(a_1, a_2, \ldots a_n)$

COMPLEX FUNCTION name $(a_1, a_2, \ldots a_n)$

If the type of a function subprogram name is not explicitly indicated in the FUNCTION statement, it will be either fixed point or floating point according to the first letter of the function's name.

The name of an arithmetic statement function may be declared by preceding the defining statement by a Type Declaration. See Program P15.5 for an illustration.

14.3   Type Declarations in a Calling Program

Suppose that a function subprogram K, whose name has been declared to be of the floating-point type, is to call one of the subprograms MATDET or TRACE. The name of the subprogram to be called is specified as an argument by the main program. The subprograms MATDET and TRACE are not shown.

Main Program	Subprogram
REAL MATDET, K	REAL FUNCTION K(T,Z)
EXTERNAL MATDET, TRACE	DIMENSION Z(25,25)
DIMENSION A(25,25)	———
———	———
———	Y = T(Z)
———	———
———	———
IF (L)3,4,3	———
3 X = Y + K(MATDET,A)	———
GO TO 8	RETURN
4 X = Y + K(TRACE,A)	END
8 ———	
END	

If L is equal to zero, the subprogram name, TRACE, is substituted for T, and A is substituted for Z. Thus, in the subprogram K the statement Y = T(Z) becomes Y = TRACE (A), and the subprogram TRACE will be called. If L is not equal to zero, the subprogram name, MATDET, is substituted for T and A is substituted for Z. In the subprogram K the statement Y = T(Z) becomes Y = MATDET (A), and the subprogram MATDET will be called.

The names MATDET and TRACE are in the list of the EXTERNAL statement because they are subprogram names which are used as arguments in a statement calling a function subprogram. MATDET and K are specified as real function names.

14.4   DATA   Statements

In a program it is often necessary to set variables equal to some initial value. This value may be a fixed or floating point constant, one of the values .TRUE. or .FALSE. for logical variables, or perhaps alphameric data. Of course, the program could be written to read these initial values from data cards or to use a series of arithmetic or logical statements to initialize the variables to some arithmetic or logical constant. However, both of these methods for setting variables to some initial value are somewhat cumbersome.

The DATA statement allows the programmer to specify data to be placed in the storage registers indicated. The DATA statement causes data to be placed into the object program at compilation time. If, during the execution of the object program, the variables are redefined, they will take on their new value regardless of the DATA statement. *The DATA statement may not be used to place data in variables located in common (blank or labeled) storage.* The block data subprogram (described in the next section) should be used for this purpose. The general form of the DATA statement is as follows:

General Form

DATA $list/a_1,a_2, \ldots a_n/,list/b_1,b_2, \ldots b_m/, \ldots/$

where *list* is a sequence of variable names separated by commas for which values are being defined. The variables may be subscripted; if so only integer constants may be used for the subscripts and $a_1,a_2, \ldots a_n,b_1,b_2, \ldots b_m$ are elements of data.

Examples of the DATA Statement

DATA X,Y/3.81,2.1416/,LV1,LV2/T,F/

DATA S(1),S(4)/17.1,3.333/

The variables in the list are assigned the values specified by the data following the list. The operation is ordered in that the first variable in the list is assigned the first data value, the second variable in the list is assigned the second data value, etc. To illustrate, consider the first DATA statement in the foregoing example. X is assigned the value 3.81, Y the value 2.1416, LV1 the value .TRUE. and LV2 the value .FALSE..

The data $(a_1, a_2, \ldots a_n, b_1, b_2, \ldots b_m \ldots)$ specified in the DATA statement may take any of the following three forms:.

1) A Fixed-Point, Floating-Point, Logical, Double-Precision, or Complex Constant

A logical constant may be specified in any of the following forms:

.TRUE.

.FALSE.

T

F

When logical, double-precision, or complex constants are specified in a DATA statement, the corresponding variables must have previously appeared in a Type Declaration statement specifying their type (see the first section in this chapter).

EXAMPLE

DIMENSION L(4)

LOGICAL L

DOUBLE PRECISION X

COMPLEX Y

DATA A,K,X,Y,L(1),L(2),L(3),L(4)/7.919,32,5.124D4,(3.1,1.2), .TRUE.,T,.FALSE.,F/

A is assigned the value 7.919, K the value 32, X the value 51240. in double precision, Y the complex number $3.1 + 1.2i$, and L(1) and L(2) the value .TRUE., and L(3) and L(4) the value .FALSE..

2) One or More Alphameric Characters

An alphameric constant is written in the following form

$$nHa_1a_2a_3 \ldots a_n$$

where n designates an integer constant specifying the number of alphameric characters following the H and the a_i's are any alphameric characters (including blanks). Starting with the first character following the letter H each group of six alphameric characters are stored in the register whose name appears next in the list. If the number of alphameric characters specified is not a multiple of six, the last *w* (where $w \leq 6$) characters are left justified in the storage register and the remaining positions in the register are filled with blanks. This action is similar to the A specification for input. If $n > 6$ the corresponding variable in the list *must* have been previously dimensioned to accommodate the alphameric characters.

EXAMPLE 1

$$\text{DATA } K,Y/6H012345,3HABC/$$

The variables K and Y will appear as follows:

$$K = 0 \ 1 \ 2 \ 3 \ 4 \ 5$$
$$Y = A \ B \ C \ b \ b \ b$$

EXAMPLE 2

DIMENSION L(5)

DATA L/26HABCDEFGHIJKLMNOPQRSTUVWXYZ/

The array L will appear as follows:

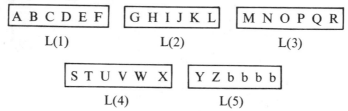

EXAMPLE 3

DIMENSION L(26)

DATA L/1HA,1HB,1HC,1HD,1HE,1HF,1HG,1HH,1HI,1HJ,1HK, 1HL1HM,1HN,1HO,1HP,1HQ,1HR,1HS,1HT,1HU,1HV,1HW, 1HX,1HY,1HZ/

Each letter of the alphabet will be stored in a separate register of the array L. The letter will be left justified in the register and the five rightmost positions filled with blanks as follows:

A b b b b b	B b b b b b	...	Z b b b b b
L(1)	L(2)		L(26)

EXAMPLE 4

DIMENSION Y(4)

DATA Y(1),Y(2)/6H456789,4HCORR/,CON/3HFIX/

The array Y and the variable CON appear as follows:

4 5 6 7 8 9	C O R R b b	F I X b b b
Y(1)	Y(2)	CON

EXAMPLE 5

DATA A/10H1234567890/

This statement is invalid since A is not dimensioned and the register can only store six characters.

3) A Series of Octal Digits

An octal constant is written in the following form

$$O d_1 d_2 d_3 \ldots d_n \quad (n \leq 12)$$

where the d_i are any octal digits. The constant may be signed or unsigned. Each octal digit is converted to three binary digits. If $n \leq 12$ the $3 \times n$ bits are right-justified in the register and the leftmost positions are filled with zeros.

EXAMPLE

DATA A/O120345701245/,K/O1236/

The registers A and K will appear as follows:

(A) = 001010000011100101111000001010100101

(K) = 000000000000000000000000001010011110

The programmer should note that there must be a direct relationship between the list and the data items. Each item of data must correspond to a nondimensioned variable or an element of an array in the list immediately preceding the data items. If data are to be placed in an entire array, the array name should appear in the list without subscripts. The number of data items must be equal to the size of the array as dimensioned.

A data item may be preceded by an integer constant k followed by an asterisk, which indicates that the data field is to be repeated k times.

EXAMPLE

DIMENSION X(5),L(5)

INTEGER E

LOGICAL L

DATA A,B,D/6.71,9.5,4HHOLL/,E, X,L/13,3*10.0,2*25.0,3*T,F,T/

Table 14.1 shows the variable and data item stored in the variable as a result of the DATA statement.

TABLE 14.1   Assignment of Variables by DATA Statement

Variable	Value
A	6.71
B	9.5
D	HOLLbb
E	13
X(1)	10.0
X(2)	10.0
X(3)	10.0
X(4)	25.0
X(5)	25.0
L(1)	.TRUE.
L(2)	.TRUE.
L(3)	.TRUE.
L(4)	.FALSE.
L(5)	.TRUE.

14.5   BLOCK DATA Subprogram

The BLOCK DATA subprogram is used to place data in variables located in labeled common storage. The subprogram may contain only the following kinds of statements:

> BLOCK DATA
>
> DATA
>
> COMMON
>
> DIMENSION
>
> TYPE
>
> END

Executable statements are not allowed in the subprogram. Blocks of common storage and the variables therein may be specified and data entered into the variables of the common blocks.

The following rules pertain to the block data subprogram.

1. The first statement of the subprogram must be the BLOCK DATA statement. The general form is

---

General Form

BLOCK DATA

---

2. The COMMON statements in the subprogram must include *all* the elements of the common blocks, although all of the elements need not be specified in the DATA statement.

3. The DATA statement must define only elements listed in the COMMON statements.

4. The DATA statement need not contain the name of the labeled blocks only the variables into which data are to be stored.

5. The last statement of the subprogram must be an END statement.

EXAMPLE

```
BLOCK DATA
DIMENSION T(3)
COMMON /A/X/TOT/SUMX,SUMY,T,U,K,N
REAL N
DATA X/7.55/,T,SUMX,K,N/1.389,1.672,2.001,75.,2HGO,100./
END
```

Problems

14.1 Examine the following sets of statements for errors. If no errors are present list the variables and their values as determined by the DATA statement.

a) DATA X,Y,Z/3.2,167.5,.01/A/75.1/

b) DIMENSION L(10),K(5)
LOGICAL K
REAL L
INTEGER H,A
DATA L/1.,2.,3.,4.,5.,6.,7.,8.,9.,10./,K,H,A/3*T,2*F,419, 6H123456/

c) DATA A,B/3.E−06,38.

d) DIMENSION L(10)
DATA C,L,K/1H0,1,2,3,4,5,38/

e) LOGICAL L
COMPLEX C
INTEGER A
DIMENSION B(3,3)
DATA L,C/.TRUE.,(3.2,−1.1)/,A,B/1000,1.,2.,3.,4./

14.2 Write the Fortran statements necessary to do the following:

a) Set up a one-dimensional array of ten elements with the following values: 2, 8, 9, 3, 95, 75, 9, 0, 49, and 1002.

b) Set up a two-dimensional array with five rows and five columns. The numbers to be stored in the elements of the array are the products of the row and column designations of the elements. For example, the element A_{34} would have the value 12(4 × 3).

14.3 A two-digit number N is punched in columns 1–2 of a card in I2 format. Write a Fortran program to read the card and print N consecutive asterisks on a line. For example, if the number punched is 32, thirty-two asterisks are to be printed. (Hint: The necessary output format statement can be defined in a data statement.)

15

Logical Operations

In addition to allowing for operations on numerical quantities, Fortran IV provides a means of manipulating logical quantities. To perform branching operations within a Fortran program conditional transfer statements containing only simple comparisons have been considered thus far. To effect branching that is based on the outcome of several conditions, nesting of transfer statements is always possible. We now consider the possibility of combining several branching conditions into a single expression. This chapter introduces the various logical operations that may be used for combining expressions into a single statement. The elements of the language required to represent these logical quantities are taken from the propositional calculus of mathematical logic.

BOOLEAN ALGEBRA

The classical two-valued propositional calculus is represented in several ways. Among the formulations of the calculus are the algebra of sets, the logic of truth functions, and the algebra of switching circuits. We shall employ the term *Boolean algebra* to designate in a general way the propositional calculus.

There exists a variety of applications of Boolean algebra in diverse fields. These include applications in switching-circuit design, methods and procedures of operations research, medical diagnosis, linguistic analysis, and programming research. With Boolean algebra it is possible to describe a set of digital computing circuits by means of a set of algebraic expressions, as well as to analyze the relationships among reactions resulting from a given set of stimuli by means of a series of logical equations. Since digital techniques for simplifying computations with Boolean variables have been developed, the use of the computer in performing Boolean computations has become commonplace. Although the study of these applications is beyond the scope of this text, a brief characterization of Boolean algebra will be given. The basic concepts of the algebra will be introduced first. A set of basic postulates for the algebra will then be presented, followed by a list of useful theorems. Several examples will be included later in the chapter to illustrate some of the applications of Boolean algebra.

15.1   The Basic Concepts of Boolean Algebra

An important characteristic of Boolean algebra is that it is a *two-valued* algebra. What this means is that underlying the algebra are two logical constants, "true" and "false", called logical (truth) values. Unlike numerical variables, which take only numbers as values, a *Boolean variable* is one that can take only the logical values true or false. Similarly, a *Boolean function* also assumes the values true or false. Thus in contrast with arithmetic expressions that take numerical constants (numbers) as values, symbolic constructions that are assigned logical values are called *Boolean expressions*. They may be thought of as denoting *propositions*, hence the name propositional calculus.

There are four possible two-valued functions of a single Boolean variable. Table 15.1 presents, in tabular form, the four functions. We will designate the values taken by the single Boolean variable X with the symbol 0 and 1, standing for *false* and *true* respectively.

Table 15.1   Functions of a Single Boolean Variable

Value of Variable X	Value for dependent function $Y = f(X)$			
	$Y = 1$	$Y = 0$	$Y = X$	$Y = \bar{X}$
0	1	0	0	1
1	1	0	1	0

The first two of these functions, $f(X) = 1$ and $f(X) = 0$, are trivial; they correspond to any logically true or logically false statement respectively. The third function, $f(X) = X$, is the identity function.

The fourth function is defined as the *negation* of X (sometimes called the *complement* of X) and is written $f(X) = \bar{X}$; the bar above the variable indicates the negation of the variable. Observe that negation is a *unary* Boolean operation; it applies to any single variable or expression serving as the argument of the function.

There are sixteen possible two-valued functions of two Boolean variables. These are called *binary* Boolean operations because they always apply to a pair of variables or expressions serving as the arguments of the function. Table 15.2 lists the truth values for five of the sixteen binary Boolean functions, and Table 15.3 identifies each operation by giving the name, symbol, and meaning associated with the usual interpretation of that function. The five functions chosen represent the more common Boolean operations. In Table 15.2 the two arguments, X and Y, can take any one of four different combinations of values. For each combination the corresponding value for each function is listed. For example, if $X = 0$ and $Y = 1$ (second row of table), the function $f(X,Y) = X \cdot Y$ has the value 0 and the function $g(X,Y) = X + Y$ has the value 1.

TABLE 15.2   Common Functions of Two Boolean Variables

X	Y	$X + Y$	$X \cdot Y$	$X \oplus Y$	$X \supset Y$	$X \equiv Y$
0	0	0	0	0	1	1
0	1	1	0	1	1	0
1	0	1	0	1	0	0
1	1	1	1	0	1	1

Table 15.3   Names, Symbols, and Meanings of Common Boolean Operations

Name of Operation	Symbol	Meaning
Negation	$\overline{X}$	not X
Disjunction	$X + Y$	X or Y or both
Conjunction	$X \cdot Y$ XY	X and Y
Exclusive disjunction	$X \oplus Y$	X or Y but not both
Implication	$X \supset Y$	X implies Y if X then Y
Equivalence	$X \equiv Y$	X is equivalent to Y X if and only if Y

The values of the function $f(X, Y) = X + Y$ listed in Table 15.2 define a binary operation called *disjunction*. $X + Y$ takes the value 1 if either X or Y (or both) has the value 1. This operation is often called *logical addition*. Observe that the plus symbol (+) has been employed to designate logical addition as well as ordinary addition with numbers. This usage will seldom result in any ambiguity so long as it is remembered that the rules of logical addition are applicable only to Boolean expressions and those of ordinary addition apply only to arithmetic expressions.

EXAMPLE 1
$$(A < B + 5) + Y > X$$

In this expression, which reads "A is less than $B + 5$ or Y is greater than X," we know that A and B must represent numerical variables or arithmetic expressions that take numbers as values. Furthermore, the occurrence of the plus sign (+) within the pair of parentheses in the example stands for ordinary addition, while the second occurrence of + is the sign for disjunction. Thus, although it is true that A and B represent arithmetic expressions, $A < B + 5$ is a Boolean expression standing for a proposition that is either true or false depending on the numerical values assigned to the quantities A and B. Similarly, since the expression $Y > X$ appears as the second argument of the binary function represented by the second occurrence of +, $Y > X$ must also be a Boolean expression taking the value true or false. Only interpreting the symbols in this manner does the example become meaningful.

Observe that if the parentheses had been placed otherwise in Example 1, a different interpretation of the symbols would have been required. For instance, consider the following:

EXAMPLE 2

$$A < B + (5 + Y > X)$$

This reads "A is less than B or $5 + Y$ is greater than X." Here A and B together with X and Y all denote arithmetic expressions, but the interpretation of each + is the opposite of that advanced in the previous example.

The values of the second function in Table 15.2,

$$f(X,Y) = X \cdot Y$$

where $X \cdot Y$ is generally written XY, define a binary operation called *conjunction*. XY takes the value 1 only when both X and Y are equal to 1. This operation is often called *logical multiplication*. Remarks similar to those pertaining to the dual use of the symbol + apply to the usage of the dot symbol ($\cdot$) as the sign for both conjunction and ordinary multiplication.

EXAMPLE 3

$$X \cdot (A \cdot B \geq C + D)$$

This reads "X and $A \cdot B$ is greater than or equal to $C + D$," where A, B, C and D are arithmetic expressions and X is a Boolean expression. This statement is true only if *both* X is true *and* the statement $A \cdot B \geq C + D$ is true.

In the next column of Table 15.2 the values of the function

$$g(X,Y) = X \oplus Y$$

define a binary operation called *exclusive disjunction*. $X \oplus Y$ takes the value 1 only when X or Y, but not both, takes the value 1. In switching circuit theory, this operation is called *sum modulo 2 addition*.

EXAMPLE 4

$$Z \oplus \text{abs} \ (W1 + W2) > M$$

This reads "either Z or absolute value of $W1 + W2$ is greater than M, but not both," where M, $W1$ and $W2$ are arithmetic expressions and Z is a Boolean expression. The statement is true only if either Z is true or abs $(W1 + W2) > M$ is true, but not both are true.

The values of the fourth function in Table 15.2, $X \supset Y$, define a binary operation called *implication*. $X \supset Y$ takes the value 1 in all cases except when $X = 1$ and $Y = 0$. That is, when X is true and Y is false, X does not imply Y. In all other cases X implies Y. X is called the *antecedent* of the implication relation $X \supset Y$, and Y is called the *consequent*. Another name for $X \supset Y$ is the *conditional* operation.

EXAMPLE 5

$$(A + B > C) \supset (C \leq D)$$

This reads "if $A + B$ is greater than C then C is less than or equal to D," where A, B, C and D are all arithmetic expressions. The statement is false only if $A + B > C$ is true and $C \leq D$ is false.

The values of the fifth function $(X \equiv Y)$ in Table 15.2 define a binary operation called *equivalence*. $X \equiv Y$ takes the value 1 only when X and Y are both equal to 1 or are both equal to 0. It can be shown that $X \equiv Y$ may be expressed as $(X \supset Y)(Y \supset X)$. For this reason, equivalence is often called the *biconditional* operation.

EXAMPLE 6

$$(A \cdot B < 1) \equiv (\text{abs } (C + 5) > M \supset Y)$$

This reads "$A \cdot B$ is less than one if and only if the absolute value of $C + 5$ being greater than M implies Y," where A, B, C, and M are arithmetic expressions and Y is a Boolean expression. The statement is true only if $A \cdot B < 1$ and abs $(C + 5) > M \supset Y$ agree in truth value.

More complex Boolean expressions are possible by allowing X and Y in Table 15.2 to be not only elementary propositions but arbitrary compound propositions containing, in addition to arithmetic operations and relations, any of the six basic Boolean operations listed in Table 15.3.

EXAMPLE 7

$$(C \equiv B) + \overline{(A \supset (X \leq Y))}$$

This reads "either C is equivalent to B or it is false that A implies that X is less than or equal to Y," where A, B, and C are Boolean expressions, and X and Y are arithmetic expressions.

15.2 The Postulates and Rules of Boolean Algebra

We shall now define a Boolean algebra in terms of complementation, logical addition, and logical multiplication.

Definition

A Boolean algebra is the set of objects $0,1,X, Y, Z, \ldots$, such that for any two elements X and Y a product XY, a sum $X + Y$, and a complement $\bar{X}$, belonging to the algebra, are uniquely defined. These operations satisfy the following basic rules:

1. *Idempotence Laws*

$$X + X = X$$
$$X \cdot X = X$$

Multiplying a Boolean quantity by itself or adding a Boolean quantity to itself leaves the quantity unchanged.

2. *Commutative Laws*

$$X + Y = Y + X$$
$$XY = YX$$

The order of addition does not affect the sum; nor does the order of multiplication affect the product.

3. *Associative Laws*

$$X + (Y + Z) = (X + Y) + Z$$
$$X(YZ) = (XY)Z$$

Hence the meaning of the product XYZ or the sum $X + Y + Z$ is unambiguous.

4. *Distributive Laws*

$$X(Y + Z) = XY + XZ$$
$$X + YZ = (X + Y)(X + Z)$$

Observe that a Boolean algebra is distributive for both the multiplication and addition operations.

5. *Zero and Unity Laws*

$$0 + X = X \qquad 1 + X = 1$$
$$0 \cdot X = 0 \qquad 1 \cdot X = X$$

The following is a list of derived rules which are especially useful in calculating with Boolean expressions.

6. *Laws of Absorption*

$$X + XY = X$$
$$X(X + Y) = X$$
$$X + \bar{X}Y = X + Y$$
$$X(\bar{X} + Y) = XY$$

These are very useful relations when expressions are to be simplified. The first two absorption laws may be derived from each other using rules 1 and 4: $X + XY = (X + X)(X + Y) = X(X + Y)$.

7. *Law of Involution*

$$\overline{\overline{X}} = X$$

The value of a quantity twice negated is left unchanged. X can take only the value 0 or 1. Since $\overline{0} = 1$ and $\overline{1} = 0$, therefore $\overline{\overline{0}} = 0$ and $\overline{\overline{1}} = 1$.

8. *Laws of Complementarity*

$$X + \overline{X} = 1$$

$$X \cdot \overline{X} = 0$$

These relations are sometimes used to define 1 and 0. Let X represent a class of objects and $\overline{X}$ represent all objects that are not members of the class X. The sum $X + \overline{X}$ will form a *universal* class (1) and the product $X \cdot \overline{X}$ will define an empty or *null* class (0).

9. *DeMorgan's Theorems*

$$\overline{(X + Y)} = \overline{X}\overline{Y}$$

$$\overline{(XY)} = \overline{X} + \overline{Y}$$

These theorems are useful in forming the complement of a given expression. For instance, the complement of an expression containing $\overline{}$'s, $+$'s and $\cdot$'s can be formed by complementing each uncomplemented variable, uncomplementing each complemented variable, and interchanging $+$'s and $\cdot$'s throughout the expression:

$$\overline{(X\overline{Y} + YZ + \overline{X}YZ)} = (\overline{X} + Y)(\overline{Y} + \overline{Z})(X + \overline{Y} + \overline{Z})$$

DeMorgan's theorems illustrate a basic duality that underlies all Boolean algebra. Each theorem has a *dual*, the basic form of which may be found by complementing each side of the equality expressed by the theorem. For example, the dual of $X + X = X$ is

$$X \cdot X = X$$

the dual of $X(Y + Z) = XY + XZ$ is

$$X + YX = (X + Y)(X + Z)$$

and the dual of $X + \overline{X}Y = X + Y$ is

$$X(\overline{X} + Y) = XY$$

Observe that by applying DeMorgan's theorem and the law of involution, logical addition can be expressed in terms of complementation and logical multiplication:

$$X + Y = (\overline{\overline{X}\overline{Y}})$$

Similarly, logical multiplication can be formed by complementation and logical addition:

$$XY = (\overline{\overline{X} + \overline{Y}})$$

Hence it is possible to define a Boolean algebra solely in terms of complementation and logical addition or complementation and logical multiplication.

15.3   Proof by Perfect Induction

The properties of a Boolean algebra may be established by deduction on a set of postulates of the algebra, such as those listed in the preceding section, or by a method of proof known as *perfect induction*. The latter approach sometimes appears more natural to one unacquainted with an axiomatic formulation of Boolean algebra. Proof by perfect induction also has the advantage that it facilitates the validation process, since it consists of a purely mechanical routine for determining validity. Applications of the method will be illustrated later in the chapter when several programming examples are discussed.

In carrying out a proof by perfect induction, the following operations on truth values will be assumed:

$$\overline{0} = 1 \qquad 0 + 0 = 0 \qquad 1 + 0 = 1 \qquad 0 \cdot 0 = 0 \qquad 1 \cdot 0 = 0$$

$$\overline{1} = 0 \qquad 0 + 1 = 1 \qquad 1 + 1 = 1 \qquad 0 \cdot 1 = 0 \qquad 1 \cdot 1 = 1$$

These operations may be viewed as an alternative set of postulates which also define a Boolean algebra in terms of complementation, logical addition, and logical multiplication. When used in conjunction with proof by perfect induction, the operations suffice to establish all the rules of the algebra listed in the preceding section. Since the logical variables used in Boolean algebra may take only one of two possible truth values at a time, all possible combinations of values for the variables may be enumerated and, using the above operations, a given expression evaluated for each combination. In this manner the validity of a rule is ascertained by evaluating each side of the equation for each set of values. If the resulting values correspond, the rule is proved.

Consider Rule 4 of the preceding section, which states that Boolean algebra is distributive over addition:

$$X + YZ = (X + Y)(X + Z)$$

There are 2^n different ways of assigning truth values to n variables. Since there are three variables (X, Y, and Z) in the rule, the rule may be verified by substituting each of the eight possible combinations of values for the variables into the equation and evaluating each side of the equation for each set of values in accordance with the operations above. A tabular representation of the values for the variables along with the resulting values for the expression being evaluated is called a *table of truth values*. Table 15.4 shows the table of truth values for the expression $X + YZ = (X + Y)(X + Z)$.

TABLE 15.4   Table of Truth Values for $X + YZ = (X + Y)(X + Z)$

Values for Variables			Left Side of Equation		Right Side of Equation		
X	Y	Z	YZ	$X + YZ$	$(X + Y)$	$(X + Z)$	$(X + Y)(X + Z)$
0	0	0	0	0	0	0	0
0	0	1	0	0	0	1	0
0	1	0	0	0	1	0	0
0	1	1	1	1	1	1	1
1	0	0	0	1	1	1	1
1	0	1	0	1	1	1	1
1	1	0	0	1	1	1	1
1	1	1	1	1	1	1	1

Since the values of both sides of the relation $X + YZ = (X + Y)(X + Z)$ agree for every possible combination of values that the variables can take, the relation holds.

In order to demonstrate further the use of proof by perfect induction and at the same time illustrate the construction of other tables of truth values, proofs for the law of absorption and DeMorgan's theorem are exhibited in Tables 15.5 and 15.6.

TABLE 15.5   Table of Truth Values for $X(\overline{X} + Y) = XY$

Values for Variables		Left Side of Equation		Right Side of Equation
X	Y	$\overline{X} + Y$	$X(\overline{X} + Y)$	XY
0	0	1	0	0
0	1	1	0	0
1	0	0	0	0
1	1	1	1	1

TABLE 15.6   Table of Truth Values for $\overline{(XY)} = \overline{X} + \overline{Y}$

Values for Variables		Left Side of Equation		Right Side of Equation		
X	Y	(XY)	$\overline{(XY)}$	$\overline{X}$	$\overline{Y}$	$\overline{X} + \overline{Y}$
0	0	0	1	1	1	1
0	1	0	1	1	0	1
1	0	0	1	0	1	1
1	1	1	0	0	0	0

LOGICAL CONSTANTS, VARIABLES AND EXPRESSIONS IN FORTRAN IV

We now turn to a study of the logical facilities of Fortran IV which make possible the programming of Boolean operations. We will consider first the basic elements of Boolean algebra that are incorporated into the language of Fortran IV. These include, first of all, the two Boolean constants *true* and *false*.

15.4   Logical Constants

Besides the two kinds of numerical constants, integer (or fixed point) and real (or floating point), Fortran IV allows a third kind — namely, two special logical constants, which may take either of the following two forms:

.TRUE.   .FALSE.

Observe that these two constants are always written with periods preceding and following the symbols.

These constants may be interpreted as new kinds of values appearing side by side with the usual numerical values represented by numbers. Every proposition represents a value from this class of logical values just as every arithmetic expression represents a numerical value.

15.5   Logical Variables

To express propositions in Fortran IV it is necessary to introduce a new type of variable, which differs in kind from integer and real variables. Called *logical* variables, these new variables correspond to Boolean variables and take as their values the two logical constants .TRUE. and .FALSE..

Variables of type LOGICAL thus represent elementary propositions and, as is the case with the two logical constants .TRUE. and .FALSE., can appear as components of compound propositions.

Logical variables are assigned Fortran names in the same general manner as integer or real variables; that is, a logical variable is named by assigning to it a maximum of six alphameric characters, provided that the first character is always alphabetic. *However, the name of each logical variable must always be declared to be logical by means of a Type Declaration statement.* †

For example, if in a particular program, F, BA, and K4 are names selected for *logical* variables, they are so declared by inclusion in the program of the following Type Declaration statement:

LOGICAL F, BA, K4

In brief, logical variables can be used freely, provided that the variables have been previously declared and assigned values. Discussion of how true and false values may be assigned to logical variables will be deferred until later in the chapter. Finally, the assignment of a logical value to an integer or real variable — as well as the assignment of a numerical value to a logical variable — is, of course, not permissible.

15.6   Logical Expressions

A logical expression in Fortran is any combination of constants (numerical and logical), variables (integer, real, logical), and operation symbols that has as its value one of the two logical constants .TRUE. or .FALSE..

A logical expression can consist of a single logical constant, or a logical variable standing alone. Where operation symbols are present in a logical expression, they belong to either of two groups: *relational operators* and *logical operators*. We consider first simple logical expressions employing only relational operators.

Relational Operators

A relational operation is a mathematical relation used to make a comparison between numerical quantities. Such comparisons may be made in Fortran by means of the following six relational operators:

Symbol	.LT.	.LE.	.EQ.	.NE.	.GE.	.GT.
Meaning	less than	less than or equal to	equal to	not equal to	greater than or equal to	greater than

General Form

A.RO.B

where the dummy symbol .RO. represents the relational operators, and A and B denote any valid Fortran arithmetic expressions of the *same mode*, both integer or both real.

---

†See Chapter 14.

The value of the expression will be either .TRUE. or .FALSE., depending upon the comparison being made and the numerical values of A and B at the time of the comparison.

EXAMPLE 1

Fortran Expression	Mathematical Meaning
X.LT.Y+7.	$X < Y + 7$

This expression will have the value .TRUE. if the numerical value of X is less than the numerical value of $Y + 7$. Otherwise the value .FALSE. will be assigned if X is greater than or equal to $Y + 7$.

EXAMPLE 2

$$3.*Y+Z.GE.W+X/5. \qquad 3Y + Z \geq W + (X/5)$$

If $3Y + Z$ is greater than or equal to $W + (X/5)$, the logical constant .TRUE. is stored in the storage register having this expression as its symbolic address. If $3Y + Z$ is less than $W + (X/5)$, the value .FALSE. is stored in the register.

EXAMPLE 3

$$7.* X+5..LE.Y*Y \qquad 7X + 5 \leq Y^2$$

Observe that when a real constant immediately precedes a relational operator, two decimal points may occur in succession in the Fortran expression.

EXAMPLE 4

$$Z.LE.1 \qquad Z \leq 1$$

Assuming the integer mode is intended here, the expression is invalid unless a prior Type Declaration statement declares Z to be an integer variable.

Logical Operators

The second class of operation symbols that may occur in logical expressions is that of *logical operators*. A major function of these operations is to allow for the possibility of combining several propositions into a more complex logical expression. Thus, for the first time, it is possible to represent in a Fortran program the outcome of several comparisons by means of a single expression.

In order to meet these objectives, Fortran IV allows for the use of three logical operators corresponding to the basic Boolean operations of negation, logical addition, and logical multiplication. The forms in which these operators may appear in logical expressions are as follows:

.NOT.X   X.AND.Y   X.OR.Y

where X and Y are themselves logical expressions. Observe that, like the relational operators, these operators are always written with periods preceding and following the symbols.

The meanings attached to the logical operators are the same as the conventional meanings for the corresponding Boolean operations described at the beginning of this chapter. Thus, .NOT.X has the value .TRUE. only if X has the value .FALSE.. Otherwise .NOT.X has the value .FALSE..

X.AND.Y takes the value .TRUE. only if both X and Y have the value .TRUE.; and it has the value .FALSE. if either X or Y, or both, has the value .FALSE..

X.OR.Y is assigned the value .TRUE. if either X or Y, or both, has the value .TRUE.. X.OR.Y has the value .FALSE. only if both X and Y have the value .FALSE..

The logical operator .NOT. must always be followed by a logical expression to its right. If the expression to the right is other than a logical variable or constant, the expression must be enclosed within parentheses in order to indicate the scope of the expression to which the .NOT. operator applies. Being binary operations, the logical operators .AND. and .OR. must always be preceded and followed by logical expressions to form more complex expressions.

Precedence of Operators

As in arithmetic expressions, the order in which operators are evaluated in logical expressions also has an effect on the meaning or result of the evaluation. In the absence of parentheses the precise evaluation of a logical expression is obtained by the rule of precedence shown in Table 15.7, which establishes a ranking of arithmetical and logical operators for each compound expression. The priority scheme of Table 15.7 defines the rank of an operation with respect to a given combination. Since arithmetic operations and relations can appear in a logical expression, the rule is valid for any of the arithmetic operations discussed in Chapter 4 (see Section 4.11 for the ranking among these operations).

TABLE 15.7   Rule of Precedence for Arithmetic and Logical Operators

Rank	Operation Symbols
1	Arithmetic operators
2	.LT., .LE., .EQ., .NE., .GE., .GT.
3	.NOT.
4	.AND.
5	.OR.

In the absence of parentheses, or within parentheses, the operations are evaluated in sequence from the highest rank (smallest number) to the lowest rank (largest number). If consecutive operations have the same rank (excluding rank 1), the result of the evaluation is independent of the order in which the operations are evaluated. As in the case of arithmetic expressions, parentheses can be used to control the order of evaluation of the operations.

EXAMPLE 1

$$Y.LE.4..OR.5..LE.Y.AND.Y.EQ.6.$$

Boolean meaning: $Y \leq 4 + (5 \leq Y \cdot Y = 6)$. In the evaluation of this expression, $Y.LE.4.$, is evaluated and assigned one of the two logical constants .TRUE. or .FALSE.. Call this variable A. In similar fashion both 5..LE.Y and Y.EQ.6. are evaluated and assigned logical truth values. Call these variables B and C respectively. At this point the original expression is equivalent to

$$A.OR.B.AND.C$$

Expression B.AND.C is evaluated next (.AND. is of higher rank than .OR.) and assigned a logical value. Call this variable D. The original expression is thus reducible to

$$A.OR.D$$

which is finally evaluated and assigned the logical value .TRUE. or .FALSE..

EXAMPLE 2

$$(Y.LE.4.).OR.((5..LE.Y).AND.(Y.EQ.6.))$$

Boolean meaning: Same as Example 1. In this example parentheses are used to control the order of evaluation of the operators. However, it will be seen that the logical operations are evaluated in the same order as in the preceding example. Hence the two expressions have the same logical truth value.

EXAMPLE 3

$$(Y.LE.4..OR.5..LE.Y).AND.(Y.EQ.6.)$$

Boolean meaning: $(Y \leq 4 + 5 \leq Y) \cdot Y = 6$. Here the introduction of parentheses produces a different evaluation of the expression, namely

$$(A.OR.B).AND.C$$

The parentheses cause the evaluation of .OR. to precede that of .AND., thus overriding the normal ranking of the two operators. That this expression differs from the two preceding examples follows from the fact if Y is assigned the value 4. then the previous two expressions assume the value .TRUE., whereas this expression takes the value .FALSE..

15.7 *Logical Assignment Statements*

As discussed at the beginning of Chapter 5, the general form of the assignment statement is as shown below, where the equality symbol ($=$) denotes replacement, or assignment, rather than equality.

General Form

$$a = b$$

where a is a variable and b is any valid expression.

We now expand the definition of the assignment statement to include *logical statements* as well as arithmetic statements. The general form of a Fortran logical statement is as shown above, where a is any logical variable and b is any valid logical expression.

In the execution of a logical assignment statement the expression to the right of the equal sign is evaluated as being .TRUE. or .FALSE. and the value of the expression is stored in the register whose symbolic name is the logical variable appearing to the left of the equal sign. Unlike arithmetic statements, mixed modes are not permissible in logical statements in the sense that if the variable on the left side of the equal sign is of logical type, the expression on the right must be a logical expression. The expression may, of course, contain arithmetic expressions of different modes as components. However, the value of the overall expression on the right must be either .TRUE. or .FALSE. if the logical statement in which the expression appears is to be a valid assignment statement.

Examples of the Logical Assignment Statement

Assume that the following variables have the values indicated:

A = 2.	D = 2.5	I = 2
B = 5.	E = −4.	J = 3
C = 10.	F = .FALSE.	K = −2

The following are examples of logical statements and the value assigned to the variable whose name is to the left of the equal sign, as a result of evaluating the expression to the right of the equal sign. In the examples all logical variables are assumed to have been previously declared by a LOGICAL Type statement.

EXAMPLE 1

Fortran Statement	Value Stored After Execution of Statement
G = .TRUE.	.TRUE.

The logical constant .TRUE. is stored in G.

EXAMPLE 2

$$H = G.AND.F.OR..FALSE. \qquad .FALSE.$$

With the given value of F and the previously assigned value for G, the Boolean expression $(G \cdot F) + $ FALSE is evaluated as .FALSE. and the result is stored in the register called H.

EXAMPLE 3

$$Y3 = A**I + B.LE.B/C + D \qquad .FALSE.$$

The two arithmetic expressions $A^I + B$ and $B/C + D$ are first evaluated and assigned the numerical values 9.0 and 3.0 respectively. Since the statement "9.0 is less than or equal to 3.0" is false, the logical expression on the right of the equal sign is assigned the value .FALSE. and the result is stored in the register called Y3.

EXAMPLE 4

$$E1 = I**J + K.GE.E + C/D - A**J \qquad INVALID$$

The expression is invalid since arithmetic expressions of *different* modes may not be joined by a relational operator.

EXAMPLE 5

$$E2 = I/J.EQ.2 + K.AND.B/C + D.GE.E + C/D - A**J \qquad .TRUE.$$

Observe that arithmetic expressions of different modes may appear in a valid logical expression provided they are not joined by a relational operator. It should also be noted that the relational operator .EQ. should be used with caution, especially in the comparison of arithmetic expressions involving real variables and where the computation is done in binary.†

EXAMPLE 6

$$W4 = C**2. + D*E - 10.E + 02.LE.B + 2.*C.AND.(H.OR..NOT.Y3) \qquad .TRUE.$$

The expression on the right has the Boolean form $a \cdot (b + \bar{c})$. Since C**2. +D*E−10.E+02 has the numerical value −910.0 and B+2.*C has the

†The situation is similar to that discussed in Section 7.3 concerning the IF statement and inexact numbers.

value 25.0, a has the logical value .TRUE.. With the previously assigned logical values for H and Y3, $b + \bar{c}$ has the value .TRUE.. Hence, $a \cdot (b + \bar{c})$ assumes the value .TRUE., which is stored in the register called W4.

15.8   Input/Output of Logical Quantities

Up to this point the input and output of numerical and alphameric data only have been considered. With the use of the L specification, Fortran IV also provides for the input and output of logical data. This specification, which is used for the manipulation of logical data, has the general form

$$Lw$$

where w is an integer representing the width of the data field.

The effect of the Lw specification in a FORMAT statement depends on whether it is being used with an input or output statement. For input, the *first* T or F encountered in the w character field of the input record results in a value of .TRUE. or .FALSE., respectively, being assigned to the corresponding logical variable. If the field of width w consists entirely of blanks, a value of .FALSE. is assumed. If any character other than T, F, or blank is encountered in the input field *before* a T, F, or blank, an error occurs and an appropriate message is indicated. For output, $w - 1$ blanks precede the single character T or F, which is inserted is the output record for a corresponding logical variable with a value of .TRUE. or .FALSE. respectively.

EXAMPLE 1

<pre>
        READ 1, A,B,C,D
    1   FORMAT (L1,L5,2L3)
</pre>

Assume that A,B,C, and D are logical variables and that the data card is punched as follows:

TbbFTbbbbbbT

The following values are assigned:

<pre>
        A = True   C = False
        B = False   D = True
</pre>

EXAMPLE 2

<pre>
        LOGICAL S1, S2, S3, S4
    12 PRINT 13, X, Y, S1, S2, S3, S4
    13 FORMAT (3H X = F8.2,2X2HY = F8.2,2X3HS1 = L2,2X3HS2 =
        L2,2X3HS3 = L2,2X3HS4 = L2)
</pre>

The following output might result:

X = b2734.86bbY = bb − 47.94bbS1 = bTbbS2 = bFbbS3 = bFbbS4 = bT

The DATA declaration statement, discussed in Chapter 14, may also be used to introduce logical constants into a program at compilation time.

EXAMPLE 3†

LOGICAL PRED1, PRED2, S

DIMENSION S(4)

DATA PRED1,PRED2/F,T/,(S(I),I = 1,4)/4*F/

As a result of these statements, PRED1 is assigned the value .FALSE., PRED2 assigned the value .TRUE., and S(1) through S(4) are all assigned the value .FALSE.. If DATA defined variables are redefined during execution, the newly defined value will be assumed.

Although logical constants are represented by .TRUE. and .FALSE. in Fortran statements, and by T and F in input and output data, no such standard convention prevails for the internal representation of logical values. The form that the internal representations of .TRUE. and .FALSE. take depends on the particular computer as well as the individual processor program.

THE LOGICAL *IF* STATEMENT

In contrast with the arithmetic IF statement, discussed in Chapter 7, the logical IF statement permits the use of logical expressions in a conditional statement. Thus by means of the logical IF statement the outcome of several comparisons can be combined in a single logical expression and used to effect branching within a Fortran program.

General Form

IF (*l*) *s*

where *l* is a logical expression and *s* is any executable Fortran statement other than a DO statement or another logical IF statement.

The logical IF statement operates as follows:

1. The expression *l* is evaluated.

2. Depending upon the value of *l* one of the following two conditions occurs:

†Indexing in the DATA statement is permitted in some Fortran systems.

a) If the value of the logical expression *l* is .TRUE., statement *s* is executed and control then passes to the statement immediately following the
logical IF statement. However, if statement *s* is an arithmetic IF or GO TO
statement, control is transferred as indicated by *s*. And if *s* is a CALL
statement, control is transferred to the first statement after the logical
IF statement only upon return from the subprogram.

b) If the value of *l* is .FALSE., *s* is not executed and control passes
directly to the next statement following the logical IF statement.

EXAMPLE 1

$$\text{IF} \ (\text{C1.AND.X.NE.Y}) \ X = Y + 2.*C$$

$$W = A*A + B**2 - C**2$$

If the value of C1 is .TRUE. *and* the numerical value of X is not equal to Y,
$Y + 2C$ is evaluated and the result is stored in X, followed by the evaluation of $A^2 + B^2 - C^2$, etc. However, if either C1 is .FALSE. or $X = Y$, or
both, control passes immediately to $W = A*A + B**2 - C**2$ without $Y + 2.*C$ being evaluated and its value stored in X.

EXAMPLE 2

$$\text{IF} \ (3.*X + Y.LE.X + Z/3..OR.MAX) \ \text{GO TO} \ (14,16,42,9), I$$

$$8 \quad W2 = \text{EXP}(X/Y**3)$$

If either of two conditions is true — $3X + Y \leq X + Z/3$, or MAX has the
value .TRUE. — control is transferred to the statement whose number is the
k^{th} statement number in the GO TO list, where the value of I is k at the time
of execution. Otherwise control passes directly to the statement numbered 8.

To illustrate further the use of the logical IF statement, we consider the
three programs P7.2, P7.3, and P7.4 presented in Chapter 7 for summing
the positive integers 1–100. Using the logical IF statement, program P7.2
becomes

$$X = 1.$$

$$\text{SUM} = 0.$$

$$8 \quad \text{SUM} = \text{SUM} + X$$

$$X = X + 1.$$

$$\text{IF} \ (X.LE.100.) \ \text{GO TO} \ 8$$

CALL EXIT

END   (P15.1)

The logical IF statement provides for the termination of the program after the integers from zero to one hundred have been summed. When the value of X is 100. or less the expression X.LE.100. has the value .TRUE.. This results in the execution of the GO TO statement, which transfers control to the statement numbered 8. As long as X has the value 100. or less, its value must be added to SUM. However, when X assumes the value 101., the expression X.LE.100. takes the value .FALSE. for the first time, which results in the execution of the CALL EXIT statement without the GO TO statement being executed. Thus, although the final value of X is 101., this value is not added to the sum.

Program P7.3 can also be rewritten to include the logical IF rather than the arithmetic IF, as follows:

$$X = 1.$$
$$SUM = 0.$$
8   $$SUM = SUM + X$$
$$X = X + 1.$$
IF (X.LT.101.) GO TO 8

CALL EXIT

END   (P15.2)

Program 15.2 differs from program P15.1 in that the logical expression in the IF statement has been changed to X.LT.101.. Observe, however, that the two logical expressions X.LE.100. and X.LT.101. both assume the value .FALSE. for the first time when X takes the value 101..

It will be recalled that P7.4 differs from P7.2 and P7.3 in that in P7.4 the IF statement *precedes* the statement which increases the variable X. Using the logical IF statement, P7.4 becomes

$$X = 1.$$
$$SUM = 0.$$
8   $$SUM = SUM + X$$
IF (.NOT.(X.LT.100.)) GO TO 6
$$X = X + 1.$$
GO TO 8

6 CALL EXIT

END   (P15.3)

When X has the value 99. or less, the expression X.LT.100. is .TRUE. and .NOT.(X.LT.100.) is .FALSE.. This condition always results in control passing to the statement immediately following the logical IF statement without the execution of the GO TO 6 statement. As a result, the variable X is increased in value by one and the incremented value is added to SUM before it is compared with the constant 100.. Since the value of X is always added to SUM *before* X is incremented, when X assumes the value 100. the program should then terminate. Otherwise X would be increased to 101. in value, and this value also added to the sum. That the program does behave as described is evident from the fact that when the value of X is 100., the expression X. LT.100. is .FALSE. for the first time, making .NOT. (X.LT.100.) .TRUE., causing control to pass to the GO TO 6 statement which results in the termination of the program. Unlike P15.1 and P15.2, the final value assumed by the variable X in P15.3 is 100..

The following use of the logical IF statement illustrates a situation in which a single logical IF statement performs a function requiring the use of several arithmetic IF statements. Suppose input to a program consisted of daily transactions relating to ten different types of wheat. Each type is indicated by a code digit, 0–9. Further suppose that types coded 3,4,6,8 are fine-grain wheat and the remaining types coarse-grain. If it were required to compile data for these two groups (fine and coarse), the following logical IF statement could be used to distinguish between the two groups. Assume the variable I in the statement contains the code digit for the type of wheat.

IF (I.EQ.3.OR.I.EQ.4.OR.I.EQ.6.OR.I.EQ.8) GO TO 90

Statement 90 is executed next if the present data relate to a fine-grain wheat; otherwise, the next statement in sequence is executed.

Terminating the Range of a DO with a Logical IF Statement

In the discussion in Section 10.5 concerning the correct use of the DO statement, it was observed that the last statement in the range of a DO cannot be a transfer statement (Rule 4).

There is one exception to this rule. The range of a DO may end with a logical IF statement. In this case the expression *I* in the logical IF statement is evaluated, and depending upon the value of *I*, one of the following two conditions occurs:

a) If the value of the logical expression *I* is .TRUE., statement *s* of the logical IF statement is executed next, and then control is transferred to the first statement in the range of the DO. However, if *I* has the value .TRUE. and statement *s* is an arithmetic IF or GO TO statement, control is transferred as indicated by *s*.

b) If the value of *I* is .FALSE., *s* is not executed and control passes directly to the first statement in the range of the DO for a repeated execution.

APPLICATIONS

We conclude the chapter with a brief account of two programming examples. The examples are intended to illustrate, at a rudimentary level, several major applications of Boolean algebra.

15.9 Analysis and Synthesis of Switching Networks

A major application of Boolean algebra is in the logical design of digital computers. Because of the on-off nature of the electronic components used in digital computers and the fact that Boolean algebra is an algebra of two-valued functions, it is natural to use Boolean expressions to represent the logical structure of digital computers. Moreover, by using algebraic techniques it is not only possible to derive the expressions for realizing the desired logical design, but it is also possible to simplify the expressions, thereby reducing the number of electronic components needed to optimize the design.

There are a number of types of electronic components which physically realize the three basic Boolean operations of NOT, AND, and OR. With such devices logical values are represented by signal levels: a high voltage or current (H) on a signal line represents the logical value 1 (truth) and a low voltage or current (L) represents the logical value 0 (falsity). It is generally convenient to use block diagrams to depict the physical devices that perform the NOT, AND, and OR operations instead of reproducing the actual circuit diagram. The table of operations and block diagram symbol for a device that performs the NOT function are shown in Fig.15.1. If we repre-

INPUT LEVEL	OUTPUT LEVEL	INPUT VALUE	OUTPUT VALUE
X	$\bar{X}$	X	$\bar{X}$
L	H	0	I
H	L	I	0

$$X \longrightarrow\!\!\!\circ\longrightarrow \bar{X}$$

FIGURE 15.1   Table of operations and symbol for device performing the NOT function.

sent the input signal to the device by the logical variable X, then the expression for the output function may be written as $\bar{X}$.

Figure 15.2 shows a two-input AND gate that physically realizes the logical multiplication operation. The inputs to the device consist of signals designated as X and Y. A table of input levels and corresponding output levels is shown, along with a table of the truth values represented by these

INPUT LEVELS		OUTPUT LEVEL	INPUT VALUES		OUTPUT VALUE
X	Y	X·Y	X	Y	X·Y
L	L	L	0	0	0
L	H	L	0	I	0
H	L	L	I	0	0
H	H	H	I	I	I

FIGURE 15.2   Table of operations and symbol for AND gate.

signals. The block diagram symbol for the AND gate is also shown in Fig. 15.2.

Figure 15.3 shows a two-input OR gate that performs the logical addition

INPUT LEVELS		OUTPUT LEVEL	INPUT VALUES		OUTPUT VALUE
X	Y	X + Y	X	Y	X + Y
L	L	L	0	0	0
L	H	H	0	I	I
H	L	H	I	0	I
H	H	H	I	I	I

FIGURE 15.3   Table of operations and symbol for OR gate.

operation. The two input signals are again designated as X and Y. If either of the inputs represents a 1, the output will represent a 1. Tables of input/output levels and corresponding truth values are shown. Figure 15.3 also shows the block diagram symbol for the OR gate.

It is possible to form networks of circuits by connecting AND gates and OR gates and negating signal lines, and to represent the outputs of such networks by logical expressions. Figure 15.4 shows the outputs from three

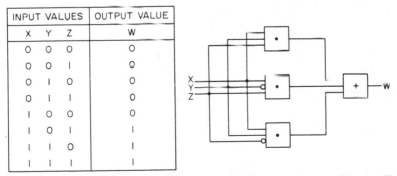

INPUT VALUES			OUTPUT VALUE
X	Y	Z	W
0	0	0	0
0	0	I	0
0	I	0	0
0	I	I	0
I	0	0	0
I	0	I	I
I	I	0	I
I	I	I	I

FIGURE 15.4   Table of operations and block diagram for $W = XYZ + X\bar{Y}Z + XY\bar{Z}$.

AND gates connected as inputs to an OR gate. There are three input signals to the circuit represented by variables X, Y, and Z, and a single output signal W. An examination of the circuit will indicate that the output will represent a 1 only when either X, Y, and Z together represent 1's, or when X and Z but not Y represent 1's, or when X and Y but not Z represent 1's. At all other times the output signal will represent a 0. The relationship between the inputs and output may be expressed by

$$W = XYZ + X\overline{Y}Z + XY\overline{Z}$$

Figure 15.4 also shows the table of operations associated with the circuit.

When a switching network is represented by a Boolean expression, it is possible to derive other equivalent Boolean representations of the network. Generally speaking, if such a Boolean representation contains fewer occurrences of variables or operators than the original expression, a corresponding reduction in the number of switching elements in the network may also be made. Minimization of switching networks by simplifying their Boolean representations constitutes an important application of Boolean algebra. The rules of Boolean algebra presented at the beginning of this chapter are useful for this purpose.

Consider the expression for the network shown in Fig. 15.4. This expression may be factored twice in accordance with the distributive law, giving

$$XYZ + X\overline{Y}Z + XY\overline{Z} = X(YZ + \overline{Y}Z + Y\overline{Z}) = X(Y(Z + \overline{Z}) + \overline{Y}Z)$$

Since $Z + \overline{Z} = 1$, the expression may be further reduced to

$$X(Y + \overline{Y}Z)$$

Applying the absorption law to $Y + \overline{Y}Z$ yields $Y + Z$. Thus the original expression finally reduces to the simplified form

$$X(Y + Z)$$

INPUT VALUES			OUTPUT VALUES	
X	Y	Z	Y + Z	X(Y + Z)
0	0	0	0	0
0	0	1	1	0
0	1	0	1	0
0	1	1	1	0
1	0	0	0	0
1	0	1	1	1
1	1	0	1	1
1	1	1	1	1

FIGURE 15.5 Table of operations and block diagram for the simplified network function $W = X(Y + Z)$.

Figure 15.5 shows the network corresponding to the simplified expression. That the simplified expression $X(Y + Z)$ and the original expression $XYZ + X\overline{Y}Z + XY\overline{Z}$ are equivalent, and hence the two networks shown in Figs. 15.4 and 15.5 are equivalent, can be established by the method of perfect induction. This consists in showing that the tables of truth values for the two expressions are identical, as can be seen from Figs. 15.4 and 15.5.

In the field of automated logical design, techniques for simulating the logical behavior of a network by means of a computer constitute an important application of switching algebra. As an illustration of how Boolean algebra can be applied to network simulation studies we shall consider a simple program for simulating the behavior of the network function $W = X(Y + Z)$. Every combination of values for the input variables is tested, and for each combination of values the program prints the values of the input variables and the resulting value of the output variable. If the output variable assumes a value of 1, a T is printed; otherwise an F is printed.

For the sake of convenience we let INPUT(1), INPUT(2), INPUT(3) and OUTPUT represent the variables X, Y, Z, and W, respectively. The program and output data are as follows:

```
      LOGICAL INPUT, OUTPUT
      DIMENSION INPUT(3)
      WRITE (6,30)
30    FORMAT (15H   X  Y  Z    W)
      DO 10 I=1,3
10    INPUT(I)=.FALSE.
      DO 22 I=1,2
      DO 21 J=1,2
      DO 20 K=1,2
      OUTPUT=INPUT(1).AND.(INPUT(2).OR.INPUT(3))
      WRITE (6,40) (INPUT(N),N=1,3),OUTPUT
40    FORMAT (1X3L3,2X,L3)
20    INPUT(3)=.NOT.INPUT(3)
21    INPUT(2)=.NOT.INPUT(2)
22    INPUT(1)=.NOT.INPUT(1)
      STOP
      END                                          (P15.4)
```

The output of P15.4 is as follows:

X	Y	Z	W
F	F	F	F
F	F	T	F
F	T	F	F
F	T	T	F
T	F	F	F
T	F	T	T
T	T	F	T
T	T	T	T

15.10   Derived Boolean Operations

In many applications of Boolean algebra it is often useful to be able to evaluate logical expressions containing Boolean operations other than negation, logical addition, and logical multiplication. We saw at the beginning of this chapter that it is possible to define any of the sixteen two-valued functions of two variables in terms of negation, logical addition, and logical multiplication. Among the derived Boolean operations, the more common ones are implication, equivalence, and exclusive disjunction. We shall concern ourselves here only with the operation of implication, which may be defined in terms of negation and logical multiplication as follows:

$$X \supset Y = \overline{(X \cdot \overline{Y})}$$

Table 15.8 establishes the validity of the above definition by perfect induction.

TABLE 15.8   Table of Truth Values for $X \supset Y = \overline{(X \cdot \overline{Y})}$

Values for Variables		Left Side of Equation	Right Side of Equation	
X	Y	$X \supset Y$	$(X \cdot \overline{Y})$	$\overline{(X \cdot \overline{Y})}$
0	0	1	0	1
0	1	1	0	1
1	0	0	1	0
1	1	1	0	1

As an illustration of how the Boolean operation of implication can be used in a computational process, we shall consider a simple program which evaluates the logical expression

$$(((X \supset Y) \supset X) \supset X)$$

This expression is known in the propositional calculus as Peirce's law and represents a logically true or valid principle of logic. This implies that for every combination of values which the variables of the expression may take, the value of the expression itself is always true. In evaluating Peirce's law the program makes use of a logical statement function to define the operation of implication. Again, for the sake of convenience we let S(1) and S(2) represent the variables X and Y, respectively, and the function name IMP in the program stands for the operation of implication. The program and output data follow.

```
      LOGICAL IMP, S, X, Y, W
      DIMENSION S(2)
      IMP( X,Y)=.NOT.( X.AND..NOT.Y)
      WRITE (6,30)
30    FORMAT (40H EVALUATION OF ((( X.IMP.Y).IMP. X).IMP.X)/
      15H   X   Y   F( X,Y))
      DO 10 I=1,2
10    S(I)=.FALSE.
      DO 21 I=1,2
      DO 20 J=1,2
      W = IMP(IMP(IMP(S(1),S(2)),S(1)),S(1))
      WRITE (6,40) (S(N),N=1,2),W
40    FORMAT (1X2L3,2X,L3)
20    S(2)=.NOT.S(2)
21    S(1)=.NOT.S(1)
      STOP
      END                                            (P15.5)
```

The output of P15.5 is as follows:

EVALUATION OF (((X.IMP.Y).IMP. X).IMP. X)

X	Y	F(X,Y)
F	F	T
F	T	T
T	F	T
T	T	T

Problems

15.1 Prove by perfect induction the associative laws, distributive laws, and laws of absorption of Section 15.2.

15.2 Find a value for Y which makes all three logical expressions at the end of Section 15.6 assume the value .TRUE..

15.3 The Fortran expressions at the end of Section 15.6 have the logical form

$$A + (B \cdot C)$$
$$(A + B) \cdot C$$

Show by perfect induction that no assignment of truth values to the variables A, B, C exists which makes $A + (B \cdot C)$ false and $(A + B) \cdot C$ true.

15.4 Write a simulation program to test the logical behavior of the network in Figure 15.6.

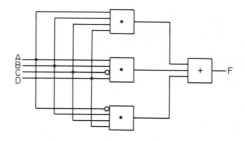

FIGURE 15.6

15.5 Find a simpler Boolean expression which is equivalent to the network function shown in Problem 15.4. Establish the equivalence of the two expressions by perfect induction.

15.6 What is the final value of the variable S(1) in program P15.4 (Section 15.9) when the program terminates?

15.7 Define the Boolean operations of exclusive disjunction and equivalence in terms of negation and logical multiplication. Write Fortran functions for these definitions.

15.8 Define logical multiplication in terms of negation and implication.

15.9   Write a Fortran program to evaluate

$$((A + B) \supset B) \supset (A \supset B)$$

15.10   Write a Fortran program to evaluate

$$(X \oplus Y) \supset \overline{(X \equiv Y)}$$

References

1.   BARTEE, T. C., I. L. LEBOW, and I. S. REED, *Theory and Design of Digital Machines*. New York: McGraw-Hill, Inc., 1962.

2.   HOHN, FRANZ E., *Applied Boolean Algebra, An Elementary Introduction*. New York: The Macmillan Company, 1960.

3.   LEDLEY, R. S., *Programming and Utilizing Digital Computers*. New York: McGraw-Hill, Inc., 1962.

16

Double Precision

In numerical computations it is often desirable to represent mathematical functions in terms of a series of simpler functions whose operations are amenable to analysis and evaluation by computers. For example, the exponential and sine functions may be expressed as follows:

$$e^x = 1 + x + \frac{x^2}{2!} + \frac{x^3}{3!} + \cdots + \frac{x^n}{n!} + \cdots$$

$$\sin x = x - \frac{x^3}{3!} + \frac{x^5}{5!} - \cdots + \frac{(-1)^n x^{2n+1}}{(2n+1)!} + \cdots$$

This technique of representing a function by expanding it in terms of what is called the Taylor series of the function is very useful. Yet it has certain inherent drawbacks. The ellipsis (...) following the expansion indicates that the series is *infinite* in the number of terms it has. This means that if the foregoing expansion formulas are used to evaluate the exponential or sine function (or any other function so represented), the value of the function can be computed *only approximately* but within a desired degree of accuracy. Thus, even though the numerical value of x itself may be exactly known, the computed value of the function e^x or $\sin x$, strictly speaking, will always be approximate. An error, however small, has been introduced into the computation.

It is common practice in numerical analysis to use approximation formulas, such as those just given, in computing many mathematical functions including the library functions first discussed in Chapter 5. The accuracy of methods based on these approximation techniques depends on many fac-

282

tors, and error analysis constitutes a large and vital topic in numerical analysis. It is outside the purpose of an elementary textbook on programming to consider any extensive treatment of this important subject. It must suffice here to consider only one major source of computing error — that resulting from round-off — and show how the effect of this error can be minimized by using double-precision calculations.

16.1 Double-Precision Variables and Expressions

We have seen that the computed values of many functions will be only approximations. So long as these values remain within desired ranges of accuracy, the fact that they contain slight errors is unimportant for it means that the magnitude of the error is small enough to cause no real concern.

It is clear that computer registers for storing numbers in computers are finite in size and that the number of significant digits that may be used in expressing a number is limited by the size of the registers. The computation errors that are caused by such limitations are called *round-off* errors.

If round-off errors prove troublesome, and no other means is available for resolving them, the problem can often be met by allocating more storage with which to represent the numbers being used in the computation. Thus, in many cases it may prove satisfactory simply to increase the precision with which the numbers being used are expressed. This can be done by allocating more storage to represent each number.

Fortran provides a facility for doing this by allowing for the declaration of certain variables to be double-precision variables. This is accomplished by means of a Type Declaration statement having the following general form:

General Form

DOUBLE PRECISION $a,b,c, . . .$

where $a,b,c, . . .$ are real variable or function names that appear within the program.

Observe that this Type Declaration statement is used only to declare *real* variables. Integer, complex, and logical variables cannot be declared to be double-precision variables. Thus, in a program, every real variable that has not been declared to be a double-precision variable may be viewed as being a single-precision variable. The effect of declaring a variable to be double precision is exactly as stated; it *doubles the precision* with which the value of the variable may be expressed. The programmer may interpret this to mean that now *twice* the number of significant digits is available to represent the value of the variable as is ordinarily the case with single-precision variables. The actual number of significant digits used to represent a real number depends, of course, on the individual computer and Fortran processor.

Double-precision variables may be combined in expressions with single-precision variables. Expressions involving double-precision quantities are formed according to the same rules presented in Chapter 5 for forming single-precision expressions. If any arithmetic expression contains a double-precision variable, the arithmetic expression itself is always a double-precision expression. In other words, the value of the expression itself is automatically calculated in double precision — that is, with twice the number of significant digits ordinarily used to represent the value of the expression.

16.2   Double-Precision Constants

Fortran provides the facility for designating constants to be double precision quantities. These constants have the following general form:

General Form

One to seventeen decimal digits written with a decimal point at the beginning, at the end, or between any two digits.

If the constant is negative it must be preceded by a minus sign; if the constant is positive a preceding plus sign is optional.

The constant may be followed by the letter D and an exponent in the form of a fixed-point constant indicating the power of ten by which the constant is to be multiplied.

When the constant consists of nine or fewer digits it *must* be followed by the letter D and an exponent (the exponent may be zero but not blank). A real constant of more than nine digits is automatically made a double-precision quantity, and use of the letter D is necessary only if the programmer wishes to use an exponent.

The decimal point may be omitted if the number is written with the D exponent. The position of the decimal point is considered to precede immediately the letter D.

Examples of Double-Precision Constants

8.12 D0

16754.981432

.17D−6

−9684.1235641D+02

86D1 (Stored as 860. in double-precision form)

Examples of Double Precision Constants Incorrectly Written

1.41D   (An integer exponent must follow the D.)

1987612321   (This is a fixed point constant,
not a double-precision constant.)

Examples of Double-Precision Expressions

Assume that the following Type Declaration statement applies to the subsequent three examples:

DOUBLE PRECISION A,B,C,D

EXAMPLE 1

$$A = B + C**2.31D1 - 4.2/X$$

The expression is evaluated in double-precision form, although the constant 4.2 and the variable X are single-precision quantities.

EXAMPLE 2

$$Y = A + B/C$$

The expression is evaluated in double-precision form, and the most significant digits are stored as the value of the single-precision variable Y.

EXAMPLE 3

$$A = (X + Y)**W$$

The expression is evaluated in single-precision form, and the result is converted to double precision and stored as the value of A.

16.3   Double-Precision Functions

Functions defined by function subprograms may have values which are double precision. The name of any double precision function called in a program must be included in a DOUBLE PRECISION statement in the calling program. Moreover, the first statement in the function subprogram defining a double-precision function must always have the following general form:

General Form

DOUBLE PRECISION FUNCTION *name* $(a,b,c, \ldots)$

where *name* is the function name, and $a,b,c, \ldots$ are the arguments of the function.

Example of a Double-Precision Function

DOUBLE PRECISION FUNCTION DET (N, M, X)

Library Functions

The library functions — sine, cosine, arctangent, logarithm, exponential, square root, etc. — are also available as double-precision functions. They are usually designated by prefixing the letter D to their names, as follows:

DSIN	DATAN	DLOG	DEXP
DCOS	DATAN2	DLOG10	DSQRT

The arguments of these functions must have double-precision values, and the value returned by the function is double precision. Certain built-in functions are double-precision functions. These are listed in Table 11.2. Among them is DBLE, a single-argument function that expresses a single-precision argument in double-precision form and DABS which evaluates the absolute value of a double-precision quantity.

16.4 Input/Output of Double-Precision Constants

Input/output of double-precision constants is similar to that of single-precision constants except that the D specification is used in the FORMAT statement for the input/output of double-precision quantities. The general form of the D specification is

$$Dw.d$$

where w designates an integer specifying complete field width including sign, decimal point, a minimum of one place to the left of the decimal point, and a four-digit exponent; d is an integer designating the number of places to the right of the decimal point.

This specification is analogous to the E specification for single-precision numbers. The basic difference is in output form: with the D specification the exponent is preceded by the letter D rather than the letter E.

D Specification for Input

The w characters on the input record are converted to a double-precision number and stored in the double-precision variable whose name appears in the list.

EXAMPLE 1

READ 7,Y

7 FORMAT (D18.8)

Assume that Y is the name of a double-precision variable and that the data card is punched as follows:

$$-75112971.28175562$$

The most significant and least significant digits of this number are stored in two adjacent storage registers which have the name Y.

EXAMPLE 2

READ 1,A

1 FORMAT (D8.2)

Assume that A is the name of a double-precision variable and that the data card is punched as follows:

12361.13

The input quantity is stored in double-precision form in two adjacent registers which have the name A.

D Specification for Output

The double-precision number whose name appears in the list is written on the output medium.

EXAMPLE

PRINT 30,A,B,C

30 FORMAT (1XD24.16/1XD11.4/1XD16.9)

The following lines of output might result:

ჼ−0.1952674388541925Dჼ05

ჼ0.2167D−02

−0.174127542Dჼ05

Problems

16.1 Assume that the formula shown below is used in computing the value of cos x for predetermined values of x. Discuss the various ways in which errors may be introduced into the computation.

$$\cos x = 1 - \frac{x^2}{2!} + \frac{x^4}{4!} - \frac{x^6}{6!} + \cdots + \frac{(-1)^n x^{2n}}{(2n!)} + \cdots$$

16.2 Show by an example how round-off error can produce incorrect results with the use of the arithmetic IF statement. Can this situation be remedied by using double-precision variables?

16.3 $a)$ Write a Fortran program using single-precision arithmetic to invert a 10×10 matrix. As input data, use the Hilbert matrix of order 10. This will be a 10×10 matrix whose elements are defined by

$$a_{ij} = \frac{1}{i + j - 1}$$

$b)$ Write the above program using double-precision calculations and compare the results.

17

Complex Arithmetic

In addition to facilities for doing arithmetic using integer and real numbers, some Fortran systems provide for the calculation of arithmetic expressions involving complex numbers. This chapter briefly introduces the subject of complex arithmetic and describes the rules available in Fortran for performing operations on complex quantities. Discussion of complex arithmetic will be at an elementary level.

17.1 Complex Numbers

All complex numbers have an imaginary component represented by the letter i, which is defined by the following relation,

$$i^2 = -1$$

If x and y are real numbers, $x + iy$ is called a *complex number;* x is its *real part* and iy is its *imaginary part.*

Addition, subtraction, multiplication, and division of complex numbers are described by the following. If we let $z_1 = x_1 + iy_1$ and $z_2 = x_2 + iy_2$, then

$$z_1 \pm z_2 = (x_1 \pm x_2) + i(y_1 \pm y_2)$$

$$z_1 \times z_2 = (x_1 x_2 - y_1 y_2) + i(x_1 y_2 + x_2 y_1)$$

$$\frac{z_1}{z_2} = \frac{(x_1 x_2 + y_1 y_2) + i(x_2 y_1 - x_1 y_2)}{x_2{}^2 + y_2{}^2} \qquad (z_2 \neq 0)$$

The complex number $z = x + iy$ can be represented by the vector (x, y). The length of the vector (x, y) is called the *absolute value* of z and is written

$|z|$. In terms of a graph, the length of the vector (x, y) is the distance of the point (x, y) from the origin $(0, 0)$. Thus $|z| = \sqrt{x^2 + y^2}$.

If $z = x + iy$, the number $x - iy$ is called the *complex conjugate* of z and is denoted by $\bar{z}$. Observe that

$$\overline{z_1 \times z_2} = \bar{z}_1 \times \bar{z}_2$$

$$\overline{z_1 + z_2} = \bar{z}_1 + \bar{z}_2$$

$$\bar{\bar{z}} = z$$

$$|z^2| = z \times \bar{z}$$

The following simple but important inequalities hold for complex numbers:

(1) $|x| \leq |z|$ and $|y| \leq |z|$

where $z = x + iy$, and x and y are real.

(2) $|z_1 + z_2| \leq |z_1| + |z_2|$

where z_1 and z_2 are complex numbers.

17.2   Fortran Representation of Complex Expressions

Complex variables are assigned Fortran names in the same general manner as integer or real variables. That is, a complex variable is named by assigning to it a maximum of six alphameric characters provided the first character is always alphabetic. However, since arithmetic operations on complex variables produce results that are different from those produced by integer or real arithmetic, it is necessary always to declare complex variables by means of a Type Declaration statement, whose general form is as follows:

General Form

COMPLEX $a,b,c, \ldots$

where $a,b,c, \ldots$ are variable or function names appearing within the program.

Complex variables may be subscripted and indexed in exactly the same manner as integer and real variables. Finally, the numerical values which complex variables may take are represented by the assignment of an ordered pair of real constants separated by a comma and enclosed in parentheses. Thus, for instance, if Z is declared to be a complex variable, a possible value which may be assigned to Z would be

$$(2.6, \ 7.)$$

COMPLEX ARITHMETIC

representing the complex number $2.6 + 7i$. Other examples of complex constants are the following:

$$(4.7, -3.46) \quad \text{representing } 4.7 - 3.46i$$
$$(8.2, 0.0) \quad \text{representing } 8.2 + 0.0i$$
$$(7.6E02, 4.35) \quad \text{representing } 760. + 4.35i$$

The parentheses enclosing the ordered pair of real constants are required regardless of the context in which the complex constant appears.

EXAMPLE

$$Y = \text{CSQRT}((4.0, +8.23))$$
$$X = Y + (2.0, -1.2)$$
$$Z = (2.0, 3.5)$$

A complex expression in Fortran is any combination of real constants, real or complex variables, and arithmetic operation symbols that has as its assigned value an ordered pair of real constants. Integer constants and variables may appear in complex expressions only as subscripts or exponents. Real or complex expressions may not appear as exponents of complex expressions; only integer quantities may so appear. Otherwise, complex expressions are formed in a manner entirely analogous to that of forming real expressions.

However, the way real and complex expressions may appear in arithmetic statements is another matter. If the variable to the left of the equality symbol is a real or integer variable, then the expression on the right cannot be a complex expression, it must be a real or integer or double-precision expression. And in similar fashion, if the variable to the left of the equal sign is a complex variable, the expression on the right cannot be an integer or double-precision expression; it must be a complex or real expression. For example, assume that the two sets of variables

$$\text{REAL} \quad \text{B, C, E, R, X}$$
$$\text{COMPLEX} \quad \text{A, D, W, Y}$$

have been declared to be of real and complex types, respectively. Then the following are valid Fortran arithmetic statements:

$$Y = B/C + D$$
$$X = (-B + (B^{**}2 - 4.^{*}R^{*}C)^{**}.5)/(2.^{*}R)$$
$$W = C^{**}2. + B^{*}E - 10.E + 02$$

However, the following expression is invalid:

$$R = E + C/D - A^{**}J$$

Complex variables may not be used in either the arithmetic IF statement or the logical IF statement. The arithmetic IF statement may not contain a complex expression and complex expressions may not be used with the following relational operators:

.LT.   .LE.   .EQ.   .NE.   .GE.   .GT.

Table 17.1 describes the library functions available for use with complex variables. Observe that the values of complex functions can be made real and the values of real functions can be made complex by the use of the built-in functions REAL, AIMAG, and CMPLX included in Table 11.2.

TABLE 17.1   Library Functions for Complex Variables $Z = X + iY$

Function Definition	Function Name	Number of Arguments	Function Type	Argument Type
$F = CABS(Z)$, where $F = \sqrt{X^2 + Y^2}$	CABS	1	Real	Complex
$F = CSQRT (Z)$, where $F = \sqrt{Z}$	CSQRT	1	Complex	Complex
$F = CEXP(Z)$, where $F = e^z$	CEXP	1	Complex	Complex
$F = CLOG(Z)$, where $F = \log_e Z$	CLOG	1	Complex	Complex
$F = CSIN(Z)$, where $F = \sin Z$	CSIN	1	Complex	Complex
$F = CCOS(Z)$ where $F = \cos Z$	CCOS	1	Complex	Complex

Table 17.2 summarizes the allowable combinations of types of variables and expressions appearing in the assignment statement.

TABLE 17.2   Allowable Forms of the Assignment Statement

Variable on Left Side of Equals Sign	Expression on Right Side of Equals Sign				
	Real	Integer	Complex	Double-Precision	Logical
Real	Yes	Yes	No	Yes	No
Integer	Yes	Yes	No	Yes	No
Complex	Yes	No	Yes	No	No
Double-Precision	Yes	Yes	No	Yes	No
Logical	No	No	No	No	Yes

17.3   Input/Output of Complex Numbers

The input/output of complex numbers is similiar to that of real numbers, except that each complex quantity consists of two distinct real numbers. Therefore, when it is desired to read or write a complex number two successive FORMAT specifications are required for each number to be processed. The specifications may be of either the E or F type. In fact, for a single complex number, one E type and one F type specification may be used.

EXAMPLE 1

PRINT 7,X,Y,Z

7 FORMAT (1X2E15,8,F10.2,E10.3,F12.4,F10.2)

Assuming the variables X, Y, and Z are names of complex quantities, the two real numbers comprising the complex number stored in X would both be written according to the format E15.8. The two real numbers making up the complex number stored in Y would be written according to the specifications F10.2 and E10.3 respectively. Finally, the two real numbers comprising the complex number stored in Z would be written according to the specifications F12.4 and F10.2 respectively. Assuming the following values for X, Y, and Z:

$$X = 204.16 + 2.2i$$

$$Y = 16.4 + 10.5i$$

$$Z = 1.542 + 120.i$$

The output line would be

b0.20416000Eb03b0.22000000Eb01bbbbb16.40b0.105Eb02bbbbbb1.5420bb
bb120.00

EXAMPLE 2

READ 6,X

6 FORMAT (F5.1,F7.2)

Assume that X is the name of a complex quantity and the data card is punched as follows:

$$-12.5b165.10$$

The complex number stored in X is $-12.5 + 165.10i$.

The DATA declaration statement, discussed in Section 14.4, may also be used to introduce complex numbers into a program.

EXAMPLE 3

COMPLEX ROOT

DIMENSION ROOT(3)

DATA (ROOT(I), I = 1,3)/(1.0,0.),(0.,1.0),(−1.0,0.)/

As a result of the foregoing statements, the following assignments of values are made at the time of compilation:

ROOT(1) = 1.0

ROOT(2) = i

ROOT(3) = −1.0

Problems

17.1 Assume that C1, C2, C3 and C4 are complex variables and R1, R2, R3 and R4 are real variables. Determine which of the following arithmetic statements are valid. State the reasons for your answers.

a) C2 = R3

b) C1 = R1*C2+R2**C3+R4

c) C4 = C2**I+R1*R2

d) R1 = R2+(R3+R4)**2

e) C3 = R1+R2*R3/R4

f) R2 = C2+R1+R3+R4

17.2 Given that $X = 2.5 + 4i$, $Y = i$, and $Z = 14.0$, write a Fortran program to compute the complex conjugate of $X + YZ$.

17.3 Based on the following statements, what assignments of values will be made to G and DET at the time of compilation?

> COMPLEX G,DET
>
> DIMENSION DET(2)
>
> DATA G,(DET(I),I=1,2)/3*(1.0,0.)/

17.4 Write a Fortran program to read the values for A, B, and C indicated below and compute X, where

$$X = A - B - C \quad \text{if} \quad (A + B) < C$$
$$X = A + (B \times C) \quad \text{if} \quad (A + B) = C$$
$$X = A^2 + B^2 + C^2 \quad \text{if} \quad (A + B) > C$$

for $A = 3.0 + 2.5i$, $B = 2.1 + 7.4i$, and $C = 3i$. Print A, B, C, and X.

18

Fortran Programs and Problems

This chapter is divided into two sections. The first consists of ten problems that have been programmed in Fortran. Flowcharts have been included with most of these problems. The programs contain many comment statements, which should aid the reader in understanding the program. The problems were chosen to illustrate the use of the Fortran language and to demonstrate some of the programming techniques useful for problem solving. The second section consists of fifteen problems which have not been programmed. They are presented as exercises for the reader.

PROGRAMMED FORTRAN PROBLEMS

Problem 18.1

Write a Fortran program to generate a table of values. Each line of the table consists of a value of X, $\sqrt{X}$, $\sqrt[3]{X}$, $\log_{10} X$, $\log_e X$, and X^2. A card is to be read with an initial value of X ($X > 0$) punched in columns 1–6, a terminal value of X punched in columns 11–16 and an increment punched in columns 21–26, all in F6.2 format.

Commentary on Program 18.1

Often the output of a program requires more than one printed page. It is the responsibility of the programmer to provide for skipping to a new page and printing the headings. Program 18.1 provides for printing fifty lines of the table on a single page and then skipping to the next page.

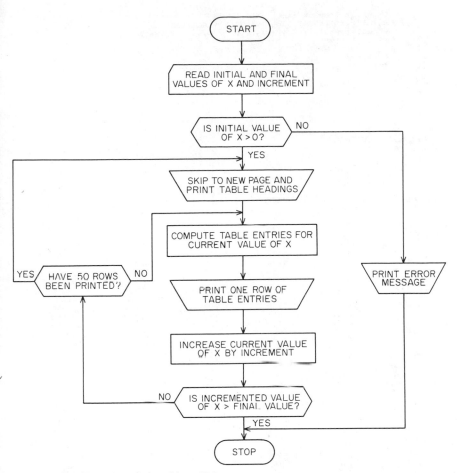

FIGURE 18.1   Flowchart for Problem 18.1.

```
C       READ FIRST VALUE OF X,THE TERMINAL VALUE OF X,AND THE INCREMENT.
C       TEST FOR NEGATIVE OR ZERO VALUE OF X.
        READ 1,XST,XFIN,XINC
      1 FORMAT(F6.2,4XF6.2,4XF6.2)
C       TEST FOR NEGATIVE VALUE OF X.
        IF(XST) 5,5,3
C       N IS USED TO CONTROL THE NUMBER OF LINES PRINTED ON A PAGE.
      3 N=0
C       PRINT HEADINGS AND SKIP THE NEXT LINE.
        PRINT 10
     10 FORMAT(1H14X1HX5X9HSQ.RT.(X)2X11HCUBE RT.(X)2X10HLOG 10 (X)4X9IILOG
      1 E (X)7X9HX SQUARED/)
C       COMPUTE ENTRIES FOR TABLE.
      7 XSQRT=SQRT(XST)
        XCUBRT=XST**.33333333
        XLOG1C=ALOG10(XST)
        XLOGE=ALOG(XST)
        XSQ=XST*XST
```

FIGURE 18.2   Program for Problem 18.1

```
C      PRINT ONE ROW OF TABLE ENTRIES.
       PRINT 2,XST,XSQRT,XCUBRT,XLOG10,XLOGE,XSQ
    2 FORMAT(1XF8.3,1XF9.4,3XF9.4,4XF9.4,3XF9.4,4XF12.3)
       XST=XST+XINC
C      TEST TO FIND IF TABLE IS COMPLETE.
       IF(XST-XFIN) 6,6,4
C      SKIP TO NEW PAGE AND PRINT HEADING IF 50 LINES HAVE BEEN PRINTED.
    6 N=N+1
       IF(N-50)7,3,3
    5 PRINT 11
   11 FORMAT(1H041HTHE VALUE OF X MUST BE GREATER THAN ZERO.)
    4 CALL EXIT
       END
```

FIGURE 18.2 Continued

005.00   050.00   000.50

FIGURE 18.3 Input data for Problem 18.1

X	SQ.RT.(X)	CUBE RT.(X)	LOG 10 (X)	LOG E (X)	X SQUARED
5.000	2.2361	1.7100	0.6990	1.6094	25.000
5.500	2.3452	1.7652	0.7404	1.7047	30.250
6.000	2.4495	1.8171	0.7782	1.7918	36.000
6.500	2.5495	1.8663	0.8129	1.8718	42.250
7.000	2.6458	1.9129	0.8451	1.9459	49.000
7.500	2.7386	1.9574	0.8751	2.0149	56.250
8.000	2.8284	2.0000	0.9031	2.0794	64.000
8.500	2.9155	2.0408	0.9294	2.1401	72.250
9.000	3.0000	2.0801	0.9542	2.1972	81.000
9.500	3.0822	2.1179	0.9777	2.2513	90.250
10.000	3.1623	2.1544	1.0000	2.3026	100.000
10.500	3.2404	2.1898	1.0212	2.3514	110.250
11.000	3.3166	2.2240	1.0414	2.3979	121.000
11.500	3.3912	2.2572	1.0607	2.4423	132.250
12.000	3.4641	2.2894	1.0792	2.4849	144.000
12.500	3.5355	2.3208	1.0969	2.5257	156.250
13.000	3.6056	2.3513	1.1139	2.5649	169.000
13.500	3.6742	2.3811	1.1303	2.6027	182.250
14.000	3.7417	2.4101	1.1461	2.6391	196.000
14.500	3.8079	2.4385	1.1614	2.6741	210.250
15.000	3.8730	2.4662	1.1761	2.7081	225.000
15.500	3.9370	2.4933	1.1903	2.7408	240.250
16.000	4.0000	2.5198	1.2041	2.7726	256.000
16.500	4.0620	2.5458	1.2175	2.8034	272.250
17.000	4.1231	2.5713	1.2304	2.8332	289.000
17.500	4.1833	2.5962	1.2430	2.8622	306.250
18.000	4.2426	2.6207	1.2553	2.8904	324.000
18.500	4.3012	2.6448	1.2672	2.9178	342.250
19.000	4.3589	2.6684	1.2788	2.9444	361.000
19.500	4.4159	2.6916	1.2900	2.9704	380.250
20.000	4.4721	2.7144	1.3010	2.9957	400.000
20.500	4.5277	2.7369	1.3118	3.0204	420.250
21.000	4.5826	2.7589	1.3222	3.0445	441.000
21.500	4.6368	2.7806	1.3324	3.0681	462.250
22.000	4.6904	2.8020	1.3424	3.0910	484.000
22.500	4.7434	2.8231	1.3522	3.1135	506.250
23.000	4.7958	2.8439	1.3617	3.1355	529.000
23.500	4.8477	2.8643	1.3711	3.1570	552.250
24.000	4.8990	2.8845	1.3802	3.1781	576.000
24.500	4.9497	2.9044	1.3892	3.1987	600.250
25.000	5.0000	2.9240	1.3979	3.2189	625.000
25.500	5.0498	2.9434	1.4065	3.2387	650.250
26.000	5.0990	2.9625	1.4150	3.2581	676.000
26.500	5.1478	2.9814	1.4232	3.2771	702.250
27.000	5.1962	3.0000	1.4314	3.2958	729.000
27.500	5.2440	3.0184	1.4393	3.3142	756.250
28.000	5.2915	3.0366	1.4472	3.3322	784.000
28.500	5.3385	3.0546	1.4548	3.3499	812.250
29.000	5.3852	3.0723	1.4624	3.3673	841.000
29.500	5.4314	3.0899	1.4698	3.3844	870.250

FIGURE 18.4 Output for Problem 18.1

X	SQ.RT.(X)	CUBE RT.(X)	LOG 10 (X)	LOG E (X)	X SQUARED
30.000	5.4772	3.1072	1.4771	3.4012	900.000
30.500	5.5227	3.1244	1.4843	3.4177	930.250
31.000	5.5678	3.1414	1.4914	3.4340	961.000
31.500	5.6125	3.1582	1.4983	3.4500	992.250
32.000	5.6569	3.1748	1.5051	3.4657	1024.000
32.500	5.7009	3.1913	1.5119	3.4812	1056.250
33.000	5.7446	3.2075	1.5185	3.4965	1089.000
33.500	5.7879	3.2237	1.5250	3.5115	1122.250
34.000	5.8310	3.2396	1.5315	3.5264	1156.000
34.500	5.8737	3.2554	1.5378	3.5410	1190.250
35.000	5.9161	3.2711	1.5441	3.5553	1225.000
35.500	5.9582	3.2866	1.5502	3.5695	1260.250
36.000	6.0000	3.3019	1.5563	3.5835	1296.000
36.500	6.0415	3.3171	1.5623	3.5973	1332.250
37.000	6.0828	3.3322	1.5682	3.6109	1369.000
37.500	6.1237	3.3472	1.5740	3.6243	1406.250
38.000	6.1644	3.3620	1.5798	3.6376	1444.000
38.500	6.2048	3.3767	1.5855	3.6507	1482.250
39.000	6.2450	3.3912	1.5911	3.6636	1521.000
39.500	6.2849	3.4056	1.5966	3.6763	1560.250
40.000	6.3246	3.4200	1.6021	3.6889	1600.000
40.500	6.3640	3.4341	1.6075	3.7013	1640.250
41.000	6.4031	3.4482	1.6128	3.7136	1681.000
41.500	6.4420	3.4622	1.6180	3.7257	1722.250
42.000	6.4807	3.4760	1.6232	3.7377	1764.000
42.500	6.5192	3.4898	1.6284	3.7495	1806.250
43.000	6.5574	3.5034	1.6335	3.7612	1849.000
43.500	6.5955	3.5169	1.6385	3.7728	1892.250
44.000	6.6332	3.5303	1.6435	3.7842	1936.000
44.500	6.6708	3.5437	1.6484	3.7955	1980.250
45.000	6.7082	3.5569	1.6532	3.8067	2025.000
45.500	6.7454	3.5700	1.6580	3.8177	2070.250
46.000	6.7823	3.5830	1.6628	3.8286	2116.000
46.500	6.8191	3.5960	1.6675	3.8395	2162.250
47.000	6.8557	3.6088	1.6721	3.8501	2209.000
47.500	6.8920	3.6216	1.6767	3.8607	2256.250
48.000	6.9282	3.6342	1.6812	3.8712	2304.000
48.500	6.9642	3.6468	1.6857	3.8816	2352.250
49.000	7.0000	3.6593	1.6902	3.8918	2401.000
49.500	7.0356	3.6717	1.6946	3.9020	2450.250
50.000	7.0711	3.6840	1.6990	3.9120	2500.000

FIGURE 18.4 Continued

Problem 18.2

Fifty numbers are punched five per card in 5F8.2 format. Write a Fortran program to determine how many of the numbers are between 25.5 and 26.0 inclusive.

```
      DIMENSION X(5)
C     INITIALIZE COUNTER TO ZERO.
      KOUNT=0
C     DO STATEMENT CONTROLS THE NUMBER OF DATA CARDS READ.
      DO 8 I=1,10
C     INPUT QUANTITIES ON A CARD ARE TREATED AS ELEMENTS OF AN ARRAY.
      READ 1,(X(K),K=1,5)
    1 FORMAT(5F8.2)
C     FOLLOWING DO STATEMENT PROVIDES FOR PROCESSING 5 NUMBERS PER CARD.
      DO 8 J=1,5
C     TEST TO DETERMINE IF NUMBER BETWEEN 25.5 AND 26.0 INCLUSIVE.
      IF(X(J)-25.5)8,7,9
    9 IF(X(J)-26.0)7,7,8
    7 KOUNT=KOUNT+1
    8 CONTINUE
      PRINT 2,KOUNT
    2 FORMAT(1H1I3,2X43HNUMBERS ARE BETWEEN 25.5 AND 26.0 INCLUSIVE)
      CALL EXIT
      END
```

FIGURE 18.5 Program for Problem 18.2

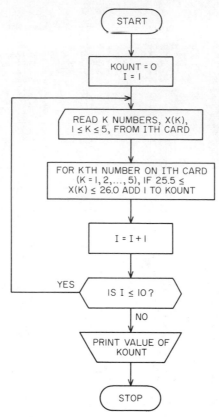

FIGURE 18.6 Flowchart for Problem 18.2

```
00025.8200038.2100025.5000028.1200028.00
00031.0900026.1000025.1800038.12  -25.00
00027.0000025.72  -26.00   -0.0100025.60
00040.20  -25.62  -25.49  +25.5000025.75
  -25.1000024.9500025.4900061.9800026.21
  +25.2300024.9600025.2100125.1200025.08
00000.0000025.2800026.0100225.6200025.01
  -2.1800025.6100026.0000725.8100025.51
00025.99  -25.9900025.2000067.19  -25.00
00026.00  -26.2000025.1900038.62  -25.99
```

FIGURE 18.7 Input data for Problem 18.2

```
11  NUMBERS ARE BETWEEN 25.5 AND 26.0 INCLUSIVE
```

FIGURE 18.8 Output for Problem 18.2

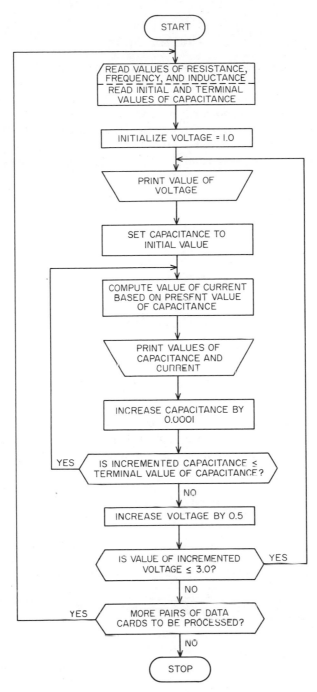

FIGURE 18.9 Flowchart for Problem 18.3

Problem 18.3

Write a program to determine the current in an a-c circuit consisting of a resistance, an inductance, and a capacitance, having been given a number of sets of values of resistance, inductance, and frequency as input data. The current is to be determined for a number of equally spaced values of the capacitance (which lie between specified limits which are input data) for voltages of 1.0, 1.5, 2.0, 2.5, and 3.0 volts. The increment for the capacitance is 0.0001. The equation for determining the current flowing through such a circuit is

$$I = \frac{E}{\sqrt{R^2 + \left(2\pi FL - \dfrac{1}{2\pi FC}\right)^2}}$$

where I = current $\quad L$ = inductance

E = voltage $\quad C$ = capacitance

R = resistance $\quad F$ = frequency.

The input data cards are punched as follows:

Card 1: A value of resistance, inductance, and frequency are punched in 3F9.4 format.

Card 2: The initial and terminal limits of the capacitance are punched in 2F8.5 format.

The input consists of sets of the two cards just described. The last set of data cards is followed by a card with 99999999. punched in columns 1–9. No data card has this number punched in columns 1–9.

```
      REAL IND
C     READ VALUES OF RESISTANCE, INDUCTANCE, AND FREQUENCY.
    7 READ 1,RES,IND,FREQ
    1 FORMAT(3F9.4)
C     TEST FOR END OF DATA.
      IF(RES-99999999.)9,15,9
C     READ INITIAL AND TERMINAL VALUES OF CAPACITANCE.
    9 READ 2, CAP1,CAPF
    2 FORMAT(2F8.5)
C     PRINT PAGE HEADINGS.
      PRINT 20,RES,IND,FREQ
   20 FORMAT(50H1DETERMINING THE CURRENT IN AN A.C. CIRCUIT WHERE //1X12
     1HRESISTANCE =F10.4,5X12HINDUCTANCE =F10.4,5X11HFREQUENCY =F10.4//)
C     INITIALIZE VOLTAGE.
      E=1.0
    5 PRINT 10,E
   10 FORMAT(10HOVOLTAGE =F4.1,8X4HCAP.7X7HCURRENT)
C     INITIALIZE CAPACITANCE.
      CAP=CAP1
C     COMPUTE THE CURRENT.
    4 CURR=E/SQRT(RES**2+(6.2832*FREQ*IND-1./(6.2832*FREQ*CAP))**2)
```

FIGURE 18.10 Program for Problem 18.3

```
C      PRINT VALUES OF CAPACITANCE AND CURRENT.
       PRINT 3,CAP,CURR
     3 FORMAT(17XF10.4,3XF11.6)
C      INCREASE THE CAPACITANCE.
       CAP=CAP+.0001
C      TEST FOR CAPACITANCE EXCEEDING ITS TERMINATING VALUE.
       IF(CAP-CAPF)4,4,6
C      INCREASE THE VOLTAGE.
     6 E=E+.5
C      TEST FOR VOLTAGE EXCEEDING 3.0.
       IF(E-3.01)5,7,7
    15 CALL EXIT
       END
```

FIGURE 18.10 Continued

```
                        100.        .005   60.
                         .00050   .00100
                       99999999.
```
FIGURE 18.11 Input data for Problem 18.3

```
DETERMINING THE CURRENT IN AN A.C. CIRCUIT WHERE

RESISTANCE =  100.0000      INDUCTANCE =   0.0050      FREQUENCY =  60.0000


VOLTAGE = 1.0       CAP.        CURRENT
                    0.0005      0.009994
                    0.0006      0.009997
                    0.0007      0.009998
                    0.0008      0.009999
                    0.0009      0.009999
                    0.0010      0.010000

VOLTAGE = 1.5       CAP.        CURRENT
                    0.0005      0.014991
                    0.0006      0.014995
                    0.0007      0.014997
                    0.0008      0.014998
                    0.0009      0.014999
                    0.0010      0.015000

VOLTAGE = 2.0       CAP.        CURRENT
                    0.0005      0.019988
                    0.0006      0.019994
                    0.0007      0.019996
                    0.0008      0.019998
                    0.0009      0.019999
                    0.0010      0.019999

VOLTAGE = 2.5       CAP.        CURRENT
                    0.0005      0.024985
                    0.0006      0.024992
                    0.0007      0.024995
                    0.0008      0.024997
                    0.0009      0.024999
                    0.0010      0.024999

VOLTAGE = 3.0       CAP.        CURRENT
                    0.0005      0.029982
                    0.0006      0.029990
                    0.0007      0.029995
                    0.0008      0.029997
                    0.0009      0.029998
                    0.0010      0.029999
```
FIGURE 18.12 Output for Problem 18.3

Problem 18.4

Write a program to evaluate the correlation coefficient given by

$$r = \frac{n \sum_{i=1}^{n} x_i y_i - \sum_{i=1}^{n} x_i \sum_{i=1}^{n} y_i}{\sqrt{\left[n \sum_{i=1}^{n} x_i^2 - \left(\sum_{i=1}^{n} x_i\right)^2\right]\left[n \sum_{i=1}^{n} y_i^2 - \left(\sum_{i=1}^{n} y_i\right)^2\right]}}$$

Each data card has a value of X and the corresponding value of Y punched in 2F8.3 format. The data cards are followed by a card with 9999999. punched in columns 1–8. No data card has this value punched in columns 1–8. Print the value of r and the value of n.

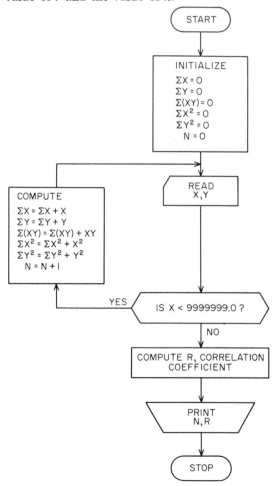

FIGURE 18.13 Flowchart for Problem 18.4

```
C      INITIALIZE COUNTERS TO ZERO.
       SUMX=0.
       SUMY=0.
       SUMXY=0.
       SUMX2=0.
       SUMY2=0.
       N=0
   13 READ 1,X,Y
    1 FORMAT(2F8.3)
C      TEST FOR END OF DATA.
       IF(X-9999999.)2,3,3
C      COMPUTE SUMS.
    2 SUMX=SUMX+X
       SUMY=SUMY+Y
       SUMXY=SUMXY+X*Y
       SUMX2=SUMX2+X*X
       SUMY2=SUMY2+Y*Y
       N=N+1
       GO TO 13
C      CONVERT N TO FLOATING POINT.
    3 T=N
C      COMPUTE THE CORRELATION COEFFICIENT.
       R=(T*SUMXY-SUMX*SUMY)/SQRT((T*SUMX2-SUMX**2)*(T*SUMY2-SUMY**2))
       PRINT 4,N,R
    4 FORMAT(1H1I5,13H OBSERVATIONS4X3HR= F7.4)
       CALL EXIT
       END
```

FIGURE 18.14 Program for Problem 18.4

```
25.000   20.000
-20.000   05.000
  10.      08.
  15.5     18.
   5.1      4.5
  10.5     15.2
   8.4      9.
  -5.12    -1.5
  10.      -1.
 100.     105.
  90.      95.
  55.      80.
  60.      88.5
-100.    -150.
  85.      80.
  15.8     20.2
  75.6    120.
 125.     140.
  -3.      30.
  10.      50.
9999999.
```

FIGURE 18.15 Input data for Problem 18.4

                    20 OBSERVATIONS   R= 0.9536

FIGURE 18.16 Output for Problem 18.4

Problem 18.5

N (where $N \leq 100$) numbers are punched one per card in columns 1–5 in F5.1 format. Preceding these data cards is a card punched with the value of N in columns 1–3 in I3 format. Write a Fortran program to find and print (a) the largest number, (b) the smallest number, and (c) the largest number in absolute value.

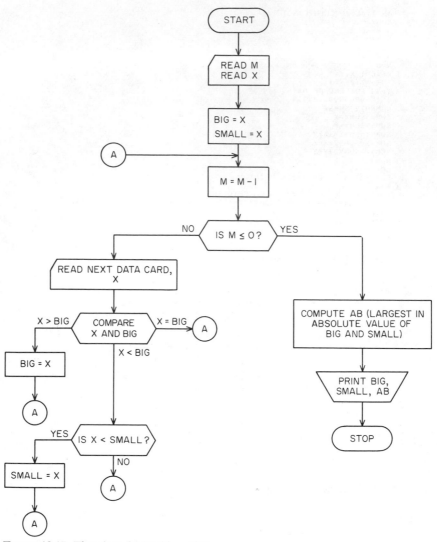

FIGURE 18.17 Flowchart for Problem 18.5

```
C       READ NUMBER OF DATA CARDS.
        READ 10,M
    10 FORMAT(I3)
C       READ FIRST DATA CARD.
        READ 11,X
    11 FORMAT(F5.1)
C       SET FIRST DATA ITEM AS BOTH THE LARGEST AND SMALLEST NUMBER.
        BIG=X
        SMALL=X
```

FIGURE 18.18 Program for Problem 18.5

```
C       SUBTRACT 1 FROM COUNT OF DATA CARDS REMAINING TO BE PROCESSED.
  15 M=M-1
     IF (M) 2,2,3
C       READ NEXT DATA CARD.
   3 READ 11,X
C       TEST FOR PRESENT DATA ITEM LARGER THAN PREVIOUS LARGEST NUMBER.
     IF(BIG-X)8,15,9
   8 BIG=X
     GO TO 15
C       TEST FOR PRESENT DATA ITEM SMALLER THAN PREVIOUS SMALLEST NUMBER.
   9 IF(SMALL-X)15,15,18
  18 SMALL=X
     GO TO 15
C       FIND LARGEST NUMBER IN ABSOLUTE VALUE.
   2 IF(BIG+SMALL) 31,30,30
  30 AB=BIG
     GO TO 6
  31 AB=SMALL
   6 PRINT 20,BIG,SMALL,AB
  20 FORMAT(1H118HLARGEST VALUE IS  F7.1/1HO19HSMALLEST VALUE IS  F7.1/
    11HO27HLARGEST ABSOLUTE VALUE IS  F7.1)
     CALL EXIT
     END
```

FIGURE 18.18 Continued

```
         15
        -52.5
        100.1
        +50.3
        987.5
        -67.2
        -99.9
        738.1
        450.0
        000.1
        738.5
        156.9
        987.6
        675.1
       -  1.0
        -91.5
```

FIGURE 18.19 Input data for Problem 18.5

```
LARGEST VALUE IS      987.6

SMALLEST VALUE IS     -99.9

LARGEST ABSOLUTE VALUE IS     987.6
```

FIGURE 18.20 Output for Problem 18.5

Problem 18.6

Ninety students have taken a quiz. The possible scores on the quiz are
0, 5, 10, 15, 20, and 25. The input data consists of ninety cards keypunched
with student number (columns 1–5) and quiz score (columns 7–8). Write a
program to determine which of the six possible scores most students received, and how many students received that score.

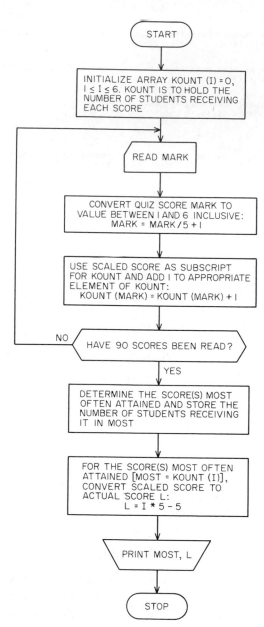

FIGURE 18.21 Flowchart for Problem 18.6

```
         DIMENSION KOUNT (6)
C        INITIALIZE ARRAY ELEMENTS TO ZERO.
         DO 8 I=1,6
       8 KOUNT(I)=0
         DO 1 I=1,90
         READ 2,MARK
       2 FORMAT(6XI2)
C        SCALE TEST SCORES TO A VALUE BETWEEN 1 AND 6 INCLUSIVE.
         MARK=MARK/5+1
C        USE SCALED SCORE AS A SUBSCRIPT AND ADD 1 TO PROPER ARRAY ELEMENT.
       1 KOUNT(MARK)=KOUNT(MARK)+1
C        DETERMINE SCORE MOST OFTEN ATTAINED AND NUMBER OF STUDENTS RECEIVING IT.
         MOST=KOUNT(1)
         DO 3 I=2,6
         IF(MOST-KOUNT(I)) 6,3,3
       6 MOST=KOUNT(I)
       3 CONTINUE
C        CONVERT SCALED TEST SCORE TO ACTUAL SCORE.
C        PRINT SCORE(S) RECEIVED BY MOST STUDENTS AND NUMBER OF STUDENTS.
         DO 11 I=1,6
         IF(MOST-KOUNT(I)) 11,13,11
      13 L=I*5-5
         PRINT 12,MOST,L
      12 FORMAT(1XI3,30H STUDENTS RECEIVED A SCORE OF I3)
      11 CONTINUE
         CALL EXIT
         END
```

FIGURE 18.22 Program for Problem 18.6

1	00	16	20	31	15	46	15	61	20	76	15
2	20	17	25	32	10	47	10	62	10	77	20
3	25	18	15	33	10	48	05	63	15	78	25
4	05	19	00	34	25	49	15	64	20	79	15
5	05	20	10	35	20	50	00	65	15	80	15
6	25	21	05	36	15	51	20	66	25	81	20
7	10	22	15	37	05	52	10	67	15	82	00
8	00	23	15	38	05	53	15	68	15	83	10
9	15	24	25	39	20	54	15	69	20	84	20
10	25	25	25	40	10	55	05	70	25	85	15
11	10	26	20	41	25	56	20	71	25	86	15
12	15	27	20	42	20	57	25	72	15	87	05
13	15	28	05	43	15	58	05	73	10	88	20
14	15	29	15	44	25	59	15	74	15	89	15
15	05	30	00	45	15	60	20	75	05	90	25

FIGURE 18.23 Input data for Problem 18.6

```
      29 STUDENTS RECEIVED A SCORE OF  15
```

FIGURE 18.24 Output for Problem 18.6

Problem 18.7

Write a Fortran program to sort a maximum of 300 numbers into ascending sequence. The sorted numbers are to be printed. The numbers are punched one per card in columns 1–5 in F5.1 format. The data cards are preceded by a card with a number punched in columns 1–3 in I3 format, which specifies the number of data cards that follow (i.e., the number of numbers to be sorted). The exchange method of sorting is to be used. In this method the first two numbers are compared. If the first number is greater than the second they are interchanged (their positions are reversed); however, if the second number is greater than the first, the procedure continues with no interchange. The second and third numbers are then compared and, if the second number is greater, they are interchanged. If the third number is greater, the procedure continues with no interchange. This procedure continues until finally the last number and the previous one are compared and an interchange either does or does not occur. At this point the largest number will be in its proper place at the end of the list of numbers. This process is then repeated beginning with the first number. At the completion of the second pass the next largest number will be in its proper place. Thus, if N is the number of numbers to be sorted a *maximum* of $N - 1$ passes will be required to put them in ascending sequence.

The following items may reduce the amount of computer time required for the complete sort:

1. The numbers are in sequence when no interchange has occurred in a complete pass.

2. During a pass all the numbers beyond the *last* interchange are in sequence. Thus, if 100 numbers are being sorted and on the first pass the last interchange is made between the 79th and 80th numbers in the list, then on the next pass the numbers in positions 80–100 need not be compared since they will be in the proper sequence.

3. At the start of a pass other than the first it is necessary only to start with the number prior to the *first* interchange of the previous pass. Thus, if the first interchange in a pass is made between the fourth and fifth numbers in the list, then on the next pass the comparisons can start between the third and fourth numbers in the list.

```
            DIMENSION X(300)
      C     READ NUMBERS TO BE SORTED.
            READ 1,N,(X(I),I=1,N)
          1 FORMAT(I3/(F5.1))
      C     INITIALIZE TO MAKE N-1 COMPARISONS ON FIRST PASS.
            K=N-1
      C     INITIALIZE TO BEGIN COMPARISONS WITH THE FIRST 2 NUMBERS.
          6 J=1
      C     L IS USED TO RECORD THE FACT THAT AN INTERCHANGE OCCURS.
         19 L=0
      C     MAKE COMPARISONS.
            DO 2 I=J,K
            IF(X(I)-X(I+1)) 2,2,3
      C     AN INTERCHANGE IS TO TAKE PLACE.
      C     IS THIS THE FIRST INTERCHANGE.
          3 IF(L) 20,21,20
      C     RECORD POINT OF FIRST INTERCHANGE LESS ONE POSITION.
         21 J1=I-1
      C     MAKE INTERCHANGE.
         20 SAVE=X(I)
            X(I)=X(I+1)
            X(I+1)=SAVE
```

FIGURE 18.25 Program for Problem 18.7

```
C       RECORD POINT OF LAST INTERCHANGE (ACTUALLY ALL INTERCHANGES).
        L=I
      2 CONTINUE
C       DETERMINE IF NUMBERS ARE IN SEQUENCE.
        IF(L) 8,9,8
C       NUMBERS ARE NOT YET IN SEQUENCE.  SET DO PARAMETERS.
      8 K=L
C       DO NOT WANT TO START AT ZERO SO TEST J1 FOR VALUE OF 0.
        IF(J1) 6,6,7
      7 J=J1
        GO TO 19
      9 PRINT 16,N
     16 FORMAT(1H13HTHE,I4,31H NUMBERS IN ASCENDING ORDER ARE/)
        PRINT 17, (I,X(I),I=1,N)
     17 FORMAT(1XI4,2XF7.1)
        CALL EXIT
        END
```

FIGURE 18.25 Continued

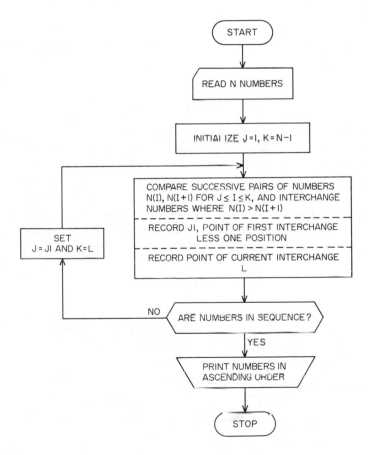

FIGURE 18.26 Flowchart for Problem 18.7

THE   25 NUMBERS IN ASCENDING ORDER ARE

1	1.0
2	2.0
3	3.0
4	4.0
5	5.0
6	6.0
7	7.0
8	8.0
9	9.0
10	10.0
11	11.0
12	12.0
13	13.0
14	14.0
15	15.0
16	16.0
17	17.0
18	18.0
19	19.0
20	20.0
21	21.0
22	22.0
23	23.0
24	24.0
25	25.0

```
25
 8.0              3.0
 9.0              4.0
10.0             24.0
11.0             25.0
12.0             20.0
13.0             21.0
14.0             22.0
 6.0             15.0
19.0             16.0
23.0              5.0
 7.0             17.0
18.0              1.0
                  2.0
```

FIGURE 18.27 Input data for Problem 18.7   FIGURE 18.28 Output for Problem 18.7

Problem 18.8

A number of students are given a questionnaire consisting of ten questions. The answer to each question is coded with one of the digits from zero to nine inclusive. The digit 0 indicates the question was not answered. A student's answers to the questions are punched on a single card in columns 1–10 respectively. The last data card is followed by a card with the digit 1 punched in column 11; no data card has a 1 punched in column 11. Write a Fortran program to tabulate and print the results of the questionnaire including the number of no responses to each question.

```
C       A 10X10 MATRIX IS USED TO TABULATE THE RESULTS OF THE QUESTIONNAIRE.
C       THE MATRIX ROWS CORRESPOND TO THE QUESTIONS, THE COLUMNS
C       CORRESPOND TO THE NUMERIC RESPONSES. COLUMN 10 OF THE
C       MATRIX WILL CORRESPOND TO A ZERO RESPONSE.
        DIMENSION N(10,10),K(10)
C       INITIALIZE MATRIX ELEMENTS TO ZEROS.
        DO 91 I=1,10
        DO 91 J=1,10
   91   N(I,J)=0
C       READ A STUDENTS RESPONSES TO THE 10 QUESTIONS. L IS USED
C       TO STORE THE DIGIT INDICATING THE END OF THE DATA.
    6   READ 1,(K(I),I=1,10),L
    1   FORMAT(11I1)
```

FIGURE 18.29 Program for Problem 18.8

```
C       TEST FOR CARD INDICATING THE END OF THE DATA.
        IF(L-1) 2,7,2
      2 DO 3 I=1,10
C       VARIABLE I CORRESPONDS TO THE MATRIX ROWS (QUESTION NO.).
C       USE THE RESPONSE AS THE COLUMN SUBSCRIPT. SINCE A SUBSCRIPT
C       CANNOT BE SUBSCRIPTED THE FOLLOWING STATEMENT IS USED.
        M=K(I)
C       FOR ZERO RESPONSE SET UP FOR COLUMN 10.
        IF(M) 4,5,4
      5 M=10
C       ADD A ONE TO PROPER MATRIX ENTRY.
      4 N(I,M)=N(I,M)+1
      3 CONTINUE
        GO TO 6
C       PRINT RESULTS.
      7 PRINT 10
     10 FORMAT(1H136HTABULATED RESPONSES TO QUESTIONNAIRE)
        PRINT 11
     11 FORMAT(1H09HRESPONSES5X1H15X1H25X1H35X1H45X1H55X1H65X1H75X1H85X1H9
        15X1H0/)
        DO 12 I=1,10
     12 PRINT 13,I,(N(I,J),J=1,10)
     13 FORMAT(1X8HQUESTION,I3,1XI4,9(2XI4))
        CALL EXIT
        END
```

FIGURE 18.29 Continued

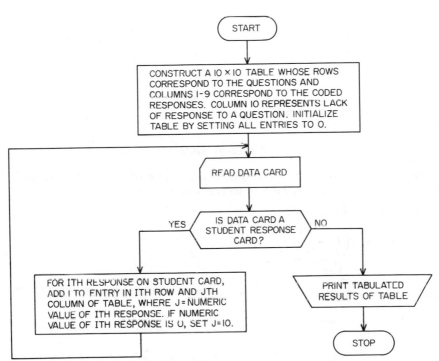

FIGURE 18.30 Flowchart for Problem 18.8

```
0123456789
1234567890
2345678901
3456789012
4567890123
5678901234
6789012345
7890123456
8901234567
9012345678
8546328179
5210876328
5628764552
0054287953
0000000000
1111111111
2222222222
0123123123
4235712985
6028413058
9850240687
4205981230
9520123574
9632085417
3245874123
                1
```

FIGURE 18.31 Input data for Problem 18.8

TABULATED RESPONSES TO QUESTIONNAIRE

RESPONSES	1	2	3	4	5	6	7	8	9	0
QUESTION 1	2	2	2	3	3	2	1	2	4	4
QUESTION 2	3	6	1	1	3	3	1	2	1	4
QUESTION 3	3	6	3	3	3	1	1	1	1	3
QUESTION 4	2	3	2	2	4	2	1	3	1	5
QUESTION 5	4	4	2	2	1	1	3	3	2	3
QUESTION 6	4	5	1	2	1	2	3	4	1	2
QUESTION 7	3	3	4	3	2	2	2	2	1	3
QUESTION 8	5	3	2	2	3	2	1	1	1	3
QUESTION 9	3	5	2	1	4	1	3	3	1	2
QUESTION 10	2	3	4	2	2	1	3	3	2	3

FIGURE 18.32 Output for Problem 18.8

Problem 18.9

Write a Fortran program to evaluate $\log_{10}(x)$ for a value of x as input data. Use the following approximation to evaluate $\log_{10}(x)$:

$$\log_{10}(x) = 0.43429448 \log_e(x)$$

$$\log_e(x) = 2\left(T + \frac{T^3}{3} + \frac{T^5}{5} + \frac{T^7}{7} + \cdots\right) + V \qquad \text{for } (1 \leq x \leq 10)$$

where $T = \dfrac{U-1}{U+1}$

$$U = \frac{x}{\sqrt{e}} \quad \text{and} \quad V = .5 \qquad \text{for} \qquad x < e$$

$$U = \frac{x}{e^{1.65}} \quad \text{and} \quad V = 1.65 \qquad \text{for} \qquad x \geq e$$

Write the program so that the series

$$T + \frac{T^3}{3} + \frac{T^5}{5} + \frac{T^7}{7} + \cdots$$

is carried out to the number of terms specified on an input card. The number for which the logarithm is to be approximated is punched in columns 1–8 in F8.3 format, the number of terms to which the series is to be carried out is punched in columns 9–10 of the same card in I2 format. Successive data cards are to be processed. These data cards are preceded by a card with the number of data cards punched in columns 1–3. Note that the approximating series for $\log_e (x)$ is valid only for $1 \le x \le 10$; therefore, it may be necessary to scale up or scale down the input number. Consider approximating $\log_{10}$ of 1231. $\log_{10} 1231 = \log_{10}(1.231 \times 10^3) = \log_{10} 1.231 + \log_{10} 10^3$. Now $\log_{10} 10^3 = 3$. Therefore $\log_{10} 1231 = 3 + \log_{10} 1.231$.

```
C       PRINT HEADINGS.
        PRINT 30
     30 FORMAT(1H111X1HX1HX15X8HLOG10(X)4X20HTERMS USED IN SERIES,5X16HFORTRA
       1IN LOG10(X)/)
C       READ NUMBER OF DATA CARDS TO BE PROCESSED.
        READ 20, NO
     20 FORMAT(I3)
        DO 21 L=1,NO
C       READ NUMBER FOR WHICH LOG IS TO BE APPROXIMATED AND THE NUMBER OF
C       TERMS TO WHICH THE SERIES IS CARRIED OUT.
        READ 1,X,K
      1 FORMAT(F8.3,I2)
        IF(X)40,40,15
     40 PRINT 41,X
     41 FORMAT(7XF11.4,4X30HINPUT DATA IS ZERO OR NEGATIVE)
        GO TO 21
C       INITIALIZE SCALE COUNT (HOW MANY TIMES THE INPUT QUANTITY
C       IS MULTIPLIED OR DIVIDED BY 10 TO PUT IT IN THE RANGE).
     15 N=0
        Y=X
C       TEST TO DETERMINE IF NUMBER IS BETWEEN 1 AND 10 INCLUSIVE.
      5 IF(Y-1.) 3,10,4
      4 IF(Y-10.) 8,8,2
C       NUMBER IS TOO LARGE, SCALE DOWN.
      2 Y=Y/10.
C       COUNT NUMBER OF DIVISIONS AND LATER ADD THIS NUMBER TO LOG.
        N=N+1
        GO TO 4
C       NUMBER IS TOO SMALL, SCALE UP.
      3 Y=Y*10.
C       COUNT NUMBER OF MULTIPLICATIONS AND LATER ADD THIS NUMBER TO LOG.
        N=N-1
        GO TO 5
C       TEST WHETHER SCALED NUMBER IS LESS THAN E AND INITIALIZE V ACCORDINGLY.
      8 IF(Y-EXP(1.)) 10,11,11
     10 V=.5
        GO TO 12
     11 V=1.65
     12 U=Y/EXP(V)
C       COMPUTE T.
        T=(U-1.)/(U+1.)
C       INITIALIZE SERIES.
        SERIES=0.
```

FIGURE 18.33 Program for Problem 18.9

```
C       SUM THE TERMS OF THE SERIES.
        DO 13 I=1,K,2
   13 SERIES=SERIES+T**I/FLOAT(I)
C       IT IS NECESSARY TO USE INTEGER EXPONENT BECAUSE T CAN BE NEGATIVE.
        YLOG=(2.*SERIES+V)*.43429448+FLOAT(N)
        W=ALOG10(X)
        PRINT 14,X,YLOG,K,W
   14 FORMAT(7XF11.4,5XF15.8,9XI3,17XF15.8)
   21 CONTINUE
        CALL EXIT
        END
```

FIGURE 18.33 Continued

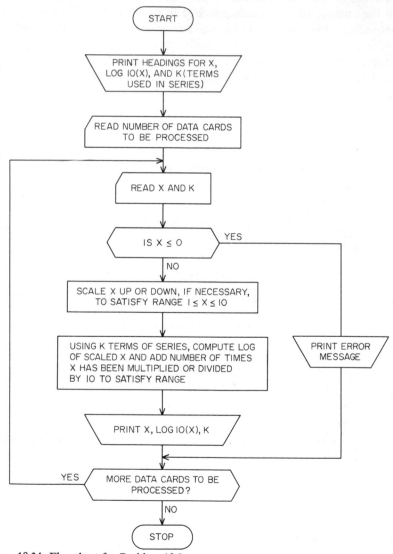

FIGURE 18.34 Flowchart for Problem 18.9

```
30
10.     05
10.     09
10.0    11
10.0    21
1.0     05
1.0'    09
1.0     11
1.0     21
5.5     08
5.5     15
2.71806
2.71811
75.0    05
75.0    09
22.15   07
22.15   13
100.    07
100.    13
352.    06
352.    11
9521    05
9521    09
.003    05
.003    09
55.     05
55.     09
1.11106
1.11111
0000.00011
-101.23111
```

FIGURE 18.35 Input data for Problem 18.9

X	LOG10(X)	TERMS USED IN SERIES	FORTRAN LOG10(X)
10.0000	0.99995841	5	1.00000000
10.0000	0.99999970	9	1.00000000
10.0000	0.99999995	11	1.00000000
10.0000	0.99999997	21	1.00000000
1.0000	0.00000688	5	0.00000000
1.0000	0.00000001	9	0.00000000
1.0000	-0.00000000	11	0.00000000
1.0000	-0.00000000	21	0.00000000
5.5000	0.74036267	8	0.74036268
5.5000	0.74036267	15	0.74036268
2.7180	0.43424257	6	0.43424945
2.7180	0.43424944	11	0.43424945
75.0000	1.87506042	5	1.87506126
75.0000	1.87506124	9	1.87506126
22.1500	1.34537370	7	1.34537372
22.1500	1.34537370	13	1.34537372
100.0000	1.99999672	7	2.00000000
100.0000	1.99999996	13	2.00000000
352.0000	2.54654392	6	2.54654266
352.0000	2.54654264	11	2.54654266
95210.0000	4.97865788	5	4.97868256
95210.0000	4.97868236	9	4.97868256
0.0030	-2.52286534	5	-2.52287876
0.0030	-2.52287870	9	-2.52287876
55.0000	1.74036266	5	1.74036268
55.0000	1.74036266	9	1.74036268
1.1110	0.04571542	6	0.04571406
1.1110	0.04571406	11	0.04571406
0.0000	INPUT DATA IS ZERO OR NEGATIVE		
-101.2310	INPUT DATA IS ZERO OR NEGATIVE		

FIGURE 18.36 Output for Problem 18.9

Problem 18.10

Write a Fortran program that includes routines for (*a*) matrix addition, (*b*) matrix subtraction, (*c*) matrix multiplication, and (*d*) developing the transpose of a matrix. Input data to the program consist of two matrices, each matrix being preceded by a card that has the number of rows and the number of columns of the matrix punched in columns 1–2 and 3–4, respectively, in 2I2 format. The first matrix *A* is punched by rows in 5F8.2 format; the first number in each row is always punched as the first number on a card. The second matrix *B* is punched by columns in 5F8.2 format; the first number in each column is always punched as the first number on a card. Allow for matrices whose maximum dimensions are 10 by 10. The input data are followed by a card that designates which matrix operations are to be performed on the matrices, as follows:

"0" in column 1 indicates no addition

"1" in column 1 indicates $A + B$

"0" in column 2 indicates no subtraction

"1" in column 2 indicates $A - B$

"0" in column 3 indicates no multiplication

"1" in column 3 indicates $A \times B$

"0" in column 4 indicates no *A* transpose

"1" in column 4 indicates A^T

"0" in column 5 indicates no *B* transpose

"1" in column 5 indicates B^T

The program should be written to process several sets of matrices. A blank card following the last matrix indicates end of data.

Commentary on Program 18.10

The reader should note the occurrences of the extra characters of output [for example, A(, B(, etc.]. This occurs because the H specification is encountered before the numeric specification that terminates the output (see page 142).

```
      DIMENSION A(10,10),B(10,10),C(10,10),K(5)
C     READ MATRIX A DIMENSIONS AND THE MATRIX ELEMENTS BY ROWS.
 9999 READ 1,M,N
    1 FORMAT(2I2)
      IF(M)9997,9998,9997
 9997 DO 2 I=1,M
    2 READ 3, (A(I,J),J=1,N)
    3 FORMAT(5F8.2)
```

Figure 18.37   Program for Problem 18.10

```
C     READ MATRIX B DIMENSIONS AND THE MATRIX ELEMENTS BY COLUMNS.
      READ 1,M1,N1
      DO 4 I=1,N1
    4 READ 3, (B(J,I),J=1,M1)
C     PRINT ORIGINAL MATRIX ELEMENTS 5 PER LINE WITH ROW AND COLUMN DESIGNATIONS
      PRINT 1100
 1100 FORMAT(1H114HINPUT A MATRIX/)
      DO 1101 I=1,M
 1101 PRINT 105,(I,J,A(I,J),J=1,N)
  105 FORMAT(1H05(3X2HA(I2,1H,I2,1H),F9.2))
      PRINT 102
  102 FORMAT(1H0//15H INPUT B MATRIX)
      DO 103 I=1,M1
  103 PRINT 104,(I,J,B(I,J),J=1,N1)
  104 FORMAT(1H05(3X2HB(I2,1H,I2,1H),F9.2))
C     READ CODES DESIGNATING MATRIX OPERATIONS TO BE PERFORMED.
      READ 5,(K(I),I=1,5)
    5 FORMAT(5I1)
      PRINT 7777,(K(I),I=1,5)
 7777 FORMAT(1H059HTHE CODES DESIGNATING MATRIX OPERATIONS TO BE PERFORM
     1ED ARE//1X5I2)
      PRINT 8888
 8888 FORMAT(1H1)
C     PROCESS THE 5 MATRIX OPERATIONS.
      DO 6 L=1,5
C     TRANSFER TO APPROPRIATE ROUTINE.
      GO TO (10,30,50,70,90),L
C     DETERMINE IF MATRIX ADDITION IS REQUESTED.
   10 IF(K(L)-1) 17,11,100
C     MATRIX ADDITION REQUIRED, CAN MATRIX ADDITION BE PERFORMED.
   11 IF(M-M1) 18,12,18
   12 IF(N-N1) 18,13,18
C     PERFORM MATRIX ADDITION.
   13 DO 14 I=1,M
      DO 14 J=1,N
   14 C(I,J)=A(I,J)+B(I,J)
      PRINT 15
   15 FORMAT(1H019HMATRIX ADDITION A+B)
      DO 16 I=1,M
   16 PRINT 19,(I,J,C(I,J),J=1,N)
   19 FORMAT(1H05(3X2HC(I2,1H,I2,1H),F9.2))
      GO TO 6
   17 PRINT 20
   20 FORMAT(1H028HMATRIX ADDITION NOT REQUIRED)
      GO TO 6
   18 PRINT 21
   21 FORMAT(1H052HMATRIX ADDITION REQUIRED BUT MATRICES NOT COMPATIBLE)
      GO TO 6
C     DETERMINE IF MATRIX SUBTRACTION IS REQUESTED.
   30 IF(K(L)-1) 37,31,100
C     MATRIX SUBTRACTION REQUIRED. CAN MATRIX SUBTRACTION BE PERFORMED.
C     NOTE THE USE OF THE LOGICAL IF STATEMENT.  A SINGLE STATEMENT OF THIS
C     FORM COULD HAVE BEEN USED IN PLACE OF THE TWO ARITHMETIC IF STATEMENTS
C     NUMBERED 11 AND 12.
   31 IF(M.NE.M1.OR.N.NE.N1)GO TO 38
C     PERFORM MATRIX SUBTRACTION.
   33 DO 34 I=1,M
      DO 34 J=1,N

   34 C(I,J)=A(I,J)-B(I,J)
      PRINT 35
   35 FORMAT(1H022HMATRIX SUBTRACTION A-B)
      DO 36 I=1,M
   36 PRINT 19,(I,J,C(I,J),J=1,N)
      GO TO 6
   37 PRINT 40
   40 FORMAT(1H031HMATRIX SUBTRACTION NOT REQUIRED)
      GO TO 6
   38 PRINT 41
   41 FORMAT(1H055HMATRIX SUBTRACTION REQUIRED BUT MATRICES NOT COMPATIB
     1LE)
      GO TO 6
C     DETERMINE IF MATRIX MULTIPLICATION IS REQUESTED.
   50 IF(K(L)-1) 52,51,100
C     MATRIX MULTIPLICATION IS REQUIRED. CAN IT BE PERFORMED.
   51 IF(N-M1) 53,54,53
```

FIGURE 18.37 Continued

```
C       PERFORM MATRIX MULTIPLICATION.
     54 DO 55 I=1,M
        DO 55 J=1,N1
        C(I,J)=0.
        DO 55 KK=1,N
     55 C(I,J)=C(I,J)+A(I,KK)*B(KK,J)
        PRINT 56
     56 FORMAT(1H025HMATRIX MULTIPLICATION A*B)
        DO 57 I=1,M
     57 PRINT 19,(I,J,C(I,J),J=1,N1)
        GO TO 6
     52 PRINT 58
     58 FORMAT(1H034HMATRIX MULTIPLICATION NOT REQUIRED)
        GO TO 6
     53 PRINT 59
     59 FORMAT(1H062HMATRIX MULTIPLICATION REQUIRED BUT MATRICES ARE NOT C
        1OMPATIBLE)
        GO TO 6
C       DETERMINE IF A TRANSPOSE IS REQUIRED.
     70 IF(K(L)-1) 72,71,100
C       THE TRANSPOSE OF A IS REQUIRED.
     71 DO 73 I=1,M
        DO 73 J=1,N
     73 C(J,I)=A(I,J)
        PRINT 74
     74 FORMAT(1H011HA TRANSPOSE)
        DO 75 I=1,N
     75 PRINT 19,(I,J,C(I,J),J=1,M)
        GO TO 6
     72 PRINT 76
     76 FORMAT(1H027HA TRANSPOSE IS NOT REQUIRED)
        GO TO 6
C       DETERMINE IF B TRANSPOSE IS REQUIRED.
     90 IF(K(L)-1) 92,91,100
C       THE TRANSPOSE OF B IS REQUIRED.
     91 DO 93 I=1,M1
        DO 93 J=1,N1
     93 C(J,I)=B(I,J)
        PRINT 94
     94 FORMAT(1H011HB TRANSPOSE)
        DO 95 I=1,N1
     95 PRINT 19,(I,J,C(I,J),J=1,M1)
        GO TO 6
     92 PRINT 96
     96 FORMAT(1H027HB TRANSPOSE IS NOT REQUIRED)
      6 CONTINUE
        GO TO 9999
    100 PRINT 101
    101 FORMAT(1H136HINCORRECT CARD CODE PROCESSING HALTS)
   9998 CALL EXIT
        END
```

FIGURE 18.37 Concluded

```
0505
   1.       2.       3.       4.       5.
   6.       7.       8.       9.      10.
  11.      12.      13.      14.      15.
  16.      17.      18.      19.      20.
  21.      22.      23.      24.      25.
0505
   1.       2.       3.       4.       5.
   6.       7.       8.       9.      10.
  11.      12.      13.      14.      15.
  16.      17.      18.      19.      20.
  21.      22.      23.      24.      25.
11111
0304
   1.5      8.      15.     250.
  10.     -10.      -5.      80.
-1000.      0.      10.5    150.25
0401
  10.      20.      30.      40.
01111
```

FIGURE 18.38 Input data for Problem 18.10

INPUT A MATRIX

A(1, 1)	1.00	A(1, 2)	2.00	A(1, 3)	3.00	A(1, 4)	4.00	A(1, 5)	5.00
A(2, 1)	6.00	A(2, 2)	7.00	A(2, 3)	8.00	A(2, 4)	9.00	A(2, 5)	10.00
A(3, 1)	11.00	A(3, 2)	12.00	A(3, 3)	13.00	A(3, 4)	14.00	A(3, 5)	15.00
A(4, 1)	16.00	A(4, 2)	17.00	A(4, 3)	18.00	A(4, 4)	19.00	A(4, 5)	20.00
A(5, 1)	21.00	A(5, 2)	22.00	A(5, 3)	23.00	A(5, 4)	24.00	A(5, 5)	25.00

INPUT B MATRIX

B(1, 1)	1.00	B(1, 2)	6.00	B(1, 3)	11.00	B(1, 4)	16.00	B(1, 5)	21.00
B(2, 1)	2.00	B(2, 2)	7.00	B(2, 3)	12.00	B(2, 4)	17.00	B(2, 5)	22.00
B(3, 1)	3.00	B(3, 2)	8.00	B(3, 3)	13.00	B(3, 4)	18.00	B(3, 5)	23.00
B(4, 1)	4.00	B(4, 2)	9.00	B(4, 3)	14.00	B(4, 4)	19.00	B(4, 5)	24.00
B(5, 1)	5.00	B(5, 2)	10.00	B(5, 3)	10.00	B(5, 4)	20.00	B(5, 5)	25.00

THE CODES DESIGNATING MATRIX OPERATIONS TO BE PERFORMED ARE

1 1 1 1 1

MATRIX ADDITION A+B

C(1, 1)	2.00	C(1, 2)	8.00	C(1, 3)	14.00	C(1, 4)	20.00	C(1, 5)	26.00
C(2, 1)	8.00	C(2, 2)	14.00	C(2, 3)	20.00	C(2, 4)	26.00	C(2, 5)	32.00
C(3, 1)	14.00	C(3, 2)	20.00	C(3, 3)	26.00	C(3, 4)	32.00	C(3, 5)	38.00
C(4, 1)	20.00	C(4, 2)	26.00	C(4, 3)	32.00	C(4, 4)	38.00	C(4, 5)	44.00
C(5, 1)	26.00	C(5, 2)	32.00	C(5, 3)	38.00	C(5, 4)	44.00	C(5, 5)	50.00

FIGURE 18.39 Output for Problem 18.10

MATRIX SUBTRACTION A-B

C(1, 1) -0.00	C(1, 2) -4.00	C(1, 3) -8.00	C(1, 4) -12.00	C(1, 5) -16.00
C(2, 1) 4.00	C(2, 2) -0.00	C(2, 3) -4.00	C(2, 4) -8.00	C(2, 5) -12.00
C(3, 1) 8.00	C(3, 2) 4.00	C(3, 3) -0.00	C(3, 4) -4.00	C(3, 5) -8.00
C(4, 1) 12.00	C(4, 2) 8.00	C(4, 3) 4.00	C(4, 4) -0.00	C(4, 5) -4.00
C(5, 1) 16.00	C(5, 2) 12.00	C(5, 3) 8.00	C(5, 4) 4.00	C(5, 5) -0.00

MATRIX MULTIPLICATION A*B

C(1, 1) 55.00	C(1, 2) 130.00	C(1, 3) 205.00	C(1, 4) 280.00	C(1, 5) 355.00
C(2, 1) 130.00	C(2, 2) 330.00	C(2, 3) 530.00	C(2, 4) 730.00	C(2, 5) 930.00
C(3, 1) 205.00	C(3, 2) 530.00	C(3, 3) 855.00	C(3, 4) 1180.00	C(3, 5) 1505.00
C(4, 1) 280.00	C(4, 2) 730.00	C(4, 3) 1180.00	C(4, 4) 1630.00	C(4, 5) 2030.00
C(5, 1) 355.00	C(5, 2) 930.00	C(5, 3) 1505.00	C(5, 4) 2080.00	C(5, 5) 2655.00

A TRANSPOSE

C(1, 1) 1.00	C(1, 2) 6.00	C(1, 3) 11.00	C(1, 4) 16.00	C(1, 5) 21.00
C(2, 1) 2.00	C(2, 2) 7.00	C(2, 3) 12.00	C(2, 4) 17.00	C(2, 5) 22.00
C(3, 1) 3.00	C(3, 2) 8.00	C(3, 3) 13.00	C(3, 4) 18.00	C(3, 5) 23.00
C(4, 1) 4.00	C(4, 2) 9.00	C(4, 3) 14.00	C(4, 4) 19.00	C(4, 5) 24.00
C(5, 1) 5.00	C(5, 2) 10.00	C(5, 3) 15.00	C(5, 4) 20.00	C(5, 5) 25.00

B TRANSPOSE

C(1, 1) 1.00	C(1, 2) 2.00	C(1, 3) 3.00	C(1, 4) 4.00	C(1, 5) 5.00
C(2, 1) 6.00	C(2, 2) 7.00	C(2, 3) 8.00	C(2, 4) 9.00	C(2, 5) 10.00
C(3, 1) 11.00	C(3, 2) 12.00	C(3, 3) 13.00	C(3, 4) 14.00	C(3, 5) 15.00
C(4, 1) 16.00	C(4, 2) 17.00	C(4, 3) 18.00	C(4, 4) 19.00	C(4, 5) 20.00
C(5, 1) 21.00	C(5, 2) 22.00	C(5, 3) 23.00	C(5, 4) 24.00	C(5, 5) 25.00

FIGURE 18.39 Continued

INPUT A MATRIX

A(1, 1)   1.50   A(1, 2)   8.00   A(1, 3)   15.00   A(1, 4)   250.00   A(
A(2, 1)   10.00   A(2, 2) -10.00   A(2, 3)   -5.00   A(2, 4)   80.00   A(
A(3, 1) -1000.00   A(3, 2)   0.00   A(3, 3)   10.50   A(3, 4)   150.25   A(

INPUT B MATRIX

B(1, 1)   10.00   B(
B(2, 1)   20.00   B(
B(3, 1)   30.00   B(
B(4, 1)   40.00   B(

THE CODES DESIGNATING MATRIX OPERATIONS TO BE PERFORMED ARE

0 1 1 1 1

MATRIX ADDITION NOT REQUIRED

MATRIX SUBTRACTION REQUIRED BUT MATRICES NOT COMPATIBLE

MATRIX MULTIPLICATION A*B

C(1, 1) 10625.00   C(
C(2, 1) 2950.00   C(
C(3, 1) -3675.00   C(

A TRANSPOSE

C(1, 1)   1.50   C(1, 2)   10.00   C(1, 3) -1000.00   C(
C(2, 1)   8.00   C(2, 2)   -10.00   C(2, 3)   0.00   C(
C(3, 1)   15.00   C(3, 2)   -5.00   C(3, 3)   10.50   C(
C(4, 1)   250.00   C(4, 2)   80.00   C(4, 3)   150.25   C(

B TRANSPOSE

C(1, 1)   10.00   C(1, 2)   20.00   C(1, 3)   30.00   C(1, 4)   40.00   C(

FIGURE 18.39 Concluded

FORTRAN PROBLEMS

The following problems are presented for the reader to solve in order to afford practice in Fortran programming.

Problem 18.11

Write a Fortran program to read an integer punched in columns 1–4 of a card in I4 format and to determine whether the integer is odd or even. Print the integer and the appropriate choice of the words *odd* or *even*.

Problem 18.12

Write a Fortran program to calculate and print the number of ways a dollar bill can be broken into change. All that is required is the total number of ways to make change — not the number of pennies, nickels, etc., making up each possible way.

Problem 18.13

N (where $N \leq 100$) numbers are punched one per card in columns 1–5 in F5.1 format. Preceding these data cards is a card punched with the value of N in columns 1–3 in I3 format. Write a Fortran program to sum the positive numbers and keep a count of how many there are, sum the negative numbers keeping a count of how many there are, and keep a count of the numbers of zeros. Print the sums and counts.

Problem 18.14

Fifty cards are each punched with three numbers (A, B, and C) in 3F8.2 format. Write a Fortran program to calculate

$$Y = \sum_{i=1}^{50} x_i$$

where

$$x_i = A^2 + B + C^2 \quad \text{if} \quad (A + B) < 0$$
$$x_i = A + 2BC \quad \text{if} \quad (A + B) = 0$$
$$x_i = B + C - A \quad \text{if} \quad (A + B) > 0.$$

Print the value of Y.

Problem 18.15

The number of combinations of N objects taken in groups of R is given by

$$C_R^N = \frac{N!}{R!(N-R)!}$$

Write a Fortran program to calculate C_R^N given values of N and R. A single data card contains a value of N in columns 1–2 and a value of R in columns 3–4 both in I2 format. The last data card is followed by a card with 99 punched in columns 1–2. No data card has 99 punched in columns 1–2.

Problem 18.16

Write a Fortran program to evaluate $\sqrt{N}$ using Newton's method of successive approximations. Each approximation is calculated by

$$X_{i+1} = \frac{1}{2}\left(X_i + \frac{N}{X_i}\right)$$

where X_{i+1} is the $(i+1)$st approximation to $\sqrt{N}$. Calculate and print all N and $\sqrt{N}$ for integer values of N in the range of $1 \leq N \leq 100$.

Problem 18.17

The Taylor series for the cosine is given by

$$\cos x = 1 - \frac{x^2}{2!} + \frac{x^4}{4!} - \frac{x^6}{6!} + \cdots$$

a)   Write a Fortran program to evaluate the cosine function based directly on the Taylor series expansion. Summation of terms of the series is to terminate when a term is reached which is less in absolute value than 10^{-8}. Compute the values of the cosine function only for 60° and 2π multiples thereof (60°, 420°, 780°,...).

b)   Write a second Fortran program to perform the Taylor series expansion using *double-precision* calculations. Compare the results of the two programs with respect to the accuracy of the computations. For additional comparison, include in the output of the second program cosine values as produced by the Fortran library function cos.

Problem 18.18

Write a Fortran program to evaluate

$$\int_a^b \frac{x^3}{e^x - 1} dx$$

by Simpson's rule:

$$\int_a^{a+2nh} f(x)dx = \frac{h}{3}[y_0 + 4y_1 + 2y_2 + 4y_3 + \cdots + 2y_{2n-2} + 4y_{2n-1} + y_{2n}]$$

where $a = x_0$

$$a + 2nh = x_{2n}$$

$$x_i + h = x_{i+1}$$

$$y_i = f(x_i).$$

Indicate in the output of the program the limits of the integration, the number of intervals, and the result of the numerical integration.

Problem 18.19

Twenty-five cards are each punched with two numbers in 2F5.2 format. Write a Fortran program to calculate and print the standard deviation of the fifty numbers where the standard deviation is given by

$$S = \sqrt{\frac{\sum_{i=1}^n x_i^2 - \left(\sum_{i=1}^n x_i\right)^2/n}{n - 1}}$$

where the x_i are the numbers and $1 \leq i \leq n$, for $n = 50$.

Problem 18.20

The elements of a one-dimensional array A are punched one per card in columns 1–5 in F5.1 format. The data cards are preceded by a card punched in columns 1–3, in I3 format with the number of elements in the array. Write a Fortran program to generate a one-dimensional array X whose elements are given by

$$X_1 = A_1$$

$$X_n = A_n$$

$$X_i = A_{i-1} + A_i + A_{i+1} \qquad 2 \leq i \leq n - 1$$

Problem 18.21

Write a Fortran program to find the largest element of an $M \times N$ matrix A of nonnegative elements. Print the value of the largest element(s) of A and indicate its position in the matrix by row and column. The matrix is preceded by a header card which indicates the dimensions of the matrix in 2I2 format (assume maximum dimensions of 50 × 50). The matrix is punched by rows in 5F8.2 format. The first element of a row is always punched as the first number on a card.

Problem 18.22

Write a Fortran program to generate a matrix A where each element is

$$a_{ij} = \frac{1}{i + j + 1}$$

The number of rows in the matrix is punched in columns 1–2 and the number of columns in the matrix in card columns 3–4, both in I2 format. The maximum dimensions of the matrix are 99 × 99.

Problem 18.23

Write a Fortran program to read a matrix A of dimensions $M \times N$ ($M \leq$ 10, $N \leq 10$). The matrix elements are punched by rows with four elements punched on each card. The data cards containing the matrix elements are preceded by a card which has the number of rows and the number of colums of the matrix punched in columns 1–2 and 3–4, respectively, in 2I2 format. Determine and print each of the following:

1. The smallest element in the matrix and its row and column number.
2. The largest element in absolute value and its row and column number.
3. The sum of the elements directly above and below and to the left and right of the element of largest absolute value. If this element is on the perimeter of the matrix the sum will consist of either two or three values.

Problem 18.24

Write a Fortran program to read a matrix of dimensions $M \times N$ ($M \leq$ 10, $N \leq 10$). The matrix elements are punched by rows with four elements per card in 4F8.2 format. The first element of each row is always punched as the first number on a card. The data cards containing the elements are preceded by a card with the number of rows and the number of columns punched in columns 1–2 and 3–4, respectively, in 2I2 format. Interchange the first element of each row with the smallest number in that row. The resulting matrix will be identical to the original matrix except that the first number in each row will have been interchanged with the smallest number in the row. Print the elements of the resulting matrix with their row and column designations.

Problem 18.25

The design equations for the ith stage of a serial binary adder may be expressed as follows:

$$S_i = X_i \oplus Y_i \oplus C_{i-1}$$
$$C_i = X_i Y_i + X_i C_{i-1} + Y_i C_{i-1}$$

where X_i and Y_i are the ith digits of the augend and addend, S_i is the ith sum digit, C_{i-1} is the carry from the previous digit addition, and C_i is the carry to the next digit addition.

Write a Fortran program to test the validity of the foregoing equations with respect to the following rules for binary addition:

C_{i-1}	0	1	0	1	0	1	0	1
X_i	0	0	1	1	0	0	1	1
Y_i	0	0	0	0	1	1	1	1
S_i	0	1	1	0	1	0	0	1
C_i	0	0	0	1	0	1	1	1

SELECTED BIBLIOGRAPHY

The following list of titles is intended to provide additional sources of information on Fortran, its implementation on specific computers, and its applications to numerical methods.

Texts on Fortran

1. GOLDEN, JAMES T., *Fortran IV Programming and Computing*. Englewood Cliffs, N. J.: Prentice-Hall, Inc., 1965.

2. HARRIS, L. DALE, *Fortran Programming (II and IV)*. Columbus, Ohio: Charles E. Merrill Books, Inc., 1964.

3. MCCRACKEN, DANIEL D., *A Guide to Fortran Programming*. New York: John Wiley & Sons, Inc., 1961.

4. ——————, *A Guide to Fortran IV Programming*, New York: John Wiley & Sons, Inc., 1965.

5. ORGANICK, ELLIOTT I., *A Fortran Primer*. Reading, Mass.: Addison-Wesley Publishing Co., Inc.. 1962.

Manufacturers' Reference Manuals on Fortran

1. *IBM 7040/7044 Operating System Fortran IV Language*, Form C28–6329–3. IBM Corporation (October 1965).

2. *IBM 7090/7094 Programming Systems Fortran IV Language*, Form C28–6274–3. IBM Corporation (November 1964).

3. *Control Data 3200 Computer System Fortran Reference Manual*, Pub. No. 60057600. Control Data Corporation (September 1964).

4. *GE-400 Series Basic Fortran IV*, Advance Information, CPB-1086. General Electric Co., Inc. (January 1965).

5. *IBM 1620 Fortran II Programming System Reference Manual*, Form C26–5876–2. IBM Corporation (1965).

ASA Standards for Fortran

1. "ASA Proposed Standards for Fortran and Basic Fortran," *Comm. ACM*, vol. 7 (October 1964) no. 10.

Texts on Numerical Methods

1. FROBERG, CARL-ERIK, *Introduction to Numerical Analysis.* Reading, Mass.: Addison-Wesley Publishing Co., 1965.

2. HARRIS, L. DALE, *Numerical Methods Using Fortran.* Columbus, Ohio: Charles E. Merrill Books, Inc., 1964.

3. KUO, SHAN, *Numerical Methods and Computers.* Reading, Mass.: Addison-Wesley Publishing Co., 1965.

4. McCORMICK, JOHN M. and M. G. SALVADORI, *Numerical Methods in Fortran* Englewood Cliffs, N. J.: Prentice-Hall, Inc., 1964.

5. McCRACKEN, DANIEL D. and W. S. DORN, *Numerical Methods and Fortran Programming with Applications in Engineering and Science.* New York: John Wiley & Sons, Inc., 1964.

6. SOUTHWORTH, RAYMOND W. and S. L. DELEEUW, *Digital Computation and Numerical Methods.* New York: McGraw-Hill, Inc., 1965.

Index